Misplaced Ideas?

STUDIES IN COMPARATIVE POLITICAL THEORY

Series editor: Diego A. von Vacano, Texas A&M University

*Consulting editors: Andrew March, Harvard University,
and Loubna El Amine, Northwestern University*

Democracy after Virtue: Toward Pragmatic Confucian Democracy
Sungmoon Kim

Tantric State: A Buddhist Approach to Democracy and Development in Bhutan
William J. Long

Misplaced Ideas?

Political-Intellectual History in Latin America

ELÍAS J. PALTI

OXFORD
UNIVERSITY PRESS

Oxford University Press is a department of the University of Oxford. It furthers
the University's objective of excellence in research, scholarship, and education
by publishing worldwide. Oxford is a registered trade mark of Oxford University
Press in the UK and certain other countries.

Published in the United States of America by Oxford University Press
198 Madison Avenue, New York, NY 10016, United States of America.

© Oxford University Press 2024

All rights reserved. No part of this publication may be reproduced, stored in
a retrieval system, or transmitted, in any form or by any means, without the
prior permission in writing of Oxford University Press, or as expressly permitted
by law, by license, or under terms agreed with the appropriate reproduction
rights organization. Inquiries concerning reproduction outside the scope of the
above should be sent to the Rights Department, Oxford University Press, at the
address above.

You must not circulate this work in any other form
and you must impose this same condition on any acquirer.

CIP data is on file at the Library of Congress

ISBN: 978–0–19–777494–6 (pbk.)
ISBN: 978–0–19–755664–1 (hbk.)

DOI: 10.1093/oso/9780197556641.001.0001

Paperback printed by Marquis Book Printing, Canada
Hardback printed by Bridgeport National Bindery, Inc., United States of America

Contents

Acknowledgments	vii
Prologue: The Laughter of the Thracian Girl: For an Intellectual History of Latin American Thought	ix

1. The History of the "History of Ideas" in Latin America and Its Critics 1

PART 1 THEORETICAL APPROACHES: THE EMERGENCE OF LATIN AMERICANIST RADICALISM: A CASE OF INVERTED ORIENTALISM?

2. Latin American Philosophy I: The Historicist Line in the Genealogical Looking Glass 27

3. Latin American Philosophy II: The Phenomenological Line and the Metaphysical Turn 58

4. Revisiting the Topic of "Misplaced Ideas": Dependency Theory and Ideological Production in the Periphery 95

PART 2 HISTORIOGRAPHICAL APPROACHES: THE SYNDROME OF ALPHONSE THE WISE: TELEOLOGISM AND NORMATIVISM IN THE HISTORY OF IDEAS

5. On the "Ideological Origins" of the Revolutions of Independence 133

6. From Tradition to Modernity? Historical Revisionism and Political-Conceptual History 156

Conclusion: The Quest for an Identity: The Pseudo-Problem as a Historical-Intellectual Problem 182

Quoted Bibliography	187
Index	199

Acknowledgments

This book gathers and synthesizes research and studies carried out over a very long period of time, in different contexts and situations, from my years as a graduate student at Berkeley to the "great enclosure" of the year 2020 due to the COVID-19 pandemic. Throughout all this time, I received advice and support from so many colleagues, friends, and institutions that it is materially impossible to do justice to them all but I offer them my heartfelt gratitude.

On this occasion I would just like to name my mentors when I was first an undergraduate, and later a graduate student: José Sazbón, Hilda Sabato, Oscar Terán, and Carlos Altamirano, at the University of Buenos Aires; Tulio Halperin Donghi, Julio Ramos, and Martin Jay, at Berkerley; Bernard Bailyn at Harvard; and Josefina Vázquez and Carlos Marichal, at the COLMEX. They were certainly not the only teachers from whose sapience I nurtured in these institutions, but indeed the closest ones.

Always present in my mind are my friends and colleagues at the Center for Intellectual History at the National University of Quilmes and at the School of Philosophy and Letters at the University of Buenos Aires, where I worked for more than two decades. Each of these individuals was a source of intellectual and creative stimulation. The list of universities in Latin America, Europe, and the United States where I participated as a visiting professor is very long, and it will not be possible to mention all of them here, as I would have wished. In all of them I found a very hospitable ambit for the exchange of ideas.

The following essays were elaborated in the framework of research groups in which I have taken part: *The Master on Conceptual History*, directed by Claudio Ingerflom-Nun at the National University of San Martín; *Iberconceptos*, directed by Javier Fernández Sebastián; *Posthegemonía*, directed by Alberto Moreiras and José Luis Villacañas, and the research programs (PICT); "Actualidad del pasado. Búsquedas y obstáculos a través de las perspectivas de Walter Benjamin y Reinhart Koselleck," directed by Lucila Svampa; and "Las identidades de América Latina. Una historia intelectual del pensamiento latinoamericano en los siglos XIX y XX," directed by Adrián

viii ACKNOWLEDGMENTS

Gorelik. These last ones were possible thanks to the funds provided by the FONCYT and the CONICET, Argentina.

Finally, I want to leave a special acknowledgement to Diego von Vacano, who gave me the opportunity to publish this book in his prestigious collection, and to Angela Chnapko and Alexcee Bechthold for taking diligent care of the edition of the present book. Finally, and definitely, to my family who have always supported me: Lola, Andrea, Andrés, Sol, Mili, Osvaldo, Sonia, Deborah, and Ruth.

Prologue

The Laughter of the Thracian Girl: For an Intellectual History of Latin American Thought

In the *Theaetetus*, Plato tells a very well-known story that is illustrative of the aim of the present book. It refers to an occasion when the philosopher Thales of Miletus was so immersed observing the sky, trying to unravel its secret, that he ended up falling into a well, unleashing the laughter of the young slave girl who accompanied him. The classic interpretation of this anecdote refers to the philosopher's lack of practical sense. Being always buried in their thoughts, the philosopher would become unable to deal with the simplest and easiest matters of everyday life. However, this story gave rise to many different versions and interpretations, which have been brilliantly recreated and analyzed by Hans Blumenberg in *The Laughter of the Thracian Woman*.[1] One of these interpretations, which I will follow here, affirms that what the Milesian whom Plato chose as the figure of the proto-philosopher (in the older version of the story no name appears) cannot perceive is the ground on which he is standing, and this is what makes him fall. Now, that soil of which the philosopher remains ignorant, that well into which he sinks inciting the mockery of the slave girl, can be understood in a peculiar sense; that is, as referring to the conceptual soil on which their thought stands, the set of assumptions that are at the basis of their perspective of the world. It is this, in effect, the conceptual dimension we intend to analyze in the present book: the hidden ground of knowledge on which discourses are founded.

Hence our approach is not addressed at investigating what the authors under consideration said, at that which lies above their heads, but at what lies below them; that is, how they could say what they said, the régime of knowledge on which their perspectives rested, and from which these took their consistency. This entails, in turn, gaining a critical distance with respect

---

[1] Hans Blumenberg, *Das Lachen der Thrackerin. Eine Urgeschichte der Theorie* (Frankfurt am Main: Suhrkamp, 1987). English translation: *The Laughter of the Thracian Woman: A Protohistory of Theory*. Translation by Stephen Hawkins (New York: Bloomsbury Academic, 2015).

X PROLOGUE

to our objects, in this case, the conceptual systems under analysis. The point is that every system of thought necessarily rests on a set of premises that are, themselves, unthinkable within that very system. What concerns us here is, then, at the same time, the closest and the most distant. Ultimately, those premises on which a given type of discourse is held can work as such only to the same extent that they are simply accepted as valid, with no reflection.[2] Only under this condition can a certain type of discourse unfold and take form.

Yet, this generates the illusion characteristic of philosophical practice: imagining that the thinker invents the concepts that they postulate, or, perhaps, that they simply inferred from the very observation of the world. And it is necessarily so because if the philosopher could penetrate what is at the basis of their way of conceiving reality, that language that secretly speaks to them, the set of knowledge that is given to them and informs their perspective, they would simply cease to be such a philosopher. Their discourse would become then inscribed into a different register, its reflection then would have moved to another terrain, to a second-order plane of discourse. In short, the philosopher would have become a metaphilosopher, and the historian of ideas a metahistorian. It is precisely this passage that we intend to carry out here; more precisely, to transfer reflection from the field of the history of ideas in Latin America to what could be called a metahistory of ideas in Latin America, a history of the history of ideas. The goal is to try to reconstruct how Latin American thought and its history were conceived, what the assumptions were from which the different views were based, and the logic that presided over their particular forms of discourse; in short, to penetrate the unapproachable dimension within these very approaches—their inherent blind spots.

---

[2] Blumenberg refers to that pre-conceptual dimension, the set of self-evident truths that, according to Husserl, are immediately given to consciousness, with the term *"neheliegend,"* literally "lying nearby," normally translated into English as "obvious." Blumenberg uses this word to describe an axiom, or belief that remains unquestioned, and distinguishes it from other German terms that can also be translated as "obvious," like *"selbstverständlich,"* literally "self-understandable." As David Carr indicates in his translation of *The Crisis of European Sciences*, Husserl, and after him, Blumenberg, uses this later term to refer to the "un-questioned but not un-questionable." See Edmund Husserl, *The Crisis of European Sciences and Transcendental Phenomenology: An Introduction to Phenomenological Philosophy* (Evanston: Northwestern University Press, 1970), 24. In *The Laughter of the Thracian Woman*, Blumenberg uses the term *"neheliegend"* everywhere to indicate those obvious surroundings that Thales ignores. He thus intends to conflate the concept of "obvious" with the bodily experience of "nearness." See Stephen J. Hawkings, "Fundamental Ambiguities, Metaphor, Translation, and Intertextuality in Hans Blumenberg's Metaphorology," PhD diss., University of Michigan, 2014.

We must be warned, however, that it is always a dangerous exercise. As Copernicus already said in what can be taken as an elliptic reference to the anecdote that we have been relating: "the elevation of our sight to stellar objects (*excelsissima*) is what separates us from the closest to us (*nobis proximal*) and leads us to the error of ascribing to the celestial bodies that which in reality is a property of the Earth." "Here, for the first time," Blumenberg concludes, "as so often occurred later in the history of science, the theoretical rupture is produced by a shift in the orientation of attention: noticing the unnoticed." However, this "shift in the orientation of attention" has its price. For Copernicus—as we have seen—noticing the unnoticed leads to discovering the illusory character of our knowledge, that it is nothing more than a projection upward of what is below us and which we ignore. And we find this out only at the moment we tumble into the well, thus eliciting malicious laughs. Ultimately, the series of idealizations that underlie a given perspective can become visible only insofar as the set of presuppositions on which that given perspective is founded becomes undermined.

The anecdote related by Plato connects with the famous tale of Icarus, who falls into the sea when he gets too close to the sun. The sea is also the environment that surrounds the city in which Thales lived and he believed to be the primordial element, that from where everything emerged. "Everything is water," he said. The smug winged who wanted to reach the heavens does not fall into a well (which, in some versions after Plato's, was full of manure), but into that formless magma of the aqueous milieu, where—in the imagination of the time—fabulous beings inhabited, and which also contained innumerable dangers. Getting away from one's own ground, from the mainland on which one is standing, and venturing into that uncertain oceanic environment, in which all our deepest certainties falter, revealing their inherent precariousness, is not an endeavor to be undertaken by just anybody.

The image of the sea is also appropriate to illustrate our own project in this book. The ground on which discourses are held, and which we will try to unravel here, is not a solid ground with clearly definable features. The aqueous substrate is where ideas come from, but it does not itself have ideas. The thinker who ventures into it thus discovers that the ideas they imagine are and are not their own. They come from the sea, but the sea does not have them. It is what allows the thinker to imagine such ideas, but this does not mean that the ideas are already pre-constituted in it and merely given to the thinker. Understanding how that formless element eventually takes shape, giving rise to a specific type of discourse—its *mise en forme*—is that other

xii   PROLOGUE

key task that we will attempt here, which sends us back, now, from the plane of metaphilosophy or metahistory, to that of intellectual history; that is, from the realm of the possible and thinkable in a given conceptual context to that of the discourses actually produced.

The point is that only at that moment when Thales stopped looking at that sky that he imagined as inhabited by a plurality of gods and started to look below him, at the primordial element of water, that philosophy would have been born. Two thousand years later, Bacon takes up this anecdote to question the Milesian who had not realized that he did not need to look up, that he could discover the secret contained in the celestial vault by observing its reflection in the water. As for the sailors of that time, who, to orient themselves in that formless mass of ocean, did no longer have to look at the stars but lower their sights to that small mass floating in oil that they called a compass, the most distant had become the closest. The point, for Bacon, is that by looking at the water Thales could have discovered the secret of heaven, but not the other way around: he could never get to know the water by looking at the sky, that element from which—for him—everything had arisen. However, the thinker, absorbed in their thoughts, would not be able to perceive this nearness of the far-away. To discover it, the thinker must first fall into the well, indeed running the risk of breaking their neck. Only in this way, assuming that challenge, will they be able to notice what remained hitherto unnoticed by them; that is, they will be able to observe the ground on which they are standing.

In Montaigne's version of this anecdote, the girl appears already considerably less naïve, and also with a tinge of perversion. In his version, the philosopher does not fall into the well, but it is the girl who puts a stone out to cause the fall. It was necessary for her to do it, according to Montaigne.[3] Only in this way could she awaken the philosopher from his illusion, make him realize that what he thinks he sees in the sky is nothing but a projection of what, in reality, is below him. Montaigne's maid is perhaps the best metaphor for the metaphilosopher-turned-intellectual historian: the one who puts stones in the way of the thinker; that is to say, reveals what is unthinkable

---

[3] "I feel grateful to the Milesian wench," said Montaigne, "who, seeing philosopher Thales continually spending his time in contemplation of the heavenly vault and always keeping his eyes looking upward, put something in his way to make him stumble, to warn him that it was time to amuse his thoughts with things in the clouds after he had seen those at his feet. Indeed, she gave him good counsel, to look rather at himself than at the sky." Michel de Montaigne, "The Apology of Raymond Sebond," *The Complete Works: Essays, Travel Journals, Letters* (New York: A. A. Knopf, 2003), 488, quoted by Stephen J. Hawkings, *Fundamental Ambiguities*, 211.

to the thinker, the blind spots inherent in their particular form of discourse, but that are at its very basis—in sum, the conceptual ground upon which they stand and from which they can scan the sky. In this way, intellectual history leads the thought of a particular time or current to confront what is inassimilable for the philosopher: the illusory nature of their knowledge, to what extent it is nothing but a projection upward of that which remains always submerged down below.

However, neither Bacon nor Copernicus perceived what Ludwig Feuerbach pointed out centuries later: that to get rid of the gods which, for Thales, the sky was populated with, would mean to lose the ground, as well. For Feuerbach, looking at the sky is precisely the most appropriate way of clinging to the ground; it is not what leads the philosopher to fall into the manure-filled well, but, on the contrary, what prevents them from doing it. Looking at the ground (*Grund*) means to become groundless, falling into an abyss (*Ab-grund*). And this, in turn, could be interpreted in two opposite ways.

For Voltaire, contrarily to the classical interpretation, the figure of the Milesian was the best metaphor of the value of philosophical knowledge: the thinker absorbed in observing the sky is the embodiment of the ideal of that who is able to see the closest, and oneself, as it were seen from Mars or Jupiter. As he said in his *Treatise on Metaphysics*, focusing on the highness entails leaving aside worldly prejudices and interests. It is thus precisely the disinterest in everyday matters that sparked the girl's mockery that allows Thales to gain access to the inner experience of the human being. Looking at the sky would be the ruse to be able to look back to oneself from the sky and see the invisible in it.

For Nietzsche, instead, the anecdote recollected by Plato was the best expression of the incompatibility between thinking and knowledge. For him, thought entails ignorance; both are inextricably tied. "Human reason is upset when it wants to investigate and trace all things back to their foundations," Montaigne said. Nietzsche would have opposed to La Fontaine's conclusion in one of his fables that states, "Poor beast, you can't even see what is at your feet and are you going to read what is above your head?"—the maxim that ignorance of what is at our feet is the very condition of thinking, the articulation of a system of knowledge that allows us to read what is above our heads. The substrate must remain invisible for the world to become visible.

However, these two opposite perspectives (Voltaire's and Nietzsche's) are not necessarily incompatible. Perhaps it is only insofar as we gain distance

xiv PROLOGUE

from our object—as we become able to observe it as if we were seeing it from Mars or Jupiter—that the ground on which said object is standing can be revealed to us, that what remains invisible in the vicinity turns visible. However, this still does not deny that it is always a risky exercise, as it undermines any pretense of truth, any illusion of truth.

Going back to the present book, it is not the desire for truth that presided over its elaboration. And this statement has an implicit warning. The reader should resign the expectation to find, at the end of this journey, the Holy Grail containing the answers to the enigmas presented above. On the contrary, if there is anything exciting in this endeavor, it lies precisely in the fact of venturing into those dark, unknown mental territories that challenge our capacities of comprehension. Making sense of the realm that resists conceptualization requires the intellectual temper for reconsidering ingrained certainties, including the very ones that allow us to think. In short, it also requires imagining the previously unthinkable, disturbing, and uncertain trajectories, even risking breaking our necks by falling into a well.

Is There a Latin American Thought?

The heaven that the historians of ideas in Latin America seek to scrutinize does not possess a clearly defined design—its contours look diffuse and blurred. It is not easy to discern the objects that are proper to it and to distinguish them from those mere reflections of distant ("foreign") constellations. And this raises a serious dilemma: do such objects really exist or are they merely illusory? What happens if we discover that the objects we see are actually only mirages? If this were the case, it would look fatuous (would provoke laughter) to persist in observing them; we should shift our gaze toward the very source from which these illusions emanate, to those distant, more consistent galaxies. Only the expectation of finding objects of its own in said sky, only the conviction that the presence in it of stars and planets is not a mere illusion, justifies persisting in its examination, in concentrating our attention on it, even if this leads to losing sight of the ground from which it is observed.

In turn, a number of new questions derive from the previous point, such as: How to identify those objects? What type of prism should we use to find them? What are the features that define these objects? What is their nature? What distinguishes them from those belonging to other universes, very different from it? The present study does not seek to find answers to these questions but, more modestly, to understand how these questions arose, and what the different answers historically proposed were. In this fashion, the present approach produces a kind of conceptual fold, turning those very questions into objects of interrogation. In effect, in what follows, I intend to reconstruct the intellectual constellation within which the question of the existence of a distinct Latin American thought became conceivable, and how it would be reformulated in the context of the various conceptual frameworks, currents of thought, and types of discourse under consideration.

I must confess, however, that the composition of the present study has been somewhat complicated regarding the mode of its disposition. The initial chapter consists of an analysis of the origins of the history of ideas in Latin America as a scholarly discipline, and what the conceptual premises on which it was originally founded were. Its emergence, as we will see, was closely associated with the definition of a particular problem: What is the point of studying intellectual formations in regions peripheral to Western culture, and that, therefore, have a "derivative" character, in Leopoldo Zea's expression? The answer to that question was not self-evident; elaborating it demanded a complex intellectual operation. Yet, Zea's answer will shortly become an object of bitter criticism. This first chapter goes on to explore some of the criticisms that the analytical model established by Zea received and which gave rise to the so-called revisionist currents. As we will see, the revisionist enterprise referred to that which Zea saw in the heaven of the history of Latin American ideas. The ground on which his perspective rested remained invisible, yet being still (although ignored) at the basis of the revisionist's own critical perspective.

From this initial chapter there emerges a kind of bifurcation. We come here to a crossroads. Two different directions derive from it, and the linear relation offered here represents only one of the possible directions. But, as in *Hopscotch*, by Julio Cortázar, the reader may eventually choose to take a different route and to reverse the direction of reading. What enables these alternative paths is the fact that reading the first part contributes to a better understanding of the second, but, conversely, reading the second part would, in turn, offer key elements for a better understanding of the first. In any case, it is an unsolvable problem because it arises from the very fact that writing and reading are, by definition, linear, although linearity is not always the most appropriate form of writing and reading, as this would be the case.

The first argumentative thread—the one adopted here—recreates the trajectory that leads from the history of ideas to Latin American philosophy

xvi PROLOGUE

(otherwise called Liberation philosophy) and, beyond it, to the criticism that it received from the perspective of the practitioners of dependency theory. The latter set into question the old topic of "misplaced ideas," which affirms the inadequacy of European ideas to represent local reality. According to that topic, the task of intellectual historians consists in searching for the forms of thinking that are proper to the region, a project from which, in addition, definite ethical-political orientations would derive. Seen from this perspective, the sky that the Latin American philosopher looks at is, as for Thales, filled with gods. They not only believe they find objects there that are proper to it, inherent in it, but also that these objects possess the attributes of the sacred, announcing a new era of redemption. Nevertheless, as we will see, the materiality of the ground is persistent and always forces our gaze down to the mud of the mechanisms of attribution of meaning to the celestial spheres. The dependency theory's criticism to Latin American philosophy can be seen as the emergence of the submerged in the latter. However, it would have revulsive consequences, even in the views of the holders of that very theory.

The other argumentative line connects the opening chapter on the history of Latin American ideas directly to the second part of the book. That first chapter, as we have seen, analyzes the traditional frameworks of the history of ideas, which had emerged from the definition of the specific nature of the problems that the study of the modes of appropriation and circulation of ideas in societies considered peripheral to Western culture posed. The second argumentative line that derived from it refers to how these frameworks were applied to the study of specific, concrete historical phenomena and processes, which is what the two chapters included in Part II respectively explore. They focus on two of these processes: the revolutions of independence and the conformation of the new political systems that emerged from them, which were founded on the basis of a new principle of legitimacy: "popular sovereignty."

More precisely stated, this second part investigates the type of problems arising from the application of the traditional schemes of the history of ideas to the interpretation of said processes. And also, how a different perspective—founded on what is currently known as a "conceptual history of the *political*"—allows for a better understanding of the debates that historically arose in the region around the core categories of modern political discourse, such as representation, nation, and democracy.

Ultimately, what we are trying to show here is why the interpretive schemes based on the topic of "misplaced ideas"—which reduce all problems to the inadequacy of European categories to local reality—lead to losing sight of the deeply dilemmatic nature of the issues under dispute at that moment. In this way, the present study aims to rescue the study of Latin American intellectual history from the place of a merely "local anomaly," with no relevance to intellectual history, at large, and to observe how its study can help us to raise theoretical issues whose relevance transcends the merely local framework, as they lead us to observe problems that are less idiosyncratic and more inherent in the very theoretical frameworks within which the discipline currently deploys. As the reader can perceive, the route that is offered in what follows is not a flat, luminous path, but rather a rough, winding one, which opens up to manifold, unexplored meanders. I do not claim to have exhausted them, but I would be satisfied if I have managed, at least, to point out some of the possible avenues, some of the different trajectories, that can be followed within that labyrinth, with the hope that eventually other, more intrepid students of Latin American intellectual history will venture to go deeper into them. In any case, what guides me in this endeavor is not the expectation of finding friendlier planets at the end of the journey, but, more simply, the desire to understand what has moved the authors and currents of thought under consideration to orient their sights in search of them, the horizon of comprehension within which that project became feasible as the proper object for local thinking.

Buenos Aires, December 2021

1

The History of the "History of Ideas" in Latin America and Its Critics

The history of ideas in Latin America has a long tradition. Its remote antecedents can be traced back to the late nineteenth and early twentieth centuries, when the first studies on local thought were elaborated. They accompanied efforts, in each country, to build an idea of its national identity, history, traditions, culture, etc., and it entailed endowing the respective nation with a proper intellectual tradition. It was, more precisely, the specific object of the histories of ideas. In fact, these early writings in the field always followed the same pattern. They described a course according to which the first works by local thinkers were only more or less faithful imitations of European models and, progressively, an authentic national expression was being forged.

The origin of these first essays was produced in a particular cultural climate, which was that of the avant-garde, that gave rise, in turn, to the so-called cultural nationalism. It first developed mainly in the marginal regions of Europe, such as Central Europe and Russia, and then spread to other regions, including Latin America (and whose most important expression is, probably, Mexican muralism). This phenomenon coincided there with the rise of the spiritualist reaction against positivism, which became widely diffused, especially after the Cuban War of Independence. At that juncture, the US intervened on the side of the Cubans, but, when the war concluded, the US troops stayed on the island and imposed a series of conditions, among which was the famous Platt amendment, giving the US the right to intervene in that country whenever its interests were supposedly under threat. This fact, and the subsequent wave of military interventions in the region, gave rise to a strong reaction in the subcontinent. In this context, spiritualism appeared as an intellectual rebellion against North American pragmatism, of which positivist thought would be its incarnation.

The best expression of this spiritual climate is the book by José Enrique Rodó published in 1900, *Ariel*, to which we will refer later. As previously

Misplaced Ideas?. Elías J. Palti, Oxford University Press. © Oxford University Press 2024.
DOI: 10.1093/oso/9780197556641.003.0001

2 MISPLACED IDEAS?

discussed, it is in this context that the emergence of the first histories of ideas in Latin America must be placed. In reality, these essays did not differ in their substance from the ones that were then elaborated in all other countries in the world. Their contents changed, but they all followed the same general pattern, the aforementioned teleological scheme. It was in the second half of the past century that a more specific problem for the region arose. This is associated with a shift in perspective. Until then, the fact that the local cultural tradition was weaker than the European cultural tradition was taken simply as denoting the "youth" of those nations, a perspective that had implicit the promise that the mere course of time would solve. Contrary to this, in the second half of the century, the marginal character of the local culture was no longer considered as resulting from circumstantial conditions, but to have structural roots. It would express the existence of fundamental asymmetries in the world system, within which said region would occupy a peripheral place. That is when the question emerged as to what kind of approaches were required to analyze the peculiar cultural dynamics in marginal regions of Western culture. The classical answer to that question leads us to Leopoldo Zea's work.

Leopoldo Zea and the Problem of Ideas in the Periphery

Zea's perspective was strongly influenced by the spiritualist currents of thought, to which he had access through José Gaos—his dissertation director. Gaos was a Spaniard exiled in Mexico who introduced Ortega y Gasset's philosophy there, the so-called circumstantialism.[1] Basically, circumstantialism stated that the thinking of a given subject was conditioned by its surrounding milieu. It is, at least, the principle that Zea followed in his approach to the history of Mexican and, subsequently, Latin American thought. And, on this basis, he introduced a fundamental shift in the studies in the region.

---

[1] On this, see G. Hernández Flores, *Del circunstancialismo filosófico de Ortega y Gasset a la filosofía mexicana de Leopoldo Zea* (México: UNAM, 2004); José Luis Abellán, *El exilio filosófico en América. Los transterrados de 1939* (Madrid: Fondo de Cultura Económica, 1998); Giuseppe Bentivegna, "Zea, Ortega y Gasset y la circunstancia hispanoamericana," *Revista de Filosofía* 142 (2017): 9–34; Andrés Kozel, *La idea de América en el historicismo mexicano. José Gaos, Edmundo O'Gorman y Leopoldo Zea* (Buenos Aires: Teseo, 2017); Tzvi Medin, *Leopoldo Zea: ideología, historia y filosofía de América Latina* (Mexico: UNAM, 1983); Tzvi Medin, *Ortega y Gasset en la cultura hispanoamericana* (Mexico: FCE, 1994); Tzvi Medin, *Entre la jerarquía y la liberación: Ortega y Gasset y Leopoldo Zea* (Mexico: FCE, 1998).

THE HISTORY OF THE "HISTORY OF IDEAS" 3

Even though, as we have seen, it would be wrong to affirm that Zea "invented" the history of ideas in Latin America, he was indeed a fundamental figure in the articulation of the theoretical and methodological premises to establish it as a particular field of scholarly research—premises that, barely modified, persist to the present, and, as we will see, *imbue indeed the views of his critics*. He was, in fact, the first to systematically approach the specificity of the demands for the study of ideas in the region, the particular problem that the writing of the history of ideas raises in the "periphery" of the West; that is, in regions whose cultures have "a derivative" nature.[2] For him, it entailed tackling a fundamental dilemma: What was the sense and object of analyzing the work of thinkers who, as he admits, did not make any contribution to the history of ideas "in general?" Insofar as its sense is not engraved in its very wording: What kind of approaches were required to make the study of these authors and their writings relevant as *cultural* objects?

In effect, once the expectation that Latin American thought could occupy a proper place in the universal history of the ideas faded, revealing that the weakness of the local intellectual tradition did not respond to a merely circumstantial situation but to a structural one, Zea and the members of his generation found themselves forced to render problematic the views that saw intellectual history as a timeless "struggle of a set of ideas against other sets of ideas." "In an interpretation of this type," said Zea in his seminal work, *El positivismo en México* (1943), "Mexico and all Mexican positivists could be spared, since they would be nothing but poor interpreters of a doctrine to which they have made no contribution worthy of universal attention."[3]

On the other hand, however, as he indicates, should these authors have made some contributions to it, discovering them would not have been relevant for the comprehension of the local culture, either. "The fact that the ones who made those contributions were Mexican positivists would have been merely an incidental happening. These contributions could perfectly have been made by men of any other country."[4] Ultimately, it is not from its eventual relation with the "kingdom of the eternally valid things" that the local history of ideas gains its sense. The question is then: From where? Thus posed, the answer to that question immediately emerges: "From its relationship with that circumstance called Mexico."[5] What really matters here

---

[2] Zea popularized that term, which appeared in a book by Samuel Ramos published some years earlier: *El perfil del hombre y la cultura en México* (Mexico: UNAM, 1934).

[3] Leopoldo Zea, *El positivismo en México*, vol. 1 (Mexico: El Colegio de México, 1943), 35.

[4] Zea, *El positivismo en México*, 1:17.

[5] Zea, *El positivismo en México*, 1:17.

4 MISPLACED IDEAS?

are not the "Latin American contributions" to thinking in general, but, on the contrary, its "failures" and its "deviations" matter. In short, the type of "refractions" that European ideas underwent when they were detached from their original habitat and became transplanted to this region.

Zea also identified the analytic unit for this type of comparative endeavor: "philosophemas" (a counterpart of the notion of "unit-ideas," which allowed Arthur Lovejoy to establish the "history of ideas" as a scholarly discipline in America).[6] According to Zea, it is in the individual philosophical units that the meaningful deviations produced by contextual displacements are imprinted, thus serving as records of them. "If we compare the philosophemas used by two or more diverse cultures," he states, "we can observe that these philosophemas, although they verbally appear alike, change their contents."[7]

We finally meet the basic design of the approach founded on the scheme of "models" and "deviations" which still dominate the discipline. This thus sprung out of the attempt to historicize ideas, the need to remove them from the abstract frameworks of generic categories around which the discipline hitherto revolved and locate them in the particular context of their enunciation. Thus considered, that is, in its fundamental premises, Zea's project is not that easy to refute. One of the problems is that it is not always possible to distinguish what Charles Hale called the "methodological aspects" of his interpretive model of the "substantive aspects" of it, which are definitively much less protected from criticism.[8] As a matter of fact, the emergence of the history of ideas as a scholarly discipline in that country was intimately associated to the diffusion of the Lo Mexicano movement,[9] and both would hitherto remain tied to the present in their shared search for the Mexican (and subsequently Latin American) "being," a point that we will consider in greater detail in subsequent chapters.

Nevertheless, there is a second reason that contributed to darken Zea's contribution. This reason is less obvious but much more important, in the context of the present chapter: the scheme of "models" and "deviations"

---

[6] See Arthur Lovejoy, "Reflections on the History of Ideas," Journal of the History of Ideas 1, no. 1 (1940): 3–23.

[7] Zea, El positivismo en México, 1:24.

[8] See Charles Hale, "The History of Ideas: Substantive and Methodological Aspects of the Thought of Leopoldo Zea," Journal of Latin American Studies 3, no. 1 (1971): 59–70.

[9] See G. W. Hewes, "Mexican in Search of the 'Mexican' (Review)," The American Journal of Economics and Sociology 13, no. 2 (1954): 209–222; Henry Schmidt, The Roots of Lo Mexicano: Self and Society in Mexican Thought, 1900–1934 (College Station: Texas A&M University Press, 1978).

readily became part of the common sense of the historical profession in the region, and this obliterated the fact that the search for "local deviations" is not a "natural object" for Latin American intellectual history, but the result of a conceptual operation which resulted from specific historical and epistemological conditions. It actually marked a theoretical *tour de force*. Yet, having shortly afterward turned into a kind of undisputable premise, the validity of which seemed immediately evident, that scheme would rob itself of its thematization. In actual fact, the criticism of Zea's approach would not really set into question his "historical-philosophical method," as he called it, but the way in which he eventually put it into practice.

According to Zea, his "historical-philosophical method" allowed him "to eliminate the contradictions whereby historians of the philosophy became trapped"; in this fashion, "those which seemed to be contradictions are now revealed as diverse stages of a single cultural development."[10] The interpretation of positivism, which had then become placed at the center of historiographical debate, served him as the leading case for his method. His attempt to historicize ideas was closely associated with his goal to integrate positivism—which, after the 1910 Revolution, had been execrated as an ideology strange to Mexico and its authentic liberal tradition—as a dialectically necessary stage in the process of Mexico's mental emancipation initiated by the independence. Thus, "although the origins of positivism were alien to the Mexican circumstances, it was adapted to them and used to impose a new order."[11]

However, this aspect of his project, unlike the methodological one, did not find fertile ground. The reaction against the "institutionalization" process of the Revolution resulted in the exacerbation of the nationalistic tendencies in the *Lo Mexicano* movement, turning all attempts of vindication of Mexican positivism (which was normally identified as the ideological sustentation of Porfirio Díaz's "dictatorship") suspicious of encouraging the most conservative wing of the PRI (*Partido de la Revolución Institucional*, the governmental party). And this led eventually Zea himself to partially revise his previous positions and to condemn the positivist movement as an ideology that managed to adapt itself to Mexico's national being but was not yet an authentic emanation of it.[12] The ideological ambiguity in Zea's perspective shortly

---

[10] Zea, *El positivismo en México*, 1:23.
[11] Zea, *El positivismo en México*, 1:48.
[12] Leopoldo Zea, *Conciencia y posibilidad del mexicano* (Mexico: Porrúa, 1952).

6   MISPLACED IDEAS?

turned him into the target of criticism, and at that moment his entire historiographical project came under attack. This would be the origin of the so-called revisionist view of the history of Latin American ideas.

The "Revisionist" Critique

In effect, in the following decades we can observe—among specialists in Latin American politico-intellectual history—an increasing uneasiness with respect of the "old" tradition of the history of ideas, of which Zea was the best representative. Particularly irritating has become its strongly dichotomic perspective, which was, ultimately, ideologically biased. As François-Xavier Guerra indicated, for Zea and his generation, the writing of history was much more "than a scholarly practice, it was a political action, in the etymological acceptation of the word: that of the citizen defending his *polis*, narrating the epic of the heroes that founded it."[13] The increasingly professional orientation of the historiographical labor and broader changes in political climate converged toward the need to develop new approaches less dependent on demands external to its particular field (basically, political ones).

Charles Hale's work set a turning point in this regard. At least for Mexico, which has served as the leading case for the whole region, all "revisionist" efforts refer back to it. As Fernando Escalante Gonzalbo remarks: "Up until the moment Charles Hale came to intervene, we could tell ourselves a delicious story: here we had an-always-assumed-as beautiful and heroic liberal tradition; which was democratic, nationalistic, republican, revolutionary and even Zapatista (and that was good); that tradition sought to counter, with patriotic vigor, an opposite one held by a minority of conservatives: monarchists, authoritarians, strangers to the nation, positivists (who were very bad)."[14] Hale himself has repeatedly indicated that his main contribution lies in having removed the local historiography of ideas from

[13] François-Xavier Guerra, "El olvidado siglo XIX," in *Balance de la historiografía sobre Iberoamérica (1945–1988). Actas de las IV Conversaciones Internacionales de Historia*, ed. V. Vázquez de Prada Vallejo and Ignacio Olábarri Gortázar (Pamplona: Ediciones Universidad de Navarra, 1989), 595.

[14] Fernando Escalante Gonzalbo, "La imposibilidad del liberalismo en México," in *Recepción y transformación del liberalismo en México. Homenaje al profesor Charles A. Hale*, ed. Josefina Z. Vázquez (Mexico: El Colegio de México, 1991), 14.

THE HISTORY OF THE "HISTORY OF IDEAS" 7

the subjective, ideological terrain (one in which, as a foreigner, he allegedly did not participate) and relocated it on the firm ground of objective history.[15]

As we will see, it is not exactly there that Hale's contribution lies. The point is that the forcefulness (and justice) of the critic on the preceding tradition of the history of ideas (unjustly) darkened the achievements by Zea and his generation—achievements on which the perspectives of his very critics still rest. In effect, Hale's criticism would point to that side of Zea's approach that, as we have seen, was the most erratic one. As Hale states, liberalism was not strange to Mexico; it had deep roots and precedents in local history. But they are not those which the historians of ideas are willing to accept. As Hale says, Zea ignores the fact that, in its attempt of "mental emancipation" from the colony, Mexican liberalism only continued the Bourbon reformist tradition.

Hale draws from this his two central theses. First, that Mexican liberalism and conservatism were less unlike each other than the Mexican historians of ideas used to believe. "There may be points of continuity in Mexican thought and policy that run deeper than political liberalism and conservatism," which consist of their shared centralist trends.[16] Secondly, the contradictory mixture of liberalism and centralism, characteristic of Mexican and Latin American liberalism, is not, nevertheless, completely strange to the European liberal tradition. Following Guido de Ruggiero,[17] Hale discovers in it two "ideal types" in permanent conflict, which he defines as "English liberalism" (incarnated in Locke) and "French liberalism" (represented by Rousseau), respectively; the former, protective of individual rights and political decentralization; the latter, instead, organicist and markedly centralist. "The internal conflict between these two ideal types," he assures, "can be observed in all the Western nations."[18] The main difference lies in that, whereas in the Anglo-Saxon countries (and the United States, in particular) both ideal types became smoothly conjugated, giving rise to a political régime of democratic representation, in the countries of the Latin basin— and in Hispanic America, in particular—they clashed, rendering the establishment of democratic systems of government impossible.[19]

---

[15] Charles Hale, *Mexican Liberalism in the Age of Mora, 1821–1853* (New Haven: Yale University Press, 1968), 6.

[16] Hale, *Mexican Liberalism in the Age of Mora*, 8.

[17] Guido de Ruggiero, *The History of European Liberalism* (Gloucester, MA: Peter Smith, 1981).

[18] Hale, *Mexican Liberalism in the Age of Mora*, 54–55.

[19] For a very different perspective, see Hilda Sabato, *Republics of the New World: The Revolutionary Political Experiment in Nineteenth-Century Latin America* (Princeton: Princeton University Press, 2018).

8 MISPLACED IDEAS?

Here we find Hale's most important contribution to the study of nineteenth-century Latin American intellectual history. It does not lie, as he affirms, in having detached it from the ideological terrain and turning it into a scholarly, objective endeavor, but rather in having turned away from the parochialism hitherto prevalent in it. Given his familiarity with the debates taking place in France around the 1789 Revolution—triggered by the neo-Tocquevillian currents that proliferated during the years in which Hale was completing his doctoral studies—he could verify that most of the dilemmas in which Latin-Americanists were entangled were less idiosyncratic than they thought. This verification allowed Hale, in *Mexican Liberalism in the Age of Mora*, to remove the debates on the supposed tensions observed in Mexican liberal thought from its local context and to locate them on a broader stage of Atlantic dimension. Nevertheless, it is also at this point that the inherent limitations of the history of "ideas"—to which the revisionist approaches initiated by Hale are still indebted—become more clearly manifest.

The "Hispanic *Ethos*" as an *Arkhē*

As we have seen, behind manifest political antagonism, Hale discovered the action of common cultural patterns that traverse Mexico's whole ideological spectrum and epochs up to the present: the "Hispanic *ethos*." "It is undeniable," he says, "that liberalism in Mexico has been conditioned by the traditional *Hispanic ethos*."[20] For him, this uniform cultural substratum constitutes a kind of *arkhē*, which contains the last key to explain and make sense of the contradictions that agitated (and still agitate) Mexican (and Latin American) history to the present day. According to him, "pursuing the question of continuity further, we can find in the age of Mora a model that will help us understand the current drift in socioeconomic policy in a Mexico emerging from revolution [...] It was again the inspiration of the late eighteenth century Spain that prevailed."[21]

Although the idea of the traditionalist, "organicist," "centralist" Mexican (and Latin American) culture is deeply rooted both in Mexican and American imaginaries, in Hale's version we can observe a more precise influence: the one from the so-called culturalist school initiated by one his

---

[20] Hale, *Mexican Liberalism in the Age of Mora*, 304.
[21] Hale, *Mexican Liberalism in the Age of Mora*, 304.

THE HISTORY OF THE "HISTORY OF IDEAS" 9

teachers at Columbia University, Richard Morse. The perspective of both Morse and Hale has, in turn, a common source which they discuss at the same time: Louis Hartz. In *The Liberal Tradition in America* (1955), Hartz fixed that which for many years had been the standard vision of American intellectual history.[22] According to him, liberalism, when translated to the United States, and lacking there a traditional aristocracy that could prevent its expansion, lost the conflictive dynamics that had characterized it in its original context (Europe) and became a unifying myth, a kind of "second nature" for Americans, thus finally fulfilling its universal vocation in that country.[23] In a later text, Hartz expanded his interpretative model to all societies arising from European expansion. Each of them, he states, would end up adopting the political culture and tradition prevailing in the occupant nation at the moment of conquest. Thus, whereas a bourgeois and liberal culture would dominate in the United States, Latin America would remain adhered to its feudal inheritance.[24]

Morse takes up this approach, but he introduces a new twist. As Claudio Sanchez Albornoz and others had already demonstrated,[25] feudalism was never really affirmed in Spain. The *Reconquista* gave rise to an early centralist impulse, incarnated in Castile, which, by the sixteenth century, following the defeat of the Cortes and the nobility (which represented older democratic traditions), was expanded to the whole Spanish peninsula and, finally, transferred in a uniform fashion to its colonies. For him, the Habsburgs are the best expressions of early absolutism. Spain and, by extension, Spanish America, would thus be victims of a precocious modernization. According to Morse: "because Spain and Portugal had prematurely modernized their political institutions and renewed their scholastic ideology in the early period of national construction and ultramarine expansion of Europe, they

---

[22] Louis Hartz, *The Liberal Tradition in America: An Interpretation of American Political Thought since the Revolution* (New York: HBJ, 1955).

[23] The readings of Hartz's work often miss his critical perspective of American liberalism. For him, the lack of an opposite ideology imbued it with a conservative character, rendering it impossible the emergence of a truly progressivist current of thought in that country. Ultimately, and paradoxically, Hartz's view of American liberalism, far from being opposite to Mexican liberalism, is not very different from Hale's view of the latter (which reveals the arbitrary character of these traditional antinomies, once again).

[24] Louis Hartz, "The Fragmentation of European Culture and Ideology," in *The Founding of New Societies. Studies in the History of the United States, Latin America, South Africa, Canada, and Australia*, ed. L. Hartz (New York: Harvest/HBJ, 1964), 3–23.

[25] Claudio Sánchez Albornoz, *España, un enigma histórico*, vol. I, (Buenos Aires: Sudamericana, 1956), 186–187.

10 MISPLACED IDEAS?

avoided the implications of the great revolutions and failed to internalize its generative force."[26]

Societies of Hispanic inheritance thus always tend to persevere in their beings, given their lack of any immanent principle of development. Paradoxically, Morse drew from this situation a positive conclusion. "A protestant civilization," says Morse, "can develop its energies in wilderness, as in the United States. A Catholic civilization stagnates when it is not in vital contact with the diverse tribes and cultures of mankind."[27] Certainly, Morse's conclusion does not seem consistent with the (rather pessimistic) historical picture he offers. This later suggests that the patrimonialist culture has remained unchanged in the region, determining all evolution subsequent to the Conquest. It would also have had rather perverse consequences in political and social terms. As another member of the culturalist school, Howard J. Wiarda, says, the result was that, "rather than instituting democratic rule, the founding fathers of Latin America were chiefly concerned with preserving existing hierarchies and the authoritarian and undemocratic institutions of the past;"[28] "in contrast to the North American colonies [. . .], the Latin American colonies remained essentially authoritarian, absolutist, feudal (in the particularly Iberian sense) patrimonialist, elitist and organic-corporatist."[29]

In *Mexican Liberalism in the Age of Mora*, Hale takes up and, in turn, discusses Morse's re-interpretation of Hartz's perspective. Whereas Hale agrees with Morse that Hispanic America has never had a feudal political tradition (although indeed a feudal society), he affirms that the centralist tendencies in local liberalism are not a legacy of the Habsburgs, but rather of the Bourbons and their reformist tradition. Thus, Hale challenges the culturalist interpretations remaining, nevertheless, within its frameworks (doubtlessly, the Bourbons appear as much more plausible candidates than the Habsburgs to the role of precursors of nineteenth-century reformist Liberalism). He simply translates the moment of the *origin* from the sixteenth century to the eighteenth century, preserving its fundamental

---

[26] Richard Morse, *New World Soundings: Culture and Ideology in the Americas* (Baltimore: The Johns Hopkins University Press, 1989), 106.

[27] Morse, "The Heritage of Latin America," 177. This paradox has an explanation. We must place it in the context of the Cold War. Morse followed here Hartz's critical perspective of American politics of isolation, which then led to the persecution of its opponents, mainly communists.

[28] Howard Wiarda, "Introduction," in *Politics and Social Change: The Distinct Tradition*, ed. Howard Wiarda (Amherst: University of Massachusetts Press, 1982), 17.

[29] Wiarda, *Politics and Social Change*, 15–16.

THE HISTORY OF THE "HISTORY OF IDEAS"   11

premise: because in every process of appropriation of ideas a selective mechanism is at work, no "external borrowing" can explain, by itself, the failure in instituting democratic governments in the region. As Claudio Véliz indicates, "there was in France or Britain sufficient complexity [of ideas] and richness of detail to satisfy the extremes of radical and conservative opinion in Latin America."[30] Therefore, its last cause should be found in its own culture, the local centralist traditions.

Anyway, Hale's translation of the original moment of Mexican liberalism from the Habsburgs to the Bourbons destabilizes that characteristic mode of intellectual procedure, insofar as it tends, in fact, to expand the selection process to the traditions themselves: paraphrasing Véliz, we could now say that local traditions are sufficiently rich to satisfy from extreme radicals to extreme conservatives. The question that this affirmation raises is, then, given such a diversity of traditions: why do Mexican liberals "choose" the Bourbons' instead of the Habsburgs', for example.

In the last instance, the expansion of the idea of selectivity to the very traditions reveals that they are not a given, but something constantly renewed, as only some of them persist, gaining new meanings in the process and fulfilling new functions, whereas others are forgotten or completely redefined. And it would render impossible distinguishing to what extent traditions are the cause of or, rather, the consequence of political history. The very relationship between past and present would become a problem; it would no longer be feasible to determine which of the two terms is the *explanans* and which the *explanandum*.

Lastly, on the concept of "culture" the same can be said as Diego von Vacano says of the concept of "race": there is no such thing as a "race" that could be established in an unambiguous manner, its determination is always a *political* attribution, contingent on the context in which these very attributions take place. Consequently, it "is not the same thing in all periods; it becomes constructed and redefined over time." According to what he calls a "synthetic paradigm," the concept of "race," and, in our case, of "culture," does not refer to any substance. It rather defines a *problematique*: how to "move beyond ossified categories" and to analyze the ways in which the concept was conceptualized and re- conceptualized in the different historical contexts.[31]

---

[30] Claudio Véliz, *The Centralist Tradition of Latin America* (Princeton: Princeton University Press, 1980), 170.

[31] Diego von Vacano, *The Color of Citizenship: Race, Modernity and Latin American/Hispanic Political Thought* (Oxford: Oxford University Press, 2011), 28.

Latin American Culture and "Saturn's Rings"

After the publication of Hale's *Mexican Liberalism in the Age of Mora*, Morse revised his previous view, as formulated in his contribution to Hartz's book, *The Founding of New Societies* (1964). Now he actually re-discovered something he had previously indicated in that work: the presence in the very origin of Latin America of two traditions in permanent conflict, the Medieval and Thomist, represented by Castile, and the Renaissance and Machiavellian, incarnated in Aragon. Although the Thomist legacy prevailed from the beginning, by the end of the eighteenth century, and, especially, after the Independence, the hidden substratum of Renaissance ideas reemerged, thus giving rise to a conflict between the two opposite traditions. At that point, Hispanic Americans "were reintroduced to the historical conflict in sixteenth-century Spain between neo-Thomist natural law and Machiavellian realism."[32] Notwithstanding, he insists that the neo-Thomist ideas would continue prevailing in the region. The Machiavellian doctrine, Morse says, could be assimilated there only insofar as "it was re-elaborated in terms acceptable" to the Neo-Scholastic matrix of inherited thought.[33] The Liberal-Reformist's and the Enlightenment's ideologies would thus be characterized there by their radical eclecticism; they would constitute "an ideological mosaic, rather than a system."[34]

Ultimately, Morse applies to the very "Bourbonist hypothesis" the *genetic method* that aims "to identify the underlying historical matrix of attitude and social action."[35] According to this method, because—as Hale himself indicates—no political development can be explained exclusively by external influences, the very reformist project of the Bourbons should be explained, in turn, and referred back to predating traditions. In this fashion, the logic of the genetic method always leads back in time to a primitive moment, which works as an *arkhē* or unfounded foundation. By referring the opposition between the Habsburgs and the Bourbons to a previous and more primitive one between the Castilian and the Aragonese, Morse's re-interpretation rescues the genetic method from the circle between "traditions" and "influences" in which Hale's proposal seemed to felt prey, but, in this fashion, he reinforces the essentialist, ahistorical character of his culturalist approach.

---

[32] Morse, "Claims of Political Tradition," 112.
[33] Morse, "Claims of Political Tradition," 112.
[34] Morse, "Claims of Political Tradition," 107.
[35] Morse, "The Heritage of Latin America," 171.

THE HISTORY OF THE "HISTORY OF IDEAS" 13

In fact, the culturalist explanations presuppose the idea of a "cultural whole," of an organic substratum of traditions and values. All questioning the existence of such a uniform, solid bedrock inevitably turns these approaches unstable and precarious. As Alan Knight remarks, cultural explanations are, in fact, circular, tautological; they have the form of "if such a Mexican village frequently rebelled during the nineteenth century, it is because it has a rebellious culture," and so back and forth. In any event, the references to culture or political culture are locked into a double bind: either, as Knight shows, they do not provide anything of interest for the comprehension of historical process that we could not already discover by empirical means, or they send us back to a level of recondite and indemonstrable essences, unable, as such, to provide any explanatory principle of complex and changing historical processes.[36] In *The Peopling of British North America*, Bernard Bailyn uses a very appropriate image to refer to the idea of a North American culture.

In that book, Bailyn compares the idea of a North American culture to Saturn's rings. When viewed from six hundred thousand million kilometers away, the rings appear as a uniform set of flat and homogenous arcs. However, in 1980, the spaceship *Voyager I* offered a very different image of them. When viewed from a mere fifty thousand kilometers away we discover an infinite myriad of celestial bodies of very diverse sizes and characteristics. The homogeneous image of the rings is then revealed as only a luminous illusion emanating from a multitude of frozen rocks and dust. It would not be even

---

[36] Alan Knight, "¿Vale la pena reflexionar sobre la cultura política?," in *Cultura política en los Andes (1750–1950)*, ed. Cristóbal Aljovín de Losada and Mils Jacobsen (Lima: Universidad Nacional Mayor de San Marcos, 2007), 45–46. What Knight omits, however, is that the same circularity can be observed in socio-economic explanations. As Pocock says: "The slogan that ideas should be studied in their social and political context is, it seems to me, in danger of becoming a shibboleth; too many of those who pronounce it assume, often unconsciously, that they already know what the relations between ideas and social reality are, and this can lead to much coarse and uncritical thinking. Most commonly it takes the form of a rather crudely applied correspondence theory, the ideas under study are assumed to be characteristic of some faction, group, class or type to which the thinker allegedly belonged, and it is then explained how the ideas express the interests, hopes, fears or rationalizations characteristic of the group. The danger here is that of arguing in a circle. It is often very difficult to identify without ambiguity the social membership of an individual, still harder that of an idea— consciousness being the contradictory thing it is—and one tends to buttress the assumption one is making about the social position of the thinker with the assumptions one is making about the social significance of his ideas, and them to repeat the procedure in reverse by a thoroughly deplorable perversion of critical method." John Pocock, *Politics, Language and Time: Essays on Political Thought and History* (Chicago: The University of Chicago Press, 1989), 105. In the end, socio-economic explanations are not less tautological than the culturalist ones. Paraphrasing Knight, they take the form of "if a revolution did not take place, it was because there were not the social and economic conditions for it to be realized (or, conversely, if it took place, it was because there were the socio-economic conditions for it)."

14 MISPLACED IDEAS?

possible to speak about a "ring" because the space between these rocks and Saturn's surface also contains infinite small bodies, not visible from Earth.[37]

Now, the same can be said of cultures. That the multitude of men and women, from diverse generations, cultural backgrounds, regions, social positions, etc., that inhabit that subcontinent, form a single culture, and share the same *ethos* may be merely a luminous illusion when seen from afar, and that, as soon as we come closer, becomes revealed as such. In any case, this is undecidable for history. As Edmundo O'Gorman indicated, whether there are richer and poorer countries, more and less democratic governments, etc., are all questions that can be discussed and analyzed on empirical bases. Instead, the affirmation that this is the result of a cultural determination is unverifiable in practice; that statement leads us beyond the realm of history to an ontological field of eternal essences and *a priori* ideas, of "entelechies":

> Little is the distance between characterizing as "spirit" what is conceived as "essence." And thus, despite its location in the historical future, Ibero-America turns out to be an entity in itself or by nature "idealistic," and Anglo-America, an entity in itself or by nature "pragmatic." Two entities, then, that although they realize their way of being in history, are [sic] as entelechies of the power of their respective essences; two entities, let's say, that like a centaur and a unicorn are historical without really being so.[38]

Nothing impedes one from postulating the presence of that kind of entelechies, but history has nothing to say about them—and, as Wittgenstein said (*Tractatus*, proposal 7), "of which it is not possible to speak, it is better to remain silent."

The "Models" in Question

The ultimate question that the history of "ideas" raises is, rather, how *not to speak* of a "local culture," how not to refer ideas in Latin America back to some supposed cultural substratum that explains the local system of its "deviations" and "distortions." The "culturalist school," as such, has actually been marginal in the field of Latin American studies. It basically represents

---

[37] Bernard Bailyn, *The Peopling of British North America: An Introduction* (New York: Random House, 1989), 47–49.

[38] Edmundo O'Gorman, *México. El trauma de su historia* (Mexico: UNAM, 1977), 69.

THE HISTORY OF THE "HISTORY OF IDEAS" 15

an attempt in American academy aimed at overcoming the prevailing prejudices with respect to Latin American culture and to understand it "in its own terms"[39] which, in last instance, only leads to uncritically replicate all the stereotypes about it. However, even though the "culturalist school" is marginal among students in the field, the reference of the Latin American history of ideas to the peculiarities of the "local culture" (that allegedly make it contradictory with the liberal principles) constitutes a universal practice. Beyond its culturalist origin, Hale's statement that "the distinctive experience of liberalism derived from the fact that liberal ideas were applied in countries which were highly stratified, socially and racially, as well as economically underdeveloped, and in which the tradition of centralized state authority ran deep"[40] appears to historians as an indisputable truth. This truism goes well beyond this school forming an essential part of the "common sense" in the profession.

This situation prevented the very interrogation on the deviations of the local culture from liberal principles from coming under critical scrutiny. The point is that such a reference to the local culture comes to meet a conceptual demand in the discipline; it fills a hole within a given grid, a nod in a theoretical network. "Latin American particularities" work in it as the objective, material substratum in which the abstract forms of the "ideal types" come to be impressed and incarnated in actual history; they presumably render concrete the generic categories of the history of ideas, thus making relevant the study of them in the local context.

In effect, within the frameworks of the history of "ideas," without "local peculiarities," without "deviations," the analysis of the evolution of ideas in Latin America lacks any sense (as Zea said, Mexico and all the Mexican authors "can be spared"). Nevertheless, as J. G. A. Pocock says, this procedure fails to rescue the historian of ideas "from the circumstance that the intellectual constructs he/she was trying to control were not historical phenomena at all, to the extent which they had been built up to by non-historical modes of inquiry."[41] On the one hand, the "models" of thought (the "ideal types"), considered in themselves, appear as perfectly consistent, logically integrated, and, therefore, *a priori* definable. Even though nobody has ever said what the

---

[39] Wiarda, *Politics and Social Change*, 353.

[40] Charles Hale, "Political and Social Ideas in Latin America, 1870–1930," in *The Cambridge History of Latin America. From c. 1870 to 1930*, ed. Leslie Bethell, vol. 4 (Cambridge: Cambridge University Press, 1989), 368.

[41] Pocock, *Politics, Language, and Time*, 11.

16   MISPLACED IDEAS?

model states, this does not affect the model itself; in any case, the problem would be of the author or authors at stake who have failed to formulate that doctrine in a consistent manner; in sum, as the old saying goes, if reality does not fit theory, too bad for reality. On the other hand, local cultures, as permanent substrata (like the Hispanic *ethos*), are, by definition, static essences. The result is thus a pseudo-historical narrative that connects two abstractions.

Ultimately, "cultural matrixes" are nothing but the necessary counterpart of the "ideal types" of the historiography of political ideas. This explains why questioning the culturalist approaches is not enough to get rid of the essentialist appellations to tradition and local cultures as the explanatory principle in the last instance. It is necessary to penetrate and undermine the epistemological assumptions on which those appellations are based; that is, to critically scrutinize the very "models" that in the local history of ideas work simply as an unquestionable premise, a given. Ultimately, the questioning of cultural stereotypes on which the scheme of "models" and "deviations" hinges inevitably leads us beyond the boundaries of Latin American intellectual history and forces us to confront that which constitutes an *inherent limit* to the whole tradition of history of "ideas": the "ideal types." At this point, we also meet the ultimate limit of Hale's revisionism.

Although Hale's approach breaks the parochialism of the local historiography of ideas and locates the contradictions observed in Mexican liberal thought on a broader context, he nevertheless preserves the same antinomies on which the old history of "ideas" was founded, introducing these contradictions at the bosom of the liberal tradition itself. All that which hitherto had been seen as clearly anti-liberal, a Latin American "oddity" (centralism, authoritarianism, organicism, etc.) comes now to integrate the definition of a liberalism-that-is-not-truly-liberal ("French liberalism"), as opposed to another liberalism-that-is-authentically-liberal ("English liberalism"). This perspective, however, would soon find itself deprived from the conceptual ground on which it had hitherto rested.

In the very same year when Hale published *Mexican Liberalism in the Age of Mora*, the American academy witnessed the initiation of the demolition process of the model proposed by Hartz, triggered by the publication of *The Ideological Origins of the American Revolution* (1967) by Bailyn.[42] As we have seen, for Hartz, the liberal and democratic principles that presided over the

---

[42] Bernard Bailyn, *The Ideological Origins of the American Revolution* (Cambridge: Harvard University Press, 1992).

THE HISTORY OF THE "HISTORY OF IDEAS" 17

American Revolution of Independence incarnated the true essence of the political culture of that country. However, when analyzing the pamphlets of the epoch, Baylin discovered in the revolutionary discourse the presence of a conceptual universe very different from the liberal one, an older and longer-lasting tradition that he defined as "civic humanist." This perspective shortly became so popular that civic humanism, redefined by Gordon Wood[43] and Pocock[44] as "classical republicanism," will end up displacing "liberalism" as the alleged matrix of fundamental thought that identifies the American universe of political ideas.

At that moment, as an echo of the debates in American academy, also Latin American historians of ideas started to appeal to the concept of "republicanism," and its opposition to that of "liberalism," as the fundamental key to understand the political-intellectual history in the region. However, and paradoxically, they believed to find in it that which supposedly identifies the most proper to Latin American thinking—an opposition to the "liberal" tradition in America. Thus, all that hitherto had been seen as organicist, antidemocratic, and so on, now would be placed under the label of "republicanism."[45]

In this fashion, these attempts to update the terms of the debate end up replicating the traditional oppositions in the Latin American history of ideas, only changing their denominations, and thereby missing the core of the transformation then produced. Ultimately, these new developments rendered problematic the traditional narratives which had remained firmly embedded in the perspective theorized by Hartz that opposed the supposedly inherently liberal tradition of that country to the postulated ill-adjustment of the liberal ideals in its Southern counterpart (an opposition that has been the matrix of the classic of "models" and "deviations").

In effect, the debate on "republicanism" ended up undermining the different definitions regarding liberalism (and its differences with republicanism), forcing successive reformulations of it—none of which are free from fundamental objections. Nevertheless, these complexities are unassimilable

[43] Gordon Wood, *The Creation of the American Republic* (Chapel Hill: University of North Carolina Press, 1969).

[44] J. G. A. Pocock, *The Machiavellian Moment: Florentine Political Thought and the Atlantic Republican Tradition* (Princeton: Princeton University Press, 1975).

[45] See Natalio Botana, *La tradición republicana. Alberdi, Sarmiento y las ideas políticas de su tiempo* (Buenos Aires: Sudamericana, 1984); Natalio Botana, *La libertad política y su historia* (Buenos Aires: Sudamericana, 1991); Oscar Terán, *Historia de las ideas en Argentina, Diez lecciones, 1810 = 1980* (Buenos Aires: Siglo XXI, 2008).

18 MISPLACED IDEAS?

for the Latin American history of ideas. It necessarily entails clearly delimited and well-defined models. Once they begin to lose their previous transparency, and their definitions are rendered problematic, the entire scheme of "models" and "deviations" inevitably crumbles. Textbook definitions, simplistic by nature, are thus uncritically taken there as valid. We thus obtain the paradox that, currently, the only ones who know (or believe they know) what, for example, "Locke's liberalism" is, are the Latin American historians of ideas, while there is no agreement on that among the specialists in the topic.[46] And this is necessarily so because, otherwise, there would be no way of discussing in what sense native liberalism departed from its premises. To put it briefly, if we no longer know what "to be liberal" means, if we question the validity of the "ideal type," we will never get to the point at stake: whether or not Mora or Alberdi were true liberals. Conversely, if we intend to discuss the latter, we cannot get into any complication regarding the models, to delve deeper into the problems that textbook definitions of them raise.

Here we get to the fundamental problem in the old tradition of the history of ideas. Ultimately, beyond the differences regarding the contents of its narratives, the goal around which the whole revisionist enterprise revolves is actually the same as that of the history of "ideas": looking for the ways in which European (particularly, liberal) ideas, once translated and superimposed on Latin American reality (one supposedly alien and, in many regards, hostile to them), "deviated" in ways not always compatible with their original models, upon which they, therefore, frequently inflicted violence. The result of the collision between the native traditionalist culture (the so-called Hispanic *ethos*) and the universal principles of liberalism was a kind of compromised ideology that José Luis Romero termed "liberal-conservative."[47]

Now, it is clear that neither conservatism nor the mixture of liberalism and conservatism are something exclusive to Latin America, an ideological formation that cannot be found in any other region. And this leads to an unsolvable problem. On the one hand, within its frameworks, if we cannot find any particular trait identifying local thought, and distinguishing it from that of any other region, its study will become pointless (Latin American thinkers "can well be spared [*salen sobrando*]," in Zea's words). But, on the other hand, it is radically unable to find their presumably particular traits. To postulate

[46] On the disagreements among the specialists, see John Dunn, *The Political Thought of John Locke: An Historical Account of the Argument of the "Two Treatises of Government"* (Cambridge: Cambridge University Press, 1995).

[47] José Luis Romero, *Las ideas políticas en Argentina* (Buenos Aires: FCE, 1975).

the finding of a "Latin American peculiarity," whatever that may be, these approaches must simplify the history of European ideas, smoothing over the intricacies of its actual course. But, even then, they could hardly find a way to describe the postulated "idiosyncrasies" with "non-European categories."

In this fashion, this tradition of the "history of ideas" generates an anxiety for peculiarity that it can never satisfy. The very approaches prevent it: if considered from the perspective of its ideological content, every system of thought necessarily falls within a limited range of alternatives. They will necessarily be either organicist or individualist, or, eventually, a mixture between organicist and individualist, either liberal or conservative, or eventually, a mixture between liberal and conservative, none of which can aspire to be exclusive to Latin America. In sum, *the history of ideas leads to a dead end*. Having to postulate a goal which is unattainable within its framework undermines the very foundations of this undertaking. Thus, in the Latin American context, a "history of ideas" appears as either unfeasible or irrelevant.

This sends us back to our original problem: If not one based on the scheme of "models" and "deviations," what kind of approaches may render meaningful the study of ideas of so-called derivative areas of Western culture? This is what we explore in the following chapters.

PART I

THEORETICAL APPROACHES

The Emergence of Latin Americanist Radicalism:
A Case of Inverted Orientalism?

In the 1960s and 1970s, contemporarily to the first "revisionist" currents, more radical approaches developed and spread over the region: "Latin American philosophy" and "dependency theory." Their points of departure were the same as the "history of ideas": the need to define the peculiar characteristic of thinking in the context of a "derivative" culture. But their conceptual references were expanded to incorporate new perspectives and approaches.

The former current of thought, Latin American philosophy, can be considered the local counterpart to the "culturalist school" in American academy. It was a kind of critical expansion of the original project of a history of Latin American ideas. As we have seen in Chapter 1, the philosophical background behind the interpretive model elaborated by Zea was Ortega y Gasset's "circumstancialism," which was a re-elaboration of German phenomenology and existentialism. Latin Americanist thinkers, in turn, will incorporate other heuristic tools taken mainly from the post-phenomenological and Marxist currents that emerged in the postwar years, rendering their views somehow more sophisticated and complex in theoretical terms than those of the history of ideas. Now, while Latin American philosophy relied on these more expanded "European" conceptual references, at the same time, it was very critical of them. From its perspective, thinking in the periphery of Western culture has a revelatory function, it undermines the rationality and unity of the ideologies prevailing at the center, laying bare their perverse (imperialistic) core. In this fashion, this current intended to detach Latin American culture and ideas from the marginal place in which the history of ideas had secluded it, thereby rendering the study of it relevant

22 THEORETICAL APPROACHES

for intellectual history at large; that is, raising questions whose relevance transcend the merely local context.

This sends us back again to our original question, the one pending from the former chapter: If not the approaches based on the scheme of "models" and "deviations," what kind of approaches may render meaningful the study of ideas of so-called derivative areas of Western culture? As we have seen in that chapter, if we intend to break with the essentialist and teleological approaches to the history of ideas in Latin America, we should first critically undermine the very epistemological grounds on which those approaches are founded. Ultimately, we should set under scrutiny the consistency and rationality of the "models" themselves. Now, it is exactly what the founders and cultivators of Latin American philosophy intended to do. Yet, paradoxically, far from breaking with the essentialism and teleologism of the history of ideas, Latin American philosophy reinforced it.

In effect, as we will see, this current reverts the terms of the antinomy, preserving the binary scheme. Instead of departing from the basic premise of the history of ideas that conceives it as a kind of eternal struggle between antagonistic models, what Latin American philosophy does is radicalize that perception. In the first two chapters of Part I (Chapters 2 and 3 of the book), we will discuss, respectively, the two main lines in which Latin American philosophy deploys: the historicist and the phenomenological. In them, I intend to unravel the structure of their discourses, to recreate both that common ground from which the two could display, and the divergent conceptual paths that they will, respectively, follow. As we will see, these trends can be seen as bifurcations from a given régime of knowledge that underlies the two of them. Yet, that régime of knowledge does not define a consistent model. Its configuration is rather labyrinth-like, as it is traversed by forking paths that intercross and diverge. Hence the lines that each author and current will follow were not pre-established, as in the case of the "model of thinking," and can only be reconstructed by analyzing their very productions. This archeological ground of knowledge sends us back to a realm from which discourses emerge but precedes them; like the sea on which Icarus fell, it allows the articulation of ideas but does not contain them.

In the third and final chapter of this Part (Chapter 4 of the book), we will analyze Roberto Schwarz's reformulation of the topic of "misplaced ideas," which postulates that foreign, European ideas are not suitable to express local reality, that they result in distorted representations of it. Actually, the dependency theory was not originally conceived to be applied to the cultural field, although it shortly expanded to encompass that realm, too. In addition, on this level, it coincided in some points with Latin American philosophy. However, the approaches to culture from the perspective of dependency theory stood in opposition to the latter. Its cultivators aimed to counter the essentialist assumptions underlying the nationalist and Latin Americanist currents of thought in all their different versions.[1]

Here lies Schwarz's fundamental contribution. He will appeal to the tenets of dependency theory to elaborate an innovative approach to the question of the problematic dynamics of ideological production and circulation of ideas in the "peripheral" areas of Western culture. Far from conceiving Latin American culture as a separate entity from it, he conceives the latter as an integral and constitutive part of the former. Hence, as he insists, we will never find in the local history of ideas any idea that is exclusive to it. And this perception radically reframes the issue of how to render meaningful the study of ideas in the "periphery" of Western culture. Once we renounce the expectation of finding "local deviations" of the "(foreign) models," our original question reemerges: What is the point of studying it? As we will see, the views based on the "dependency theory" provide some clues to re-elaborate the issue from a perspective removed from the scheme of the "models" and "deviations," one that, conveniently reformulated, could eventually help us to break with the essentialist and teleological assumptions permeating the old tradition of history of ideas, as well as its sequel, Latin American philosophy. Lastly, the latter can be seen as a kind of "inverted Orientalism."

Latin Americanism as an Inverted Orientalism

In *Critique of Latin American Reason*, Santiago Castro-Gómez establishes a relationship between his proposal and that of Edward Said's in *Orientalism*, which, I understand, expresses very well the object to which the chapters included in this first part is oriented.[2] In *Orientalism*, Said shows how a discourse regarding the East was produced in Europe as its "other," or that which is located outside of modern Western rationality, and in contrast to which it will define itself. Castro-Gómez, in turn, takes up this idea, but inverted

---

[1] For a criticism of it, see Oscar Terán, "Sobre la historia intelectual," in *De utopías, catástrofes y esperanzas. Un camino intelectual* (Buenos Aires: Siglo XXI, 2006).
[2] Santiago Castro-Gómez, *Crítica de la razón latinoamericana* (Bogota: Pontificia Universidad Javeriana, 2011).

24 THEORETICAL APPROACHES

it. His aim is to analyze how an orientalist discourse is produced in the East itself, the phenomenon of self-exoticization, the self-construction of itself as the other in Europe, although, in this case, in reference not to the East, but to Latin America.

As Said says, "the Orient is not an inert natural fact, just as the Occident is not just there either"[3]—it is a conceptual construction. Yet, Karl Marx's statement, on which Said relied, that "they cannot represent themselves, they must be represented," would not be completely true.[4] The "Orient" would indeed represent itself as the "Orient." Nonetheless, the recreation of the series of conceptual operations by which, in this case, Latin America was constructed as the "other" of Europe indeed entails taking a critical distance from its very object, from the idea of the existence of a Latin American "being," and the assumption that it is "natural fact," something that is "just there." It thus implies transcending the level of the explicit contents of the discourses under consideration, avoiding simply reproducing what their very authors affirm in their texts, their self-representations, and penetrating and reconstructing that epistemic ground on which this particular type of discursivity is sustained. In short, it is necessary to disclose the contingent nature of its foundations, and to recreate the historical-conceptual conditions that made it possible.

More precisely stated, we should unravel the mechanisms by which a certain place of *Truth* is instituted, that which will function in each case as an *arkhē*, the alleged instance in which the own identity becomes fully revealed, in which the meaning and sense of the inner being becomes transparent to itself.[5] But also, and above all, what would prevent these narratives from stabilizing its discursive régime, the lines of fissure that run through it. And, eventually, we may propose possible reformulations of the traditional approaches to the mechanisms of appropriation and circulation of ideas in

---

[3] Edward Said, *Orientalism* (London: Routledge and Kegan Paul Ltd., 1980), 12.

[4] Karl Marx, *The Eighteenth Brumaire of Louis Bonaparte* (London: Pluto Press, 2002), 155; quoted by Said, *Orientalism*, 8.

[5] As Edmundo O'Gorman stated: "Those who ask about their identity already know who they are, but for some reason are not satisfied with what they are, with the beings they are, and from that unbearable uneasiness rises the desire for identification and, in consequence, the anxiety of searching for another form of being which certainly cannot help but fully satisfy them and in whose regard there is no room for any doubt, that is, an essential mode of being. Thus, what lies behind that eager search is the search for an essence, the Latin American essence, the solid bedrock, impregnable before any contingency in the mode of being that is wanted to be." Edmundo O'Gorman, "Latinoamérica: así no," *Nexos* 123 (1988): 13; quoted by Carlos Altamirano, *La invención de Nuestra América. Obsesiones, narrativas y debates sobre la identidad de América Latina* (Buenos Aires: Siglo XXI, 2021), 23.

peripheral areas that permit integrating the local and regional processes within a broader stage, and analyzing the system of transnational, symbolic exchange in a more problematic, and more productive, fashion than the views founded on the topic of "misplacedideas," which is, in the last instance, the one that underlies all the different versions of philosophical Latin Americanism.

2

Latin American Philosophy I

The Historicist Line in the Genealogical Looking Glass

In 1971, Cuban Roberto Fernández Retamar published a text proposing an interpretation of Shakespeare's *The Tempest* that was very different from that offered by Rodó in 1900. His re-interpretation is symptomatic of the historical-conceptual transformations undergone in the meanwhile. As we have seen, Rodó's work had arisen in the context of the reaction against the advance of the US imperialist policy in times of the "Big Stick." Rodó then revisited *The Tempest* to posit the idea of an opposition between the figures of Ariel and Caliban. In his interpretation, *Ariel* was the incarnation of Latin American spiritualism in opposition to the pragmatic and materialistic worldview, the North American desire for domination, that was embodied in Caliban. Seventy-one years later, Fernández Retamar took up these same figures but inverted their relationship. Caliban, an anagram for cannibal, would refer, for Fernández Retamar, to the (cannibal) natives that the first conquerors met on the Caribbean coasts. He considers that it is this, the subjected and humiliated slave, condemned to an animal condition and despised as monstrous, and not Ariel, who would truly express the Latin American being.

Fernández Retamar's reading synthesizes the changes produced in the transition from the history of ideas to Latin American philosophy. The latter not only looked for what distinguishes Latin American thought from European thought, its "local deviations" vis-à-vis "imported models." It radicalized its approach interpreting these presumed deviations as manifestations of a rebellion against its dominated condition, and also as an expression of popular feeling in opposition to the literate elite's abstract mind (which stands in contrast with the aristocratic bent in Rodó's text).

From this perspective, the liberation of Latin America would be the revenge of Caliban. In *The Tempest*, Prospero, the conqueror, exiled and condemned the brute Caliban to slavery. But Prospero also imposed his tongue on Caliban, and, in this way, Caliban also learned to curse his master.

Misplaced Ideas?. Elías J. Palti, Oxford University Press. © Oxford University Press 2024.
DOI: 10.1093/oso/9780197556641.003.0002

28   THEORETICAL APPROACHES

In the same fashion, for Latin Americanist philosophy, it will not be about despising European knowledge and rejecting it, but of appropriating it, engulfing it, cannibalizing it, and thus turning European knowledge against itself, converting it from an instrument of oppression into a weapon for its own liberation.

This project will become very attractive for an important segment of the Latin American *intelligentsia*, which will give rise to "Latin American philosophy," otherwise called "Liberation philosophy." Its diffusion is closely associated with the triumph of the Cuban revolution and the anti-colonialist movements in Africa and Asia. It must thus be inscribed within the political and intellectual climate of the time, although, as is always the case with each new current of thought, its cultivators will posit it having deeper roots in local culture. They will thus search for its origins back in time, placing them especially in the spiritualist tendencies of the first decades of the twentieth century, although some of them indeed will affirm that the foundations of a proper Latin American philosophy were already prefigured in the pre-Hispanic past.

The formal beginning of this trend was the result of a series of meetings organized in Argentina. The first took place within the framework of the Second National Congress of Philosophy in 1971 (which followed the First National Congress of Philosophy in 1949, which closed with the presentation of a document by Juan Domingo Perón, *The Organized Community*).[1] The second meeting was the so-called Encuentro de San Miguel, organized that same year by Enrique Dussel and Juan Carlos Scannone at the Universidad del Salvador (since its inception, Latin American philosophy has been closely linked to Liberation theology). These annual meetings continued until 1975, and it was in the third one that the controversy between Zea and Salazar Bondy took place, marking an important milestone in the definition of the program to be followed by the historicist line, as we will see later.

In the following years, various meetings were organized in other countries, the most important of which was the "Morelia Encounter" in 1975, that culminated in the drafting of a manifesto, the "Declaration of Morelia." In it converged the different trends present in that group, which then tried to reconcile their differences. However, these differences will subsequently

---

[1] On this, see Marcelo González, "El año-evento 1971 y sus ondas expansivas," in *La explosión liberacionista en la filosofía latinoamericana. Aportes iniciales de Enrique Dussel y Juan Carlos Scannone 1964–1972*, ed. Marcelo González and Luciano Maddonni (Buenos Aires: Teseo, 2020), 269–400.

become more noticeable, giving rise to a series of controversies. These different trends can be grouped into two major categories: the historicist, whose main representatives were Leopoldo Zea and Arturo Roig; and the phenomenological, embodied especially in the figures of Rodolfo Kusch and Enrique Dussel.[2]

The emergence of Latin Americanist philosophy was an important event in Latin American intellectual history, although it has been largely neglected by scholarly students, in part because it will shortly lose its prestige in the academic milieu. Hence, most of the available studies on it tend to replicate the image that this very current forged of itself, to reproduce its own particular ideology without trying to penetrate the conceptual premises on which it was founded, which is what we will intend to do in the following pages.

From the History of Ideas to Latin American Philosophy

A key figure in the transition from the history of ideas to Latin American philosophy was, once again, Zea.[3] His subsequent trajectory to *El positivismo en México* illustrates this transition. In 1948, Zea founded the *Hiperión* group, together with Ricardo Guerra, Joaquín Macgregor, Jorge Portilla, Salvador Reyes Narváez, Emilio Uranga, Fausto Vega, and Luis Villoro, a group that gathered from 1952 on at the Center for Latin American Studies, at the UNAM. These institutional achievements were possible, largely, thanks to Zea's closeness to the PRI, the governing party, from which he received fundamental support. This institutional setting served as a basis to carry out the project of recovering and giving expression to the "authentic" Latin American intellectual tradition.

As I indicated above, an important milestone in the definition of his intellectual project was the controversy that arose after Zea's publication in 1969 of *Filosofía americana como filosofía sin más*,[4] in which he responded to a book that had appeared a year earlier, *¿Hay una filosofía de Nuestra América?*, by Peruvian Augusto Salazar Bondy.[5] In this later book, Bondy deployed a

---

[2] For a minute description of the different currents, authors, and perspectives in Latin American philosophy, see Carlos Beorlegui, *Historia del pensamiento latinoamericano. Una búsqueda incesante de la identidad* (Bilbao: Deusto, 2010).

[3] See Adriana Arpini, *Tramas e itinerarios. Entre la filosofía práctica e historia de las ideas en Nuestra América* (Buenos Aires: Teseo Editores, 2020).

[4] Leopoldo Zea, *La filosofía latinoamericana como filosofía sin más* (Mexico: Siglo XXI, 1969).

[5] Augusto Salazar Bondy, *¿Existe una filosofía de Nuestra América?* (Mexico: Siglo XXI, 1968).

30   THEORETICAL APPROACHES

rather pessimistic view on the intellectual potential of local thinking, at least, in its present state. He distinguished then between dependency and domination, as the latter involved not only a political but also a mental colonization. The dominated condition thus generated "masking myths" in the local population that prevented it from perceiving its actual situation, rendering it impossible to elaborate a proper tradition of thought.

In *Filosofía americana como filosofía sin más*, Zea contended with Bondy, arguing that the reflection on the dependent condition does not preclude local philosophy to gain a universal dimension. For Zea, Bondy's position replicated the typically Eurocentric view that denied Latin Americans the capacity to develop a proper, authentic thought, or whose worth could be comparable to the thought of any other region.[6] And, for him, this problem went beyond the merely theoretical realm, having practical consequences whose reach transcended the local context. An authentic Latin American thinking, says Zea, will spring from our capacity "to face our problems, and from trying to find a solution to them which can increase the feasibility of realizing the *New Man*."[7]

This is also Zea's answer to the revisionists' criticism. For Charles Hale, in his shift from "history of ideas" to "Latin American philosophy," Zea deepened the characteristic *pathos* of the former tradition that resulted from the immaturity of local thinking and the weak professionalization of intellectual labor in the region: the subordination of the demands of historical accuracy and objectivity to current, practical (mainly political) considerations.[8] For Zea, instead, it is precisely in it that the superiority of Latin American philosophy lies vis-à-vis Western rationalism, the canonical forms of (European) thinking: its vocation and capacity to not merely comprehend local reality, but also to put that knowledge at the service of the

---

[6] "What kind of men are we," asked Zea, "that we are not able to create a system, that we are not able to originate a philosopher similar to those that have been and are fundamental in the history of philosophy? This question will be at the center of the problem." Zea, *La filosofía latinoamericana como filosofía sin más*, 11.

[7] Zea, *La filosofía latinoamericana como filosofía sin más*, 153.

[8] A similar criticism was realized by Luis Villoro in *Perfil de México en 1980* (Mexico: Siglo XXI, 1972), although, in a later work, he introduced some nuances in his criticism of Zea. See Luis Villoro, *Sobre el problema de la filosofía latinoamericana* (Mexico: Siglo XXI, 1983), William D. Raat, instead, was more drastic. For him, Zea's embracement of philosophical Latin Americanism entailed a metaphysical turn. "What started as a modest attempt to understand historical thinking," he said, "turns into a speculative activity in which the presence of a superior entity is affirmed that is not subordinated to an objective analysis of the role of ideas in history." William D. Raat, "Ideas e historia en México, un ensayo sobre metodología," *Latinoamérica. Anuario de Estudios Latinoamericanos* 3 (1970): 175–188, quoted by Leopoldo Zea, *Filosofía de la historia americana* (Mexico: FCE, 1978), 23.

LATIN AMERICAN PHILOSOPHY I   31

transformation of said reality. Actually, Latin American philosophy resulted from the combination of the anxiety over the disclosure of the authentic "Latin American being" with the "ethic of engagement" which was widespread in the intellectual milieu of the time.[9] In any case, it is true that the allegedly "objective" and "neutral" vantage point of American scholars did not prevent them from relapsing into the very metaphysical terrain which they denounced as marring the views of their Latin American counterparts, as is the case of the idea of a "Hispanic *ethos*," in which, as we have seen in the first chapter, they believed to have found the last explanation for all historical developments in the region up to the present. However, it does not mean that their criticism of Zea's project was totally invalid.

Latin American Philosophy: Its Main Premises

There was a basic tension in Zea's project of a history of Latin American ideas that he left unsolved and, as we will see, would become critical in the process of its transformation into Latin American philosophy. On the one hand, Zea affirmed that the object of the history of Latin American ideas was to identify what particularizes them vis-à-vis European ideas. And, on the other hand, he insisted that it was not alien to universal (Western) thinking, but a particular manifestation of it.[10] For Zea, these two statements were not contradictory, but rather complementary. We meet here the first topic established by him that will serve as a basis for Latin American philosophy: that the elaboration of a proper thinking did not entail the rejection of Western, canonical thinking, but demanded its appropriation.[11] This topic will subsequently be replicated over and over, under different rubrics. Indeed, the most radical

---

[9] See Leopoldo Zea, *La filosofía como compromiso y otros ensayos* (Mexico: FCE, 1952).

[10] As he already stated in his seminal essay, "En torno a una filosofía americana" (1942): "The American must not be considered as an end in itself, but as the limit of a broader end. Hence the reason why any attempt of doing an American philosophy with the sole pretense that it is American was doomed to failure. We must do philosophy pure and simple, that the American will be given by addition." Leopoldo Zea, "En torno a una filosofía americana," in *El ensayo mexicano moderno*, ed. José Luis Martínez (México: FCE, 1958), 296. Zea's text originally appeared in *Cuadernos Americanos* 1 (1942): 63–78.

[11] This point was articulated in different fashions. Francisco Miró Quesada defined it as a middle point between "Latin Americanism" and "Universalism." Francisco Miró Quesada, "Universalismo y latinoamericanismo," *Isegoría* 18 (1998): 61–78. Luis Villoro took up Ortega y Gasset's opposition between "alterity" and "*ensimismamiento*." The conciliation of the two terms he called "*parasimismamiento*." Luis Villoro, "¿Es posible una comunidad filosófica iberoamericana?," *Isegoría* 18 (1998): 53–60].

32   THEORETICAL APPROACHES

impugners of Western knowledge, such as Rodolfo Kusch, insisted on its necessary "phagocytation."[12]

This leads to the second premise he established. For Zea, it is in this very process of assimilation of "foreign" ideas that the Latin American being is revealed. Going back to the case of positivism, which then turned into a kind of *sinecdoque* of Western rationalism at large, Zea states that, despite their imitative drive, Latin American positivists were, in their own fashion, "authentic." He finds the expression of authenticity, "paradoxically, in the affirmation that adoption could have originated bad copies of the adopted models."[13] The fact of being "bad copies," of "not faithfully replicating the proposed models," reveals that "over this supposed imitation, again and again, was imprinted the reality of the one who imitates."[14]

Thus, the very reading of the Western cannon from the periphery would already entail a work upon it.[15] It is thus that from the reflection on the universal emanates the particular. Conversely, from the reflection on the particular condition emanates the universal. Latin American thought thereby could find a proper place within Western philosophical tradition. This was, precisely, Zea's point of contention with Bondy. For him, there was an intimate (dialectical, he would say) connection between the two terms of the equation, which operates in a double direction: from the universal to the particular and from the particular to the universal. Yet, all his elaborations were addressed to explain how the particular emerges out of the universal. As Luis Villoro remarked, he never explained how this dialectic works the other way around, how from the very reflection from the perspective of the Latin American condition emerges a universal thought, and what the alleged place of local thinking was within Western philosophical tradition.[16] If he did not,

---

[12] See Rodolfo Kusch, *América profunda* (Buenos Aires: Biblos, 1999).

[13] Zea, *Filosofía de la historia americana*, 18.

[14] Zea, *Filosofía de la historia americana*, 18.

[15] On this, see Silviano Santiago, *Uma Literatura nos trópicos* (São Paulo: Editora Perspectiva, 1978).

[16] As Luis Villoro remarked: "But that movement was left in a conceptual dilemma. Achieving an authentic Latin American philosophy was conceived in terms of a contraposition of concepts: the proper versus the foreign, or the particular versus the universal. It seems that only a thought of what distinguishes us could be authentic, a thought referring to our 'circumstance,' but the particular would be a way of reaching the universal. Unfortunately, it was never sufficiently clear what the relationship was between the circumstance and the 'universal.' The way in which something universal would be achieved from the examination of a concrete object was never specified. It cannot be through an inductive operation because in no logic is it valid to induce the universal notes of a class of objects from a singular case. Nor can we think of an eidetic abstraction, in which an essence is captured from the examination of a single specimen, because Zea expressly rejected an 'essence' of man. The opposition between the singular-concrete and the universal is not resolved." Luis Villoro, "Leopoldo Zea: La posibilidad de una filosofía latinoamericana," in *México, entre libros. Pensadores del siglo XX* (Mexico: El Colegio Nacional/FCE, 1995), 93.

it was because he simply took it for granted; paraphrasing him, it "will be given by addition."[17]

However, the connection between these two terms would shortly become problematic. The anxiety in finding a proper place for Latin American philosophy within Western philosophical tradition would be denounced as a typical expression of a "colonized" mind. In fact, Latin American philosophy was founded on the assumption of a radical, irreconcilable antinomy between "alienation" and "authenticity," terms which would express, respectively, the "discourse of oppression" and the "discourse of emancipation." Zea himself then denounced what Antonio Caso called "Bovarism"; that is, the anxiety of Latin Americans to be something different from what they actually are. Whereas for authors such as Alfonso Reyes, who postulated in *La última Tule* that the fact that the mind of Latin Americans was oriented to the future (the promise of a future liberation) made it the place of utopia, for Zea it led them to reject their present state and to ignore their past.[18]

As we have seen, Zea's conclusion, unlike Bondy's, was not pessimistic regarding the prospect of the achievement of a proper thinking in Latin America. Anyway, at this point, it became clear that it could not be a spontaneous emanation from the local reality itself, as he had formerly insisted in connection with the case of Mexican positivism. If the elaboration of a proper thought was still not impossible, it indeed demanded an intellectual effort aimed at breaking the chains of foreign categories and elaborating their own ones, which would be, more precisely, the self-imposed mission of Latin Americanist philosophers.

This, besides, was not conceived as a merely intellectual endeavor. The whole destiny of the subcontinent was, presumably, at stake. Here, we find the second fundamental tension that traverses this project of a Latin American philosophy. The first was that between the particular and the universal. The second is between expression and transformation, immanence and transcendence.[19] On the one hand, the thinkers associated to this current claimed to merely echo the voices of the local population. On the other hand,

---

[17] Leopoldo Zea, "En torno a una filosofía americana," 296.

[18] Leopoldo Zea, *El pensamiento latinoamericano* (Barcelona: Ariel, 1976), 23.

[19] On this topic, see an interesting comparison between Ezequiel Martínez Estrada's and Leopoldo Zea's views by Andrés Kozel, "Dos tratamientos de lo trascendente en el latinoamericanismo clásico: Ezequiel Martínez Estrada y Leopoldo Zea" [online]. Presentation at the Congress: "Diálogos. Literatura, Estética y Teología. La libertad del Espíritu" (Buenos Aires: Universidad Católica Argentina, 2013). https://repositorio.uca.edu.ar/bitstream/123456789/4818/1/dos-tratamientos-trascendente.pdf

34 THEORETICAL APPROACHES

however, they considered these societies as alienated and locked within the cage of dominant, foreign ideologies. And it is necessarily so, as otherwise the very emancipatory project would be pointless.

This latter tension will shortly prove indeed more crucial than the former, giving rise to the emergence of its different internal trends. In the last instance, it would make manifest the simultaneous necessity and impossibility of a proper thinking in the context of a culturally dependent society (Zea's and Bondy's postures, respectively). The entire production of both the historicist and the phenomenological lines of Latin American philosophy can be considered as a series of different attempts to tackle that double impasse: between the particular and the universal, and between immanence and transcendence. This is what we will see in the following discussion, beginning with the historicist line. However, we must first observe a third premise established by Zea that connects directly with this latter trend in philosophical Latin Americanism.

As seen in the previous chapter, one of the fundamental problems that the project of a Latin American history of ideas faced was the impossibility of finding any idea that particularized local thinking. Zea then tried to solve the issue by moving it to a different terrain. As he says in *La filosofía latinoamericana como filosofía sin más*, the fundamental difference between a history of ideas in Latin America and Latin American philosophy is that the latter did not seek merely to study the adaptation of European ideas to local reality but the very logic of this adaptation process.[20] And it is here that he found its originality.

Zea then goes back to Hegel's philosophy of history, which he considers unsuitable to understand the dynamics of local intellectual history. While European intellectual history follows the Hegelian logic of *Aufebhung*, in Latin America it follows a logic of *juxtaposition*. That is, the different conceptual frameworks follow and overlap one another without being sublated by a superior synthesis that comprehends them. This will be a recurrent topic among the authors in this tradition. Yet, Zea's view was still ambiguous in this regard. In his first elaborations he saw it as a liability rather than an asset. In any case, he still hoped that, in the near future, Latin America would

---

[20] In a subsequent book, *Dialéctica de la conciencia americana* (1976), Zea replied to his critics, especially to Willian Raat's "Ideas e historia en México. Un ensayo sobre metodología," justifying the anachronistic transposition intrinsic to his project of searching for a Latin American thinking as a kind of transhistorical entity, arguing that he did not look for facts but tried to understand their meaning. Leopoldo Zea, *Dialéctica de la conciencia americana* (Mexico: Alianza, 1976), 11.

overcome that situation so that the dynamics of local ideas would adjust to the Hegelian dialectical pattern.

The cultivators of Latin American philosophy will instead endorse a more radical view claiming that the differential logic of ideas in Latin America is not merely different from European ideas, and certainly not a deficient expression of it, but indeed superior to it. What concerns us here is that this view will have methodological consequences. In its attempt to overcome the fundamental problem in the tradition of history of ideas (determining which ideas particularized local thinking), Latin American philosophy will replicate and deepen a fallacy that was inherent in the former. In effect, it will produce an intellectual operation selecting—in an inevitably arbitrary manner—one particular philosophical system (Hegel's, Descartes', or whichever) and positing it as *the* expression of European thinking. It will thus be postulated as the epitome of the—allegedly perverse—modern rationality to which Latin American thinking comes to oppose. Lastly, all these essentialist views of Latin American thinking need to construct a similarly essentialist concept of European thinking as its counterpart, a "model" in opposition to which the former could define itself, be it as a "deviation" or an "overcoming" of it.

We come here to the core of the historicist project within Latin American philosophy. It will display simultaneously in a double direction. Basically, it intends to trace its own genealogy, to recover the precursory works of Latin Americanist thought. But, to do that, it will also have to elaborate a vision of the Western tradition which the former came to oppose, defining what its distinguishing features are, who its best representatives have been, etc. And both tasks are inextricably associated because the two philosophical traditions (European and Latin American) are defined here by their mutual opposition.

In the following exposition we will focus on the work of one of the most influential members (and founders) of the "historicist" trend in Latin American philosophy, the one who most systematically attempted to combine philosophical insights and historical approaches: Arturo Andrés Roig ("Latin American philosophy and History of Ideas," he said, "are two faces of the same task").[21] Thus, his work becomes revealing beyond the concrete contents of his historical narratives, of the conceptual ground on which such

---

[21] Arturo Andrés Roig, *El pensamiento latinoamericano y su aventura*, vol. 2 (Buenos Aires: CEAL, 1994), 141.

36 THEORETICAL APPROACHES

genealogical narratives were founded, and of the series of the intellectual procedures at work in their elaboration.

Arturo Roig and the Historicist Trend in Latin American Philosophy

As I have said, Arturo Roig was the one who proposed to reformulate the history of ideas in Latin America based on the premises of Latin American philosophy. And the basis for this was provided, in his view, by Zea himself. For Roig, in his subsequent work to *El positivismo en México*, Zea introduced three fundamental reformulations. Firstly, his search for a proper, authentic thinking transcended the national framework to encompass the subcontinent as a whole. Secondly, he found its expression in the work of a series of thinkers who reflected on it. This labor of self-knowledge, he says, was initiated in the transition from the nineteenth to the twentieth century by figures such as Ugarte, Vasconcelos, Rodó, and "so many other visionary heirs of the Bolivarian message."[22] And thirdly, even though this stance prolonged the "circumstantialism" to which Zea adhered in his early work, it then transcended the field of thought to project itself into that of action as well. The knowledge of the Latin American being now appears at once as the condition for overcoming the neocolonial order.

In Roig, the last statement contained implicit a criticism of the process of institutionalization of the history of ideas as a scholarly discipline, a longing for a time when there was still a close relationship between knowledge and practice, and which was later lost. "Neither in [José] Ingenieros nor in [Alejandro] Korn," says Roig, "was the history of ideas a matter of pure scholarly research. For them, as we have already said, the task was associated with the question of the national being and its destiny."[23] Historians, however, shortly became professional academics and this altered their way of conceiving the sense of the history of ideas: "with [Coriolano] Alberini and [Francisco] Romero, the history of ideas turns into a merely technical tracing of influences."[24]

---

[22] Arturo Roig, "De la historia de ideas a la filosofía de la liberación," in *Historia de ideas, teoría del discurso y pensamiento latinoamericano* (Bogota: Universidad Santo Tomás, 1993), 25.

[23] Roig, *Historia de ideas*, 28.

[24] Roig, "De la historia de ideas a la filosofía de la liberación," 28. On Francisco Romero's concept de "philosophical normality," see Francisco Romero, *El hombre y la cultura* (Buenos Aires: Espasa-Calpe, 1950) and M. Donnantuoni Moratto, "La categoría de 'normalidad filosófica' en Francisco Romero y su dimensión histórica," *Cuyo. Anuario De Filosofía Argentina y Americana* 33 (2020): 93–115.

For Roig, this very project was tainted with a certain idealism, in the sense that, although it seeks to understand the specificity of Latin America, it had not yet managed to break away from Eurocentric schemes. By the time Roig wrote this, the project of a Latin American philosophy had become more radical. Its cultivators now affirmed that the interpretive pattern of the "models" and "deviations" that resulted in the erudite labor of searching for "influences" was still indebted to the exoticism typical of intellectuals. The goal now, for him, was to overcome the anxiety about discovering the "European influences" and to look for the roots of an alternative thought.

In the local historiography of ideas, and also in Latin American philosophy, the paradigm of Eurocentric thought was, precisely, positivist philosophy. Hence, the great dispute that arose in those years revolved around its interpretation. As we have seen, in his book, cited previously, Zea tried in some way to rescue positivism from the stigma of being an ideology strange to the Mexican national being. For Zea, once transferred to Latin America, positivism became adjusted to local reality, although it would not yet be an authentic expression of it. For Roig, Alberini's position represented an overcoming of Zea's because his critique of positivism contained, at the same time, an alternative proposal. That is, it revealed the presence in the region of a current of thought opposed to positivism, and allegedly more akin to Latin American sensibility.

The axis around which this controversy revolved was actually connected with Alberdi's figure and its meaning. While, for Alejandro Korn, Alberdi was an *avant la lettre* positivist, for Alberini there was in Alberdi a whole spiritualist metaphysical system. Thus, they both sought to appropriate Alberdi's legacy, although in opposite ways. For Korn, Latin American positivism was not at all a mere copy of European ideas because Alberdi was already positivist before positivism emerged in Europe. There is certainly an obvious anachronism in his perspective.[25] However, this was not Roig's concern.

In actual fact, Roig's "historicism" was not very sensitive to conceptual anachronisms (which Zea, who participated in this "historicist" trend,

---

[25] It is clear that, to draw this conclusion, Korn had to first dehistoricize the forms of thinking and make of positivism something so vague (the orientation "toward practical necessities") that, in effect, it could be found in any historical-conceptual context, at any place and time. According to Arturo Ardao, Alberdi and the members of the Argentinean "Generation of 1837," "shortly freed themselves from romantic ideals and speculative concerns in order to orient themselves toward the practical activities required by the national organization." This, he said, "reveals a spontaneous positivist inclination." Arturo Ardao, *Espiritualismo y positivismo en el Uruguay* (Montevideo: Universidad de la República, 1968), 73.

38   THEORETICAL APPROACHES

indeed vindicated).[26] His rejection of positivism pointed in a different direction, a more radical one. He no longer tried to see whether positivism was indigenous or not. It is at this point that he appealed to Alberini's discovery that positivism was not dominant in Latin American thought. For him, what identified it was the opposite: a certain spiritualist tendency of thought. According to Roig, it was in positivism where the traces of the Francophile *intelligentsia* could be perceived, while the anti-positivist, spiritualist currents were the ones that effectively departed from their European matrices of thought, becoming an authentic expression of local culture.

The old dichotomy between liberalism and conservatism then paved its way to another between positivism and spiritualism. Besides, the latter had—not only for Roig, but for the cultivators of Latin American philosophy at large—a clearly social content. The recent history of Mexico provided the basis for this interpretation. While positivism was considered to be the expression of the local bourgeoisie's attempts to assert its domination (which, in Mexico, identified with the Porfiriato), spiritualism was associated with its resistance by the oppressed sectors of population, which became manifest in Mexico during the 1910 revolution.

In sum, for this historicist trend, the history of Latin American thought was that of the eternal struggle between a Europeanizing positivist mentality and the spiritualist currents closer to the authentic Latin American being. It was the core of Roig's historiographical project. Basically, his aim was to trace the genealogy of Latin American spiritualism, and, as we anticipated, Alberdi occupied a central place in his genealogy of Latin Americanism. In Alberdi's 1840 writing, *Ideas para presidir la confección del curso de filosofía contemporánea*, Roig believed he found already defined the intellectual project that nineteenth-century spiritualism would later adopt and would end up giving rise to "Latin American philosophy."

As Roig said, it was during his research for the elaboration of his first major work, *Los krausistas argentinos*,[27] that he found the basis for stating the presence of a spiritualist substratum of thought in Latin America. Its main traces could be perceived in the influence of K. Ch. F. Krause. As he assured:

> In this way, something that at first seemed of little significance to us began to gain preeminence in our research, not only because of its presence at

[26] See note 71.
[27] Arturo A. Roig, *Los krausistas argentinos* (Puebla: José M. Cajica, 1969).

University, but also in other fields, including politics. We are referring to Krausism, which, according to traditional historiography, was an almost exclusively Spanish event within the Hispanic world. . . . However, there were significant facts that allowed us to infer the weight and extension of the influence of Krausism in Latin America.[28]

Krause was a mystical thinker who participated in the German idealist movement of the early nineteenth century. He is known as the creator of "panentheism." Mostly forgotten in Germany, his work had its most important reception in the Hispanic world, mostly thanks to the labor of Julián Sanz del Río. The influence of Krausism in Spain has an explanation. The Hispanophile fury resulting as a reaction to the defeat in the war of Cuban independence in 1898 led to the search for a proper philosophical tradition also in Spain. And a group of thinkers considered Sanz del Río's proposal to look at Krause's philosophy as an attractive alternative. They thus dedicated themselves to rescuing that largely forgotten figure, taking him as a guide for their own elaborations.[29]

Roig, in turn, found in it a philosophical model that was highly influential in Latin America, albeit it was, for him, unjustly forgotten by historians.[30] He remarked the fact that Argentine president Hipólito Yrigoyen (1916–1922 and 1928–1930) read Krause's works and was influenced by his ideas.[31] This gave him the key to affirm the existence of a Latin American spiritualist tradition and to give it, in addition, a specific ideological sign. He thus affirmed that Krausism served in Argentina as an instrument for the struggle against the oligarchy, inspiring the great popular movement of Argentine radicalism. Krausism would then have been an emancipatory ideology.[32]

---

[28] Roig, *Historia de ideas*, 38.

[29] See J. López Morillas, *El krausismo español* (Mexico: FCE, 1956).

[30] Actually, Roig overstates the influence of Krausism in Argentina. And, beyond Argentina, its influence was indeed more uneven. In Cuba, it was adopted by young José Martí, although he later abandoned it due, in large measure, to the fact that the Spanish Krausists refused to support Cuban independence. Puerto Rican Eugenio María de Hostos was another important figure in its diffusion, although his thought was actually a mixture of Krausism and positivism. On the influence of Krausism in Latin America, see D. Rodríguez de Lecea and T. Koniecki, eds., *El krausismo y su influencia en América Latina* (Madrid: Fundación Ebert/Fe y Secularidad, 1989).

[31] Although, for Roig, Krause's influence on Yrigoyen's thought was fundamental, he also admitted that it was difficult to measure that influence because Yrigoyen did not cite his sources. See Roig, *Los krausistas argentinos*, chapter III, "Krausismo y política."

[32] Roig referred to the revolutionary character of the Krausist ideology in Latin America, in opposition to the "evolutionism" of positivism. As he said: "In the face of the oligarchy that, positivist or not, leaned towards an evolutionary conception of progress, radicalism [Yrigoyen's Radical Party, EP] upheld the legitimacy of revolution. The philosophical justification for the use of force is developed in almost the same terms as those of Krause or Ahrens, Gumersindo de Azcárate or Eugenio

40 THEORETICAL APPROACHES

Actually, as we can see, Roig did not break here with the scheme of "influences." In any case, what guided him, he says, was the characterization of "oppressive discourse" and the "liberating discourse" as universal forms. The struggle between positivism and spiritualism—that is, between European and North American ideologies on the one hand, and Latin American philosophy, with Hispanic and spiritualist roots on the other— would be merely the local expression of a confrontation that would cross through the whole history of thought.

In a later work, *El pensamiento latinoamericano y su aventura* (1994), Roig developed that idea by inscribing the internal struggle in Latin America between two opposing intellectual currents into a broader scenario, one of universal–historical dimensions. The emergence of spiritualism would ultimately make manifest the crisis of conscience that had been corroding Western thought since the First World War. Oswald Spengler's work, *The Decline of the West* (1918) was its best expression, although, for him, it obtained its most systematic formulation in the work of the so-called philosophers of suspicion: Marx, Nietzsche, and Freud.

Roig was thereby reacting against postmodern criticism which, he says, ignored the long process of deconstruction of the modern subject; that is, it omitted the presence in Europe of a tradition of thought opposed to Cartesian rationalism (we can perceive here Roig's attempt to overcome the unilateral vision of European thought by a large number of the cultivators of philosophical Latin Americanism who rejected European thought *en bloc*). It would therefore be an antagonism exceeding the Latin American context. However, this alternative tradition, he said, remains marginal in Europe. Only in Latin America and the colonial world does the critique of the *ego cogito* find an appropriate place to develop insofar as it is there that it reveals its hidden face as an *ego conqueror*. Latin America and its philosophers thus have the task of completing this work of de-centering the values of modernity and rescuing this other alternative tradition present in it. Through its intercession, the project of human emancipation from oppressive rationalism would finally achieve its realization in "our America."

Basically, Roig's and Latin American historicism's project in general consisted in locating the place of Latin America within a historical teleology,

---

María Hostos, to Yrigoyen," Roig, *Los krausistas argentinos*, 117; here we based on the digital version at https://ensayistas.org/filosofos/argentina/roig/krausismo/3.htm. Roig then clarified that the "revolution" the Krausists talked about was understood in moral terms and sought to restore institutional order rather than destroy it.

LATIN AMERICAN PHILOSOPHY I   41

determining what role it allegedly had to play in the realization of those ends
to which its course was supposed to be oriented. However, this type of historical teleology had already lost by then its conceptual ground. This generated
a series of tensions that this historicist line of Latin American philosophy
would no longer be able to solve.

Latin Americanism and its Historical Methodology

The fundamental shortcoming in the historical reconstruction provided by Roig
was that the contributions to this field were rather poor and inconsistent. The
great revelation that resulted from his historical-philosophical elaborations was
the discovery of Krausism, which was, in fact, a marginal current of thought,
both in Europe and in Latin America, and whose importance Roig thus had
to overemphasize.[33] On the other hand, he did not seem perplexed by the fact
that his search for the ultimate essence of Latin American thought ended up
referring him to a figure like Krause, who probably knew little or nothing about
Latin America, its history, and its culture. The point, however, is that beyond
the objections to which his historical reconstruction of the genealogy of Latin
Americanism gave rise, what underlaid it were deeper problems of a theoretical-
methodological order.

The first of these problems referred to the schematism of its theoretical
framework. The historical reconstructions based on the assumptions proper
to Latin American philosophy followed a characteristic pattern. As we have
seen, from this perspective, the history of Latin American thought appeared
as a permanent oscillation between positivism and spiritualism; that is, between those intellectual formations that remained locked within European
mental categories and those that expressed the authentic Latin American

---

[33] See note 84. Besides, the ideological character Roig attributes to it at that point was rather du-
bious. On the ideological ambiguities of Argentine Krausism, see Hugo Biagini, "Presentación," in
Orígenes de la democracia argentina. El trasfondo krausista (Buenos Aires: Legasa, 1989), 7–20. In
the text by Arturo Roig included in that book, he also qualified his previous statements regarding the
ideological radicalism of Krausism in that country. "For a correct assessment of Krausism as an ideology of the Radical Civic Union," he said, "it is necessary to start from an important fact: that it was
actually a way of thinking shared by various sectors and indeed assumed by important intellectuals
who were part of the liberal-conservative movement that radicalism called 'The Regime.' We understand that this has already been duly proven." At this point, the sense of the opposition between
"spiritualism" and "positivism" blurred. "For the rest," continues Roig, "the comparison between 'The
Regime' and positivism must be questioned." Roig, "La cuestión de la 'eticidad nacional' y ideología
krausista," 61.

42 THEORETICAL APPROACHES

being.[34] In the last instance, it merely replicated, under different names, the classical antinomies of the old history of ideas (Enlightenment versus Romanticism, mechanism versus organicism, cosmopolitanism versus nationalism, etc.). Alberini, whom Roig claimed to be one of the forerunners of philosophical Latin Americanism, provides a good example of this. In his studies of French doctrinarism, Alberini assigned relative percentages to the different authors according to the coordinates Enlightenment–Romanticism.[35] He thus stated that this author was eighty percent Romantic and twenty percent Enlightened, whereas some other author was forty percent Romantic and sixty percent Enlightened, and so on and so forth.

The truth is that the dichotomous approaches typical of the history of ideas—and that Latin American philosophy preserved and indeed reinforced—inevitably led to this kind of schematism, making historical research a rather unstimulating task insofar as its results are predictable. What we always find are forms of thought that are either more in line with our own being or more alien to it; that is, closer either to spiritualism or to positivism. The only discussion that this interpretative scheme can give rise to is, eventually, about where the thought of a given author or current should be placed within this binary classification grid. All analyses exhaust in it. Eventually someone may reply that such an author or such a current of thought was a little more authentic than stated, whereas others would insist that it was not so much, that it was rather mentally foreign, and so on. But not much more can be said about it.

Ultimately, this perspective eliminates history itself, which would then revolve around a pre-established pattern, within which frameworks the only distinctions that can be established are merely quantitative, matters of degree, as Alberini makes explicit. In this fashion, nothing can emerge from historical research that we do not know beforehand, except *factual* clarifications, such as whether this or that thinker was on this or that side within the authenticity/alienation coordinate axis, but nothing of a *conceptual* order.

---

[34] Eduardo Devés Valdés took this historical approach to its last consequences. He intended to trace the trajectory of all Latin American thinking according to the coordinates identitary/modernizing thoughts. In a recent work, he presented a timeline, which would allegedly describe the curve followed by local thought. SeeEduardo Devés Valdés, "El pensamiento latinoamericano a comienzos del siglo XX: la reivindicación de la identidad," *Anuario de filosofía argentina y americana* 14 (1997): 12.

[35] Coriolano Alberini, *Precisiones sobre la evolución del pensamiento argentino* (Buenos Aires: Docencia, 1981).

Even more seriously, the need to fit all the various ways of thinking into this grid inevitably entails a selectivity process. To take the case of the figure that Roig postulated as a kind of founding father of Latin Americanist thought, Alberdi, it is clear that presenting him as such results in an arbitrary operation upon his work and his thought. As we have seen, Roig and his followers considered Alberdi's 1840 writing, *Ideas para presidir a la confección del curso de filosofía contemporánea*,[36] as the best expression of proto-Latin Americanism. In effect, in that text Alberdi spoke of the need of an "American philosophy." However, as soon as we go just a little deeper into the analysis of that text, we immediately perceive that Alberdi's idea had nothing in common with the Latin Americanism that emerged more than a century later.[37] In fact, we can find in that text statements affirming exactly the opposite ideas to those that Roig intended to attribute to Alberdi. For example, he assured that "the people of Europe who, according to their intelligence and character, are destined to preside in the education of these countries is without contradiction the French [. . .]; we, also southern in origin and situation, belong by right to its intelligent initiative."[38] Roig simply decided to leave aside all of Alberdi's thinking that was not compatible with his own perspective, and to focus exclusively on those expressions of Alberdi's which, out of context, could be interpreted as anticipating the kind of discourse he proposed to rescue and whose genealogy he intended to trace. To put it in Eric Hobsbawn and Terence Ranger's words, it is a typical example of an "invention of traditions."[39]

[36] This text can be found in Leopoldo Zea, ed., *Pensamiento positivista latinoamericano*, vol. 1 (Caracas: Ayacucho, 1980), 61–67. Let's say that the inclusion in this compilation of Alberdi's text, along with others such as José María Luis Mora's "Revista Política," as "precursors" of Latin American positivism, is curious and suggestive. For Zea as well as for Roig, Alberdi was a precursor of Latin Americanism, although for opposite reasons: for Zea, because he was positivist; for Roig, instead, because he was spiritualist. In truth, both interpretations are equally arbitrary. If we read the content of the above-mentioned texts it is impossible to understand the criteria that led Zea to place them within the category of "positivists." Nothing in them seems to authorize conceiving them as such, unless we conceive positivism in such a vague and generic way (as in the case, already analyzed, of Arturo Ardao) that practically all writing could be considered as such. But the same could be said of "spiritualism." In both cases, such operations involved a degree of simplification that ended up confusing more than it clarified.

[37] On this, see Javier Sasso, *La filosofía latinoamericana y sus construcciones históricas* (Caracas: Monte Ávila Editores Latinoamericana, 1997). In the section entitled "El programa de Alberdi y sus admiradores contemporáneos" (131–137), Sasso dismantled the "mitological amalgamation" woven around Alberdi's 1840 text.

[38] Alberdi, "Ideas para presidir el curso de filosofía contemporánea," 62–63. It should be remembered here that a few years later Alberdi would call for French military intervention in Argentina, requesting the establishment of a monarchy there, just like what was happening in Mexico at the same time.

[39] See Eric Hobsbawm and Terence Ranger, eds., *The Invention of Tradition* (Cambridge: Cambridge University Press, 1992).

44   THEORETICAL APPROACHES

Furthermore, focusing exclusively on that text, which was actually very minor in Alberdi's production,[40] entailed a very drastic and rather captious trim of his work and thought.[41] In this fashion, Roig incurred in the kind of fallacies or "mythologies" that Quentin Skinner denounced as typical of the old history of ideas.[42] One of them is the "mythology of coherence" in which the studied author is endowed with a system of thought that, in actual reality, never existed as such in that author. This is usually the means of making their ideas fit within the "model" which they supposedly belong to. Now, as soon as all that does not fit the putative model is discovered in their work, it is either discarded, affirming that it would not form a part of the "doctrinal core" of their system, or attributed to their "contradictions"; that is, that they would be an inconsistent thinker who combined ideas taken from incompatible models. Models themselves thus appear as always irrefutable. If the ideas of the analyzed authors do not match them, the problem would be of the authors, not of the models. There is no room here for suspecting that perhaps such supposed "incongruities" could be revealing, not that the ideas of said authors were inconsistent, but more simply that the incongruous ones are the frameworks with which they are interpreted; that is, that they are not appropriate for understanding complex discourses, which do not lend themselves to become reduced to such simplistic schemes.[43]

The point is that this kind of anachronistic projections were characteristic of the historical reconstructions from the perspective of Latin American philosophy—it was a systematic method in them. The schematism of its perspective, founded on eternal or quasi-eternal antinomies, inevitably leads to conflation and unification under the same label conceptual formations that, in actual reality, were very different from each other. Within the schemes that are proper to it, there is no way of discovering what separated, for example, nineteenth-century Romantic thought from twentieth-century spiritualism,

---

[40] On the other hand, it had no impact at that time. These were the guidelines for a course that was never given due to lack of interested students.

[41] In fact, Roig could not ignore this fact because Alberdi's "Europeanism" was undeniable. It was already present in his first major writing, *Fragmento preliminar al estudio del derecho* (1837), in which he stated: "We have had two existences in the world, one colonial, the other republican. The first was given to us by Spain, the second by France. The day we stopped being a colony, our connection with Spain fell: from the Republic on, we have been children of France." Juan B. Alberdi, *Fragmento preliminar al estudio del derecho* (Buenos Aires: Biblos, 1984), 153.

[42] Quentin Skinner, "Meaning and Understanding in the History of Ideas," *History and Theory* 8, no. 1 (1969): 3–53.

[43] See Elías J. Palti, *Intellectual History and the Problem of Conceptual Change. Skinner, Pocock, Koselleck, Blumernberg, Foucault, Rosanvallon* (Cambridge: Cambridge University Press, forthcoming).

except, as we have seen, by mere matters of degree or of an empirical order. Both Romanticism and Spiritualism, although very distant both in chronological and conceptual terms, would thus appear as parts of one and same line of thought. This misses the fact that, as we will see in the next chapter, they participated, respectively, in completely different conceptual horizons and that, over the course of the century that separated them, the ground of knowledge on which each one was based had mutated.

In fact, Roig took up Wilhelm Dilthey's idea of "horizon of understanding," which referred to epochal conceptual universes. With it, Dilthey intended to indicate how the conditions for the articulation of ideas change over time. These horizons of understanding were, for him, specific historical formations. However, Roig dehistoricized them by placing them on an anthropological plane (what he called "anthropological *a priori*"). Thus redefined, these horizons of understanding became reduced to two fundamental ones (the "oppressive discourse" and the "emancipatory discourse"), which in turn expressed two opposite projects whose antagonism allegedly traverse the whole of Western history. In short, they appeared to Roig as two transhistorical substances engaged in a perennial struggle, like good and evil in ancient cosmologies.

This view assumed, in turn, the existence of a secret complicity between facts and values, the idea of a kind of pre-established harmony between the spontaneous development of history and their political project, the principles to which these authors claim to adhere. For this historicist current, from the very study of history emanates an ethic, and, ultimately, defined political program. Historical development would not be a blind becoming, but it would bear a meaning; it would participate not in the order of *chronos* but of *kairos* (meaningful time). However, this teleological view of history, which was typical of the nineteenth-century philosophies of history, had already lost its conceptual ground. In fact, all the fundamental categories that Latin Americanist philosophers took up—and which they relied on to develop their ideas (and that refer, basically, to German phenomenological and neo-Kantian thought of the late nineteenth and early twentieth centuries)— represented, precisely, a rebellion against the idealistic (evolutionist-teleological) philosophies of history, which would be embodied in the figure of Hegel (who would then be placed at the center of the criticism). These Latin Americanist philosophies would thus not be able to avoid oscillating permanently between historicism and voluntarism. This paradoxical mixture of historicism and voluntarism (immanence and transcendence) will parallel

46 THEORETICAL APPROACHES

an equally paradoxical mixture of intellectualism and anti-intellectualism, of messianism and populism.

The ethics of engagement has it implicit. On the one hand, we find the idea that the intellectual, by being able to grasp what the Latin American being is, has the mission of revealing their true identity to its compatriots. It thus addresses a society that is considered alienated by forms of knowledge strange to its own being and that oppresses it. Otherwise, the emancipatory project would not make sense. On the other hand, this messianic or redemptive vocation coexists with a distrust toward intellectuals considered as those most prone to be influenced by foreign ideologies. That would lead, in turn, to a new dichotomy, the vindication of the spontaneous insights of the people versus the abstract knowledge of intellectuals. As we will see, this inconsistent mixture of intellectualism and anti-intellectualism, of messianism and populism, will no longer find a balance. The process of undermining teleological certainties that had permeated the thought of the nineteenth century would prevent it, depriving these philosophies of a ground on whose basis to "dialectically" reconcile these two contradictory drives (the reliance that history itself would take care of it, that it would convey their fusion).

Between the *A Priori* and the *A Posteriori*

In *Teoría y crítica del pensamiento latinoamericano* (1981) Roig developed the theoretical framework that guided his historical interpretation. In it, he exposed the fundamental concept that articulated his perspective: that of "anthropological *a priori*," which he also called "historical *a priori*."[44] In it we can see again the characteristic oscillation of this current of thought between expression and transformation (immanence and transcendence). In this case, it becomes manifest in the uncertainty of the nature, at once *a priori* and *a posteriori*, of the postulates that articulates Roig's horizon of understanding, his hesitant oscillation between "being" and "ought-to-be."

This tension can be observed in the philosophical references on which he relied. With his concept of "historical *a priori*," Roig took up, on the one hand, the Kantian idea of transcendental subject and, on the other, the Hegelian idea of the subject as a historical product. The *a priori* indicates a mode of conceptualization of reality, prior to all knowledge, as it refers to the realm

---

[44] Arturo Roig, *Teoría y crítica del pensamiento latinoamericano* (Mexico: FCE, 1981).

of its conditions of possibility. But the realm of the *a priori*, unlike Kant's view, does not refer to a universal subject (i.e., a set of capacities innate in the human subject) but to a contingent result, in each case, of a certain historical development. It is what Roig called the "empirical subject," which in this case was the "Latin American being." As he said:

> The axiological is necessarily posited and understood as an *a priori*. The experience, we know, is not possible without this anticipation. But the empiricity of the subject is not the [transcendental, EP] experience, but something prior to it and to the universals that make it possible, and, in this sense, the axiological is an *a posteriori* by means of which each historical "we" opens itself to the understanding of the world in its very process of becoming and gestating, whether in an authentic or inauthentic way. From this we must necessarily conclude that the axiological, which always has the characteristics of a "taking a position," is based on our empiricity or, at least, must be based on it as "proper."[45]

In this (rather confusing) statement, we can see that oscillation, characteristic of this current of thought, between expression and transformation, immanence and transcendence, being and ought to be, the *a priori* and the *a posteriori*. As we will see, all Roig's discourse displayed as a series of attempts to try to reconcile both terms, without ever succeeding.

On the one hand, Roig affirmed that the unity of the subject was given in the *a priori* realm, it entailed a horizon of understanding in whose framework it could be constituted as such:

> It is not difficult to see that the exercise of "positing ourselves as valuable" involves a horizon of understanding according to which, with a different sign, the discursive level is elaborated, which always takes the "positing ourselves" as its premise. As we have tried to show, in each case it provides us with [the basis to grasp] the meaning of the "we" and the "ours."[46]

The question posed by the conception of a type of being that is no longer generically human is in each case: How to delimit it? What are its defining features? The point is that this is not something that can be drawn from reality

---

[45] Roig, *Teoría y crítica del pensamiento latinoamericano*, 143.
[46] Roig, *Teoría y crítica del pensamiento latinoamericano*, 19.

48   THEORETICAL APPROACHES

itself. What we have in front of us are always plural subjects. The empirical being is diverse; unity is produced only on the discursive level, it entails a criterion to determine which, of all the features that can be observed in reality itself, are the ones that identify a given people, that define their identity. Ultimately, for Roig, this referred us to the level of the "ought-to-be"; that is to say, it was a project to be carried out, rather than something given. As Roig said:

> Diversity is always thought of in terms of unity, which is understood at the same time as actual and possible, aspects that can be seen, in different degrees, depending on the weight we give to "being" or to "ought-to-be."[47]

Thus, if we put the weight on being, we will have pure diversity, which is what we observe in actual reality; only if we put the weight on the ought-to-be do we get unity, which is not something real but something to be built. Here, we meet the Kantian side of Roig's thought, his constructivism. The synthesis occurs here exclusively in the realm of the *a priori*, of the observing subject. To produce it, it is necessary to inscribe the plurality of the empirical within a horizon of understanding that produces its unity and renders it intelligible, granting it a given identity. Yet, in this case, constructivism was not limited to the gnoseological field, as in Kant, but was projected onto the practical realm as well; what is posited as an *a priori* of knowledge is postulated, at once, as a project to be carried out, to become materialized in actual reality. We observe here a fundamental difference with Kant's concept, which disentangled the gnoseological and the practical, the sphere of knowledge and the sphere of ethics—"being" and "ought-to-be." For Kant, an ethics (a project) could not be derived from knowledge, nor could it be founded on reality itself, but on pure reason. This leads us to the second term in Roig's concept: the *a posteriori*.

Immediately after that, Roig's argument rotates and moves it in the opposite direction. At that point, Roig insists that the emphasis on the *a priori*, the ought-to-be, has implicit the danger of a relapse into pure subjective voluntarism, into utopianism. "It is," he assures, "a historicism that indicates, as a regulating idea, a duty, a goal, which is not alien to the attitude that mobilizes utopian thought."[48] It raises the need to seek for an anchor in actual reality to

---

[47] Roig, *Teoría y crítica del pensamiento latinoamericano*, 4.
[48] Roig, *Teoría y crítica del pensamiento latinoamericano*, 5.

such an emancipatory project, to find roots for the ought-to-be at the bosom of being. Hence, Roig argued that, although subjects are constituted as such in the realm of the ought-to-be, the *a priori*, (and it entails a certain horizon of understanding) conversely, the horizons of understanding from which a given concept of the subject arises derive, in turn, from actual subjects, which, therefore, would be pre-constituted, with precedence to every horizon of understanding, that is, its unity as such subjects would pre-exist their own discursive conditions of possibility:

> Certainly, the ought-to-be, as a possibility given at hand, is not absolute, a position that can lead to a negative utopian extreme, but somehow its conditions are already given in being; in multiplicity there is unity and at the same time there is not.[49]

This means a reversal of the previous statement: the ought-to-be, the horizon of understanding, Roig said, is what turns the empirical being into a subject (reduces plurality to unity, provides it with an identity), but, at the same time, he now added, that ought-to-be emanates from the empirical being. The project would thus no longer be a mere *a priori*, its coming into being would consist merely in the bringing to consciousness what already exists before its formal constitution as such, what predates every horizon of understanding because the latter is the emanation of the former, which leads us back to the Hegelian motive of the transit from the in-itself to the for-itself. This is what he expresses in the apparently contradictory phrase that "in multiplicity there is unity and at the same time there is not." This should be understood in the sense that it does not exist as an actual reality but only as a project. But this "project" is no longer situated in the *a priori* realm, that of subjective consciousness, but in the *a posteriori* realm, it would already be present in the empirical subject as a kind of immanent *telos*.

There is an ambiguity here regarding the nature of the emancipatory subject: as we have seen, for Roig, this would be both things at the same time, a project and a reality. Ultimately, all Roig's discourse oscillates indecisively between the ought-to-be and the being, the *a priori* and the *a posteriori*. As he himself admitted, "this fact would come to pose an apparent vicious circle that would spring out of the affirmation of the subject's priority in respect of

---

[49] Roig, *Teoría y crítica del pensamiento latinoamericano*, 6.

50   THEORETICAL APPROACHES

the reception of cultural forms and at the same time the acceptance that they are constituent parts of that subject's own consciousness."[50]

In the last instance, this circularity, this indecisive oscillation between the *a priori* and the *a posteriori* springs from the fact that neither the Kantian path nor the Hegelian path would be transitable, and, in the attempt to combine the two, Roig overlaps problems rather than solves them. On the one hand, the horizons of understanding by which a subject is instituted as such, the *a prioris*, unlike Kant, are no longer conceived as natural but as contingent formations; that is, they themselves are also diverse, plural, which would have implicit the danger of relativism. The solution, in this case, will consist in transferring the whole issue to an ethical sphere. However, the ethical realm is also the realm in which pure subjectivity emerges, and in which pluralism prevails. Thus, to avoid that relapse into subjectivism, pluralism had to be severely reduced and limited to antinomic options, whose axiological content could be immediately graspable. It is at this point that all the horizons of understanding are reduced to two fundamental ones: the "emancipatory discourse" and the "oppressive discourse." Every possible form of thought would thus be inscribed within one or other horizon. And·they would refer, respectively, to two orders of subjectivities: the modern European rational subject and the Latin American oppressed subject.

In this way, although these *a prioris* no longer have a natural foundation but a contingent one, they will not be properly historical entities either. They will transcend their condition as such, appearing as two transhistorical substances in perpetual antagonism, respectively bearing a manifest ethical content. They will constitute what Reinhart Koselleck called "asymmetric counterconcepts,"[51] which are defined by their mutual opposition, one being only the negative side of the other, and together exhaust the universe of possibilities (A or ~A); within this framework *tertium non datur*. However, this permanent struggle between these two terms would have a meaning, an end toward which it would be oriented, and which would find its ultimate expression in Latin America. It is here where we find the point toward which Roig's whole argument converges. Its underlying assumption is that the *a priori* that postulates an emancipatory horizon and the *a posteriori* of the Latin American empirical man, the ought-to be and the being, are, in this case, coincident. From the Latin American being would emanate an axiology

---

[50] Roig, *Teoría y crítica del pensamiento latinoamericano*, 23.

[51] Reinhart Koselleck, "The Historical-Political Semantics of Asymmetric Counterconcepts," in *Futures Past: On the Semantics of Historical Time* (Cambridge, MA: MIT Press, 1985), 159–197.

that would coincide with the political project itself of the Latin Americanist philosopher. Thus, there would be a spontaneous convergence between the two—a kind of pre-established harmony.

This supposes the abandonment of Kantianism to embrace a posture of Hegelian reminiscences. Ultimately, the idea of a "historical *a priori*" is, in reality, a terminological contradiction, an oxymoron. The only way to reconcile the two terms is by placing an Absolute below them; that is, ontologizing history, turning it into an at once immanent and transcendent entity, which is the concept that, as Koselleck showed, emerged during the period that he calls *Sattelzeit* (1750–1850), and that paved the way to the emergence of the philosophies of history of the nineteenth century. It is then that the idea emerged of the existence in the historical course of a hidden rationality that operates independently of the empirical consciousness of the subjects and leads them toward the realization of a universal ideal. Thus, the ultimate end of reason (the *a priori*) would be built-in in the very subject as an immanent *telos*; in short, the *a priori* would also be an *a posteriori*, the ought-to-be would incarnate in the being. Hence Roig defines Latin American philosophy as "a science understood as 'a knowledge in me of what is in me,' "[52] which is, again, a translation of the Hegelian passage from the "in-itself" to the "for-itself."

We come here to the characteristic syndrome of this form of discourse. It affirms, in principle, the contingency of the empirical subject, as well as of its knowledge, which supposes a departure from Kantian apriorism, only to immediately deny it and identify it with an Absolute. The Latin American being would thus be a subject at once empirical and transcendent; historical and contingent, but one in which a universal value comes to incarnate the bearer (*Träger*) of a historical mission, inscribed in its very being. This supposes, in short, a relapse into a form of teleologism of an idealistic matrix, an evolutionary view of history, which, however, as we have said, had already become theoretically untenable. As a matter of fact, Roig himself demolished it, showing its inconsistencies (what he calls "The demolishing of Hegelian ontologism"), which leads us to the problem of "rupture."[53]

[52] Roig, *Teoría y crítica del pensamiento latinoamericano*, 144.
[53] Roig, *Teoría y crítica del pensamiento latinoamericano*, 142.

52 THEORETICAL APPROACHES

The Problem of "Rupture"

According to Roig, in the "Introduction" to his *Lessons on the Philosophy of History*, Hegel invoked the idea of a "subject," but then relapsed into the metaphysical terrain, putting in its place an Absolute. However, said Roig, such an invocation immediately reveals its metaphysical nature. It was here that Roig introduced his fundamental concept of "rupture," which is the effect that—he assured—Latin American knowledge produces within modern rationality:

> Now, this "perfect" image of State, in which the reformulating function assumes the form of a social demand is, in fact, brutally demolished by the presence of human groups that reject their integration. They no longer constitute the "people" but the "mob" (*Pöbel*) [. . .]. The whole Hegelian concept, and that of its integration function, goes to bankruptcy before this scandalous fact of the populace, leading it to inevitable contradictions [. . .]
> . In this way, the concept, which in Hegelian logic only fulfills a function of integration, comes to demand, in the name of such integration, an act of rupture.[54]

The "people" referred to by Hegel as the incarnation of a universal was, in actual fact, a metaphysical entity that should not be confused with the empirical "people," the "mob," which was a merely contingent entity, alien to reason. As Roig pointed out, the introduction of the idea of "populace" fissured the Absolute of reason, introducing a gap that separated the ought-to-be from the being, the *a priori* and the *a posteriori*. Now, what Roig did not notice was that the same happened in the philosophies of Latin American identity with the introduction of the idea of "alienation." In this case, the "Latin American being" that they invoked was no longer confused with the empirical subjects, ignorant of their authentic being. The idea of "alienation," which was at the basis of this philosophy, was at the same time destructive of it. It produced in it the same "rupture" effect as the introduction of the concept of the "mob" in the Hegelian discourse, as Roig remarked, without perceiving how this was also replicated in his own perspective. To put it in his own words, "its integration function goes to bankruptcy before this scandalous fact."

---

[54] Roig, *Teoría y crítica del pensamiento latinoamericano*, 54.

Roig's argument then becomes trapped into a double bind. On the one hand, he must affirm the people's alienation because, otherwise, if the people were not in such a state, the emancipatory project will become pointless and it will lose its purpose. The very logic of its own discourse demands it. "It is 'philosophy,' as a subject," said Roig, "the one that 'demands a people,' just as it needs its decline."[55] But, on the other hand, in this case, it would lack an empirical ground, it would reveal itself as a merely subjective projection without a sustentation in actual reality, a pure ought-to-be, a mere *a priori*. In sum, the attempt to escape from the sheer *a priori* that had been revealed as contingent, which—unlike in Kant's time, had lost its foundations in nature or pure reason—led him to transfer the whole question to the empirical realm, the *a posteriori*. But, unlike in Hegel's time, this no longer provided a firmer foundation, either, which, in turn, sent Roig's argument back to the *a priori* realm. This argumentative circularity, this undecisive oscillation between the *a priori* and the *a posteriori*, was the defining feature of this form of discourse.

A Specular Logic

Let's review what we have seen so far. In the first instance, Roig affirmed that the conformation of a people, the reduction of the plurality of individuals into the whole of the community, is not something that simply arises from reality itself, that its concept is not the result of a mere empirical verification of an actual fact, but it rather entails a given horizon of understanding from which to identify what that people is, what its essence is, its nature, in sum, what provides it with an entity as such a people. This, then, leads us to the realm of the *a priori* determinations.

The question that this raised, in turn, was how that horizon of understanding was constituted. At this point, his argument took a turn, producing a kind of reversal. Just as the formation of a people presupposes a certain horizon of understanding, this, in turn, presupposes the existence of a people. A horizon of understanding is not an abstract, generic rationality, but the concrete emanation of a given type of subject. And this brings us back to the question of how the people from which this horizon of understanding emanates is constituted. The answer, in this case, is that this would be a historical product. History would thus be entrusted to break this circularity

---

[55] Roig, *Teoría y crítica del pensamiento latinoamericano*, 45.

54   THEORETICAL APPROACHES

between the *a priori* and the *a posteriori*. It would be in charge of constituting that subject, conferring an identity upon it and providing a unitary sense to its development. The problem is that, as we have seen, this evolutionary-teleological concept, typical of the nineteenth-century philosophies of history, had already lost its conceptual ground—it had become theoretically untenable. Roig's entire discourse is based on the assumption of its bankruptcy—which is what led him to postulate the idea on which his argument was based—that constituted its point of departure: that the formation of a people required an *a priori*, presupposed a certain horizon of understanding. The idea of horizon of understanding that Roig borrowed from Dilthey arose, precisely, out of the dissolution of the evolutionary concept of history (it was a central category in his project of a "critique of historical reason").[56] The two were mutually incompatible.

In effect, either the horizon of understanding is the one that constitutes the subject, or it is the subject that constitutes the horizon of understanding. At this point, the only solution that remains consists in unfolding the planes, positing the existence of two different orders of subjectivity, which would be what phenomenology would postulate: on the one hand, the *thetic* subject, in Husserl's words, who would take on a determinate identity within a system of references and, on the other hand, the *non-thetic* subject, a subjectivity prior to the constitution of the subject, a kind of primordial being situated in a more primitive realm of reality and from which the senses of reality emanate. But the historicist trend could not accept this either, as, from the perspective of this trend, it supposed a relapse into the metaphysical terrain, which was precisely what it criticized to its opposite trend within Latin American philosophy—the phenomenological.[57]

It explains why Roig's argument remained attached to a concept of history that had nevertheless become untenable. Lastly, at that moment it was clear that history does not speak by itself, that someone must speak on its behalf, disclose what its meaning is, the logic that presides over its development. And this brings us back to the starting point, although the question is now not how to reduce the plurality of subjects to the whole of the community, but another one, different in its content albeit analogous in its form: how

---

[56] See Wilhelm Dilthey, *The Formation of the Historical World in the Human Sciences* (Princeton: Princeton University Press, 2002).

[57] One of the central topics of Roig's criticism of the phenomenological line refers to the "idea of the existence of a mythical 'cultural continent' from which what we receive as a 'legacy' arises or flows" (Roig, *Teoría y crítica del pensamiento latinoamericano*, 23).

LATIN AMERICAN PHILOSOPHY I   55

to produce the reduction of the plurality of singular events—which is what is given in actual reality—to the unity of history. This demanded, once again, a given horizon of understanding in order to determine, from the plurality of events that occur in actual reality, which ones are the properly "historical" ones, which ones bear a historical sense, and which do not (which was, precisely, what gave birth to Dilthey's concept of "horizon of understanding"), with which his argument is sent back to its starting point. In sum, once the teleological assumptions had been broken, once the "demolishing of Hegelian ontologism" was produced, the appellation to history only transferred the question to another terrain (from the *a priori* to the *a posteriori* realm) in which it could no longer find a solution either. Thus, the historicist trend refused to produce an escape toward transcendence, to invoke the idea of some sort of metaphysical entity, an immaterial, ahistorical being, as the phenomenological trend would postulate, but it could no longer rest on a historical teleology either. Hence, it ended up trapped in an argumentative cycle, a perpetual oscillation between the *a priori* and the a *posteriori*.

From this first argumentative circularity derived a second one, much more fundamental because it would bring about consequences of not a merely conceptual but also of a practical-political nature. As we have seen, the invocation to history and the people would then have been revealed as such, that is, as an invocation necessarily produced from within a particular horizon of understanding, which entailed a kind of knowledge. It was not a spontaneous emanation of reality itself, but it demanded a labor of reflection. As Roig says in his criticism of the concept of "ideology":

> The doctrine of ideology, according to which this would be a "reflection" of the social relations considered in their pure facticity, has led to ignoring the phenomenon of mediation, creating the illusion that extralinguistic reality and its expression in language can be immediately confronted, since access to the former would be direct. But this is not the case, because, in order to establish the desired confrontation, that reality must also be expressed at a discursive level. There are no raw economic or social facts without the mediation of discursive forms. The confrontation therefore does not occur between a naked reality and the theories or doctrines, scientific or not, but among discursive forms.[58]

---

[58] Roig, *Teoría y crítica del pensamiento latinoamericano*, 19.

56 THEORETICAL APPROACHES

It was here that philosophy found its role, and that it gained a sense. It plays the role of the "evanescent mediator" (which, as we will see in the next chapter, constitutes a key concept in the Latin Americanist discourse), the one who must intercede between the essence and its manifestation to reveal its "true" being to the empirical subject. The philosopher was thus posited as the one who would have access to a hidden knowledge, the possessor of an arcane. According to Roig:

> In relation to this programmatic value of the normative—which allows us to discover the value of a guideline possessed by any norm that functions as an anthropological *a priori*—there is undoubtedly an understanding of philosophy as auroral knowledge and not as evening knowledge. The normativity of philosophy receives, according to what has been said, its unity and meaning—whatever the levels at which it is indicated—from the self-affirmation of the philosophizing subject, which makes its "beginning" possible.[59]

As he states, philosophical knowledge, the horizon of understanding from which it unfolds, unlike what Hegel postulated, is not something that comes to the saga of history, it is not placed at its end, but rather constitutes its point of departure. It is, as he says, an "auroral" knowledge, the condition of possibility of historicity. It is an *ex-ante* kind of knowledge. The question that it raises, in turn, is how this *ex-ante* knowledge—that is not, by definition, an *ex-post* result from history—is, itself constituted. To put it otherwise, what is that subject, behind the subject, that establishes that horizon of understanding from which philosophical knowledge displays? A question that inevitably leads to an infinite regress. To stop it, the Latin American philosopher must appear as a *causa sui*, an uncaused cause. In the last instance, it becomes placed in the site of the *arkhē*, the last foundation and the premise on which this whole discourse rests.

In sum, it becomes the authentic subject and Latin American philosophy is ultimately revealed as a discourse about itself, thus remaining locked within the circle of its own self-referential logic. What is then produced is, paraphrasing Emmanuel Lévinas, the curvature of its space for reflection. The Latin Americanist discourse folds upon itself turning into the subject and the object of itself. In fact, all the historical reconstructions produced

---

[59] Roig, *Teoría y crítica del pensamiento latinoamericano*, 5.

by the historicist trend of Latin Americanism only refer to itself, to its own genealogy.

In this fashion, the argumentative circularity between the *a priori* and the *a posteriori* replicates itself on the level of the second-order discourse, the meta-discourse; that is, the specular logic in the way of conceiving the people is reproduced in the ways of conceiving the ways of conceiving of the people, or, to put it in other terms, of the ways that the Latin Americanist philosopher conceives themself and the nature of their own knowledge. In the former case, on the level of the discourse-object, the specular logic worked in this fashion: the horizon of understanding constructed its object, the people, and then proceeded in reversal asserting that *that horizon of understanding was the emanation of that very object which was its own creation*. In the latter case, on the level of the meta-discourse, the Latin American philosopher also constructed its own object, in this case, its own genealogy, and then *claimed to be themself the emanation of the genealogy they themself had retrospectively created*.

The point is that it is only in this way that this type of discourse can produce a certain closure effect in logical terms. It thus ended up at its point of arrival finding what it itself had posited at the beginning of it as its premise, from which, in turn, that very discourse would claim to take its meaning and have its foundations. This circular logic was inherent in Latin American philosophy as a whole, and, as we will see in the next chapter, it was the one that articulated the discourse of the phenomenological trend as well.

3

Latin American Philosophy II

The Phenomenological Line and the Metaphysical Turn

As seen in Chapter 2, the historicist line of Latin American philosophy oscillates indecisively between the *a priori* and the *a posteriori*, between immanence and transcendence, without being able to reach a point of equilibrium; that is to say, without finding what would have allowed it to reconcile both contradictory poles (the empirical and the transcendental): the idea of an Absolute (be it Nature or History). Now, this oscillation spreads throughout Latin Americanist thought under different fashions, encompassing the different fields in which it unfolds itself. The basic antinomy that articulates it can thus be observed indeed in the "analytical," "scientist" current, represented by Francisco Miró Quesada.[1]

Miró Quesada's perspective can be considered a translation of Roig's concept of "historical *a priori*" into the epistemological field. The opposition between the two discourses that Roig talked about (the "oppressor" and the "emancipator") for Miró Quesada was not, properly speaking, an *ideological* opposition. The ideology of the oppressed subject, although it is founded in a contingent, historical form of knowledge, would transcend its condition as a merely particular ideology, identifying itself with a Truth. What defines its epistemological status, however, is not its content but the nature of the subject of its enunciation (the "saying" rather than "what is said"). According to Miró Quesada, only the oppressing subject must appeal to the masking of reality, while the knowledge of the oppressed subject necessarily has an

---

[1] The field of Latin Americanism is rather vague, encompassing very different fields of intellectual production. Its scope ranges from Miró Quesada's "hard," "analytical" perspective, to the "weak" genre of the identity-essay, one "in between" philosophy and literature. The latter does not participate in the anxiety for an objective, impersonal Truth, but rather seeks to make room for subjective expression, in which the moral, the aesthetic, the cultural and the political are intertwined. For the theory and the trajectory of this genre in Latin America, see Liliana Weinberg, *El ensayo entre el infierno y el paraíso* (Mexico: FCE/UNAM, 2001); Liliana Weinberg, *Situación del ensayo* (Mexico: CCYDEL-UNAM, 2006); John Skirius, ed., *El ensayo latinoamericano del siglo XX* (Mexico: FCE, 1981).

Misplaced Ideas?. Elías J. Palti, Oxford University Press. © Oxford University Press 2024.
DOI: 10.1093/oso/9780197556641.003.0003

LATIN AMERICAN PHILOSOPHY II   59

unmasking effect. This, therefore, presupposes the possession of some kind of privileged access to reality by the latter, one that would not be caught within the meshes of ideology.[2] Thus, Miró Quesada's "analytical" philosophy connects with that metaphysics of the subject which the phenomenological line sought to elaborate.[3]

Unlike the historicist trend, the phenomenological or populist trend of Latin American philosophy did not seek to reconcile the *a priori* with the *a posteriori*, but, on the contrary, it radicalized their opposition. It did not aim at establishing a link between what is given, the empirical realm, and what is sought for, the transcendent realm, but, on the contrary, to make manifest the existence of an irresolvable contradiction between the two. Both instances (the ontic and the pre-ontic or ontological) represented, for this trend, two different realms of reality, which followed contradictory logics. For the phenomenological line, the point is to transcend the former instance (the ontic) and to gain access to the latter (the pre-ontic), where the inner Latin American being allegedly resides.

Lastly, once the conceptual foundations of the evolutionary-teleological concept have been undermined, once the "rupture" of the teleological assumptions of history that Roig spoke about had been produced, the only alternative that remained available to break the circularity between the *a priori* and the *a posteriori* consisted in assuming the apriorism of its *locus* of enunciation, and from there to find an escape toward transcendence, toward the metaphysical terrain, positing the presence, under the empirical (alienated) being, of a deeper and more authentic level of subjectivity, an inner being seeking to manifest itself from behind the carapace of its actual material existence; in short, ontologizing, reifying, this time, not History, but the Subject. This is precisely the project that the "phenomenological"—also called "populist"—trend would follow.

The kind of intellectual operation produced by this trend can be seen as analogous to the case studied by Ernst Kantorowicz of "the king's two

---

[2] As Beorlegui points out, Miró Quesada's statement does not really match the "objective," "scientific" pretensions of that author: "his liberating option," states Beorlegui, "is merely a voluntaristic position, which is not explained or justified by him." Beorlegui, *Historia del pensamiento latinoamericano*, 63.

[3] See Rodolfo Kusch, *Esbozo de una antropología filosófica latinoamericana* (Buenos Aires: Castañeda, 1991), 20.

60   THEORETICAL APPROACHES

bodies."[4] In the medieval imaginary, the sovereign was inhabited by two bodies, the material body of the sovereign (its empirical incarnation) that died, and his mystical body (the royal investiture) that did not die. Something similar happens in this case with the figure of the people. The people to which the phenomenological line of Latin American philosophy seeks to give expression is not the empirical people, immersed in an inauthentic life resulting from their state of alienation. The people to which Latin American philosophers refer is situated on another plane, it is an immaterial being, the mystical body of the people, which will never become confused with the actual people, the alienated subject whom they want to liberate. The question that arises here is: What is this being? Where can it be found? How can it be defined? How can entity be given to that immaterial substance, which has a rather phantasmatic existence? Ultimately, these problems have deeper conceptual roots, which are associated with the régime of knowledge here at work.

However, the critical point, as we will see, is that the very same thing that determined the relapse into a metaphysical terrain, the need to escape to a transcendent sphere—the rupture of the teleological view of history—at the same time deprived it of a foundation. As we have seen, the phenomenological trend would detach the empirical subject of the inner being and thereby identify the latter, without further ado, with its immaterial substance, which lacked, by definition, all corporeity, all historicity, and appeared as an ethereal, timeless entity. However, it would end up facing aporias that were insoluble within their frameworks, and would end up reproducing, on that metaphysical level, the same type of logical circularity in which the historicist concept of Latin Americanism became locked, although it would get there along a very different path. While the historicist trend would fail to conciliate the opposite poles of the *a priori* and the *a posteriori*, conversely, the phenomenological trend would fail to avoid its collusion, to preserve the former from being polluted by the materiality of latter. Thus, it would transfer the aporias present in the historicist trend from one level of reality to another without really solving them yet. Rodolfo Kusch's perspective illustrates both the nature of the conceptual operations that the phenomenological trend of philosophical Latin Americanism had to produce in its attempt to break the argumentative circularity of the historicist trend, and the reasons why it could not do that, how its very categorical framework prevented it.

[4] See Ernst Kantorowicz, *The King's Two Bodies: A Study in Mediaeval Political Theology* (Princeton: Princeton University Press, 1981).

LATIN AMERICAN PHILOSOPHY II   61

Rodolfo Kusch and the Pre-Ontic Turn

Rodolfo Kusch was a peculiar character. Most of his production took place in a small town in the mountains in Jujuy, Argentina, where he affirmed to be in immediate contact with the Latin American being, thus being able to gain insight into it. His work unfolds through a wide range of fields, although we will focus on his essayistic texts, particularly on the two which summarize his perspective: *América profunda* (1962 and 1975) and *Esbozo de una antropología americana* (1978).

In these two works we find already defined the fundamental tenets of the program of the "phenomenological" trend of Latin Americanist thought, which proposed to move beyond the empirical plane and enter that more primitive realm of reality where the fundamental determinations of every historical development would be located. This leads us to the basic antinomy around which Kusch's discourse revolves—that between "ser" (*being*) and "estar" (*being-there*), a kind of translation of the Heideggerian concept of *Dasein*. The concept of *being-there* came thus to replace the "anthropological *a priori*" in Roig. It indicates that more primitive (pre-ontic) realm of reality, which is not a historical product but gives origin, and provides a meaning to history, its ultimate foundation. In short, an *arkhē*. It is not a project either, but it leads us to the realm from which projects emanate, a realm that is therefore conceptually elusive, impossible to define according to rational categories because it does not belong to the sphere of reason, it preexists it.[5] In short, it is neither a pure *a priori* nor an *a posteriori* but rather a kind of *vanishing mediator*, whose entity is ungraspable.[6] We cannot gain access to it through reflection or language; it reveals itself through symbols and gestures, which is the milieu in which native cultures move:

> The demand and use of the archaic is—whether we like it or not—the renewing principle to which natural thought resorts to expand the area

---

[5] "And if the archaic unites opposites, it is because it refers to a foundation. It occurs in the area of what is not thought, because it is left aside." Kusch, *Esbozo de una antropología filosófica americana*, 79.

[6] "This paradoxical relationship between subject and substance, where the subject emerges as the crack in the universal Substance, hinges on the notion of the subject as the 'vanishing mediator' in the precise sense of Freudian-Lacanian Real, i.e., the structure of an element which, although nowhere actually present and as such inaccessible to our experience, nonetheless has to be retroactively constructed, presupposed, if all other elements are to retain their consistency." Slavoj Žižek, *Tarrying with the Negative. Kant, Hegel, and the Critique of Ideology* (Durham: Duke University Press, 1993), 33.

62 THEORETICAL APPROACHES

of thought and to renovate its contact with the absolute, and this cannot be achieved with language. Not for nothing does popular thought prefer gestures to words. Gestures reactivate the demand of the sacred, regardless of words.[7]

Kusch claims to have managed to penetrate that more primitive realm of reality, to have finally found that Latin American *arkhē* in the Quechua and Aymara cultures. He affirms to have discovered it during his trip to Bolivia, which, for Kusch, was tantamount to a kind of "descent into hell,"[8] in the presence of which, as Dante stated, all meaning fades away, that is, all our (Western, rational) knowledge finds that ultimate limit that it cannot trespass ("an unthought area, impossible to be thought").[9] It is in the natural conscience of the natives that that "anti-discourse" is forged, as opposed to the philosophical discourse that is inevitably distorting; that is, abstract, reflexive, thus missing the primitive whole in which meaning is nested.[10] *América profunda* is the product of that journey, the diary of his discovery. The following paragraph summarizes his finding:

> The intuition I outline here oscillates between two extremes. One is what I call "being," or "being someone," in which I discovered in the bourgeois activity of sixteenth-century Europe, and the other, "being-there," which I consider to be the profound modality of pre-Columbian culture and that I tried to elicit from the chronicle of the Indian Santa Cruz Pachacuti. They are the two deep roots of our mestizo mind—in which white and brown

---

[7] Kusch, *Esbozo de una antropología filosófica americana*, 79. Gesture, which is the way in which *being* is expressed, and the natural consciousness of the natives, which is manifested in their spontaneous behavior, is defined by Kusch as a "liturgy," whose meaning can only be accessed through symbolic thought, which is what becomes manifest in it. "Wisdom," he says, "implies a form of radicalized cunning, and therefore a liturgy that can only be justified by means of symbolic thinking." Rodolfo Kusch, *Estar siendo*, in *Obras completes, vol. III* (Rosario: Fundación Ross, 1975), 481.

[8] "It could be thought that what is given and makes of the being-there a foundation, is the hell where reflection should descend. In it there is death, non-life, disorder in the sense of the unusual. It is the descent of thought to the bottom of the philosophical place, where what I am, the being I cling to, becomes diluted, and where I cannot determine what it is, but where everything that is weighs with all its mystery." Kusch, *Esbozo de una antropología filosófica americana*, 113.

[9] Kusch, *Cuando se viaja desde Abra Pampa*. Pamphlet edited by Salma Haidar, San Salvador de Jujuy, Argentina, June 25, 1988. Quoted by Iván Ariel Fresia, "La filosofía de la liberación como filosofía del pueblo. La experiencia del grupo argentino: La línea Kusch, Cullen, Scannone," *Cuadernos de Filosofía Latinoamericana* 39, no. 118 (2018): 83.

[10] The passage from symbolic thinking to critical thinking, he says, "implies the rupture of the meaning that the absolute provides, and a deficit that is not of the object itself, but of the subject." "There is then," he continues, "an existential fall, or rather, a transition from a symbolic consciousness to a critical consciousness, where the 'outside of the thinking globality' is posited." Kusch, *Esbozo de una antropología filosófica americana*, 75.

participate—and can be found in the culture, politics, society and psyche of our milieu. From the conjunction of *being* and *being-there* during the Discovery, *phagocytation* arises, which constitutes the concept resulting from the other two.[11]

The *being-there* to which Kusch intended to get access is condensed into a type of knowledge that is immediately given to consciousness, without having to go through the structures of language, through the distorting prism of reason; in short, it is there where meaning fully presents itself and from where all possible discourses emerge, what underlies all of them:

> Although language can be viewed as the consequence of a combinatorial that results in a structure, simultaneously, there is also another level, a saying, from where an ontology of language can be traced, or rather an ontography of discourse, in the sense of something that visually specifies what might have consistency in it.
>
> In the method I used, the latter was important. As a result of a phenomenology of existence it is possible to justify the existence of a symbolic horizon that structures the discourse. Thus, saying a word does not point to the word, but rather occurs first, as Heidegger affirms, in the articulation of meaning.[12]

Being-there, the object of "a phenomenology of existence," is thus associated to that "symbolic horizon that structures the discourse." This means that *being-there* does not refer exclusively to Latin America. It is a universal category, an "existential" (*existezialen*), in Martin Heidegger's words. Consequently, it could also be found in Europe, although there it was subdued and subjugated by *being*. This very same confrontation can also be found in Latin America between *being* and *being-there* expressed in Peru in the traditional antinomy between the Coast and the Sierra. The Coast is "the excess of form," while the Sierra is that of the "under-lying;" the Coast is the "neatness," the Sierra is the "stench" that expels the visitor; the Coast is the place of reification, the world of the merchant and the Sierra that of "pure subjectivity," "pre-objective," prior to the distinction between subject and object, in which both are still fused. That is precisely what was obscured in the

---

[11] Kusch, *América profunda*, 20–21.
[12] Kusch, *Esbozo de una antropología filosófica americana*, 20.

64 THEORETICAL APPROACHES

West and of whose vestiges can only be found by it in the "East" or through psychoanalysis; at the Coast an abstract, mechanistic vision of the world is displayed, while the Sierra finds itself in immediate communion with the living, the "Lifeworld" (the Husserlian *Lebenswelt*); in short, the Coast is the realm of reflection; the Sierra, that of wisdom.

However, in the struggle between *being* and *being-there*, the former can never end up imposing itself, as, assured Kusch, the former is parasitic of the latter, *being* always presupposes the *being-there* ("everything that is," he said, "is immersed in being-there"). To the process of "acculturation" of *being-there*, Kusch opposes that of "phagocytation" of *being* by the *being-there*. Kusch distinguishes here the "cultural" from "culture" (the "process" and its "institutionalization").[13] This pre-ontic realm, that of "the cultural," is indeterminate, it remains in a magmatic state. But it is precisely in its formlessness that lies the source of its fecundity. It is in the magmatic background of the popular that the primitive substratum of humanity from which the different civilizations successively emerged is condensed and preserved.[14] And it is also from there that the awareness of the relativity of the living arises, where life and death, order and chaos, are fused, inseparable, constituting a meaningful whole—its disaggregation, the establishment of distinctions, is the result of a subsequent work of abstraction produced by reason.[15] According to Kusch, it is this that was transmitted to him by his informant, Santa Cruz Pachacuti. And this leads us to the other fundamental category that Kusch introduced: that of "ground."

Latin American Philosophy and the Problem of the "Ground"

The category of *being-there* in Kusch is closely associated with that of *ground*. The *ground* is precisely where one is, where one stands. It does not refer to a geographical place, but to an existential one; it is, in short, the name of the *arkhē*:

---

[13] Kusch, *Esbozo de una antropología filosófica americana*, 136.

[14] Here Kusch takes up a point by Arnold Toynbee regarding the emergence, throughout history, of around twenty different civilizations that developed and disappeared in succession. But, says Kusch, after the disappearance of each one of them, "the basic magma of the popular that rescues the human until the next civilizing experience is preserved." Kusch, *Esbozo de una antropología filosófica americana*, 144.

[15] Kusch, *América profunda*, 179.

The idea of foundation in philosophy is actually a derivation of the concept of ground, in the sense of "not falling," of standing on the ground, like *stare* or standing on our feet (*Stehen*, in German). And this being, standing, is ready before the circumstance in order to be able to install existence.[16]

The *ground* gives gravity to thought, it always places thought within that *being-there* from which it derives, thus introducing a deformation that frustrates its claim to universality. As he says in relation to the Hegelian system, it can thus be seen "to what extent it also consists of a local deformation of a philosophizing that transcends it," that "was pulled down by the gravitation of the ground."[17]

Here we find an analogue to the idea of "rupture" in Roig, that which dislocates the Absolute. It is, in fact, one of the central topics of philosophical Latin Americanism. The *ground*, as a foundation (*Grund*), forms and deforms at the same time. "The ground," he says, "is not about the empirical, like the River Plate, but about the function of forming, or better, deforming, and ultimately corrupting the intuition of the absolute." "Hence," he continues, "what reason thinks to put *a priori*, suffers a rupture and, therefore, a deformation."[18]

Now, it is worth asking here what the *ground* is on which Kusch's own perspective and, ultimately, Latin Americanist philosophy, in its different versions, stand. For Kusch, as we have seen, it is not about an empirical, a material soil, like physical geography, but a cultural ground.[19] However, the question stands whether it is really from there that his philosophy derived; more precisely, to what extent it is the native culture that founds his discourse, or, conversely, his discourse that shapes his vision of native culture. And, if the latter were the case, what is the structure of that discourse, or more precisely, what is this régime of knowledge on which it itself is based. The first hypothesis (that the Latin Americanist discourse is the emanation of a "Latin American being") is, in actual fact, indemonstrable because it sends us back to a metaphysical sphere, presupposing the existence of a transcendent subjectivity, a hidden, inaccessible essence. On the contrary, the second hypothesis (that the "Latin American being" is, in reality, a construction that takes place in the Latin Americanist discourse itself) can be

---

[16] Kusch, *Esbozo de una antropología filosófica americana*, 18.
[17] Kusch, *Esbozo de una antropología filosófica americana*, 9.
[18] Kusch, *Esbozo de una antropología filosófica americana*, 20.
[19] Véase Kusch, *Geocultura del hombre americano*, in *Obras completas, vol. III*, 5–240.

66 THEORETICAL APPROACHES

assessed through the analysis of the work of these authors, and the conceptual operations present in it. This leads us to the view of one of the most lucid critics of Latin American philosophy, Santiago Castro-Gómez.

The Critique of Latin American Reason

In his book, now a classic in the field, *Crítica de la Razón Latinoamericana*, Castro-Gómez systematically unravels the series of operations that underlie the conceptual constructions of the different trends in this current of thought. And this marks a fundamental turn in the ways of approaching the issue. As he says, "it is not the history of Latin American ideas that interests us, but the genealogy of Latin Americanism."[20] Taking up Foucault's proposal in *The Order of Things* (1966), he states:

> The genealogical approach does not claim to "represent" those voices [the "people's"]. On the contrary, it seeks to excavate the soil of the Latin Americanist discourses that have tried to speak on behalf of the people and show the heterogeneous layers on which they are built.[21]

Seen from this perspective, Latin American philosophers suffer from epistemological naïvety, insofar as they remain blind to the series of presuppositions that make up their own discourse, which is what the genealogical approach intends to recreate. By projecting on an ontological plane, the categories that, in fact, are constitutive of its own discourse, Latin American philosophy reifies them, thus foreclosing the possibility of interrogating its conceptual foundations, the ground of knowledge on which they stand, and that have made those categories conceivable. We meet here the crucial difference between a "history of ideas" and an "archeology of knowledge." The latter does not seek to trace the "influences," which normally are made explicit in the very texts under consideration, but rather to dig deeper to investigate the articulating logics that underlies them (and to show, eventually, how mutually opposed views can, however, be different orientations deriving from one and the same conceptual matrix). While the "influences" are no secret, and

---

[20] Santiago Castro-Gómez, *Crítica de la razón latinoamericana* (Bogota: Pontificia Universidad Javeriana, 2011), 116.
[21] Castro-Gómez, *Crítica de la razón latinoamericana*, 117.

are accepted by the authors at stake, the ground of knowledge refers to that unthought and unthinkable from within their own horizon of thinking.

Penetrating it is, more precisely, the task of an archaeological approach. As Castro-Gómez points out with reference to Zea's and Roig's historical . narratives:

> [These narratives] function appealing to all the motifs and figures defined by that archaeological network of knowledge that Foucault called the modern *episteme*. There is a logic of history, a transcendental subject, some objectifications of consciousness and critical intellectuals who discover themselves as valuable and incidentally reveal the secret of what is ours.[22]

On that pre-conceptual level, we could find what founds a given form of discourse and also what prevents its consistency. The fundamental inconsistency to which anticolonial narratives, in general, give rise to consists, for Castro-Gómez, in that "from the rules of enunciation of the modern episteme there emerges a discourse that enunciates an exteriority to it."[23] In sum, the Latin Americanist philosopher would not be able to perceive to what extent the denunciation of modernity does not place his discourse outside modernity, but inscribes his discourse within it. His discourse thus unconsciously reproduces that régime of knowledge inherent to it. "All the figures that his discourse uses [Castro-Gómez refers here to Dussel, but it could well be extended to other members of the Latin Americanist philosophy] are possible thanks to the same rules that make it the Truth of the discourses in the modern episteme possible."[24]

According to Castro-Gómez, this also explains the instability inherent in Latin American discourse, the oscillation between historicism and phenomenology, between the *a posteriori* and the *a priori*, between *being* and *ought-to-be*; in short, between immanence and transcendence. To him, this is related to the doubling that, for Foucault, is the defining feature of the concept of the subject in the modern episteme. As Foucault shows in *The Order of Things*, the modern subject is a transcendental and empirical duplicate. For Castro-Gómez, it is this ambiguity in that concept that underlies the

---

[22] Castro-Gómez, *Crítica de la razón latinoamericana*, 118–119.

[23] Castro-Gómez, *Crítica de la razón latinoamericana*, 168.

[24] Castro-Gómez, *Crítica de la razón latinoamericana*, 173. "Between Dussel and Gadamer there is no epistemic externality, as Mignolo wrongly states in his Introduction to *The Darker Side of the Renaissance*." Castro-Gómez, *Crítica de la razón latinoamericana*, 173.

68   THEORETICAL APPROACHES

aforementioned oscillation in the Latin Americanist discourse. In fact, as a constituent part of the modern episteme, philosophical Latin Americanism cannot help but reproduce that aporia that is intrinsic to it. However, it is at this point that we must take distance from Castro-Gómez's perspective. As we have said, although his work marks a true turning point in our perspectives of Latin American philosophy, it still demands precision of a historical-conceptual nature.

Latin American Philosophy and the "Age of Forms"

One of the strong points in Castro-Gómez's critique of Latin American philosophy, and, more precisely, of the historicist trend, is that its perspective of (Western) modernity is too vague and generic, which leads to dehistoricized discourses. That is, it leads to placing under the same label (that of "modernity") very different forms of thought, such as nineteenth-century Romanticism and twentieth-century Spiritualism. In this fashion, these perspectives miss that, in actual fact, both are inscribed within two very different régimes of knowledge. And this leads, in turn, to tracing an artificial line of continuity in Latin American thought, one clearly arbitrary (as we have seen in connection with Roig). In the last instance, to make all these very different types of discourses fit the pre-established schemes, these approaches must leave aside precisely that which specify them: their distinguishing features.[25]

However, Castro-Gómez's vision of the "modern episteme" is still very vague, too. It does not allow us to discern what separates Romantic thought from twentieth-century Spiritualism either, and, therefore preventing anachronistic projections like, for example, placing Alberdi and Vasconcelos in the same line of thought. To understand what separates them, we must analyze the nature of the epistemic mutation that occurred in the intervening years,

---

[25] Dussel responded to Castro-Gómez's criticism in *La posmodernidad a debate* (Bogota: Universidad Santo Tomás Aquino, 2002). In a similar vein, Damián Pachón Soto rejects that Latin American philosophers affirm the presence of " 'a thing-in itself' called 'Latin America.'" As he says: "I do not believe that naivety has spread over the continent and that the historicity of what we are and our historical processes has been ignored." Damián Pachón Soto, *Filosofía de la liberación y teorías descoloniales. Textos reunidos.* Colección Nuevas Ideas 5 (Bucamaranga, 2018), 145. Yet, the question here is not whether "Latin America" is a (fixed) "thing-in-itself" or a "historical entity." The critical point in Pachón Soto's statement is that of "what we are." It assumes the presence of a subject underlying the changes it historically undergoes. As we can see, it is simply taken for granted, it remains as the unthought-of and unthinkable premise of this discourse.

which was precisely what made room for the emergence of Latin Americanist philosophy.

In effect, the emergence at the end of the nineteenth century of a new régime of knowledge was what established the conceptual ground from which it arose and stood. Unlike what Kusch and Latin American philosophers affirm, that to which they gave expression was not any illusory "Latin American being," but a given form of discourse, only within whose frameworks the existence of such a being became conceivable.

As I have anticipated, the different trends of philosophical Latin Americanism must be framed in the context of the breakdown of teleological evolutionary conceptions of history that had taken place up to the end of the nineteenth century. In fact, this epistemic mutation that then followed would encompass the whole thinking of the *fin de siècle*, including the natural sciences. Ultimately, it is revealing of the emergence in the West of a new paradigm of temporality, which was founded on a stronger idea of the contingency of historical developments: the presence in them of ruptures that break the linearity of evolutionary processes.

A new discipline that then emerged, electrodynamics, is indicative of the transformations undergone at that moment in the ways of thinking about the historicity of physical (and, by extension, social) systems. In the theory elaborated by Maxwell and Faraday, magnetic fields are not mere aggregates of elements but, as Ferdinand de Saussure said about language, they are sets of relations that make up integrated systems of interacting forces. However, such systems appear as constellations of elements whose composition and re-composition are sudden events, following no genetic pattern of progressive formation. The notion of totality (structure) then became detached from that of finality (function), thus dissociating diachrony from synchrony, the evolutionary processes from the inherent system dynamics, oriented only toward their own self-reproduction, toward the preservation of their internal balance or *homeostasis*.

Once teleological assumptions dislocated, and systems became deprived of any inherent impulse for self-transformation, change could now only come to them from a transcendent instance, placed outside them. Historicity would be the emanation of a being that pre-exists systems, an ego prior to the distinction between subject and object. According to Husserl, this kind of subjectivity prior to the constitution of the subject (which can constitute as such, gain an identity, only in the interior of a given system of references, a structure), leads us back to the pre-categorical instance of institution of

70 THEORETICAL APPROACHES

the primordial senses of reality.[26] What we see here, in short, is the emergence of a new régime of knowledge, a new episteme, in Foucault's words, that will be articulated around the opposition between self-regulating systems and intentional action, between structures and transcendental subjectivity. Adopting the terminology of the time, between "forms" and "life." It is, briefly stated, what elsewhere I have called the "Age of Forms."[27]

In it, "life" works as the generic name to designate that transcendent sphere, that generative force (which would be translated into different figures) prior to any formal configuration, and that eventually emerges disrupting the systems, its empirical crystallizations. The title of the essay dedicated to Sören Kierkegaard that Geörgy Lukács wrote around those years and was included in a book whose very title is already telling, *Soul and Forms*, condenses this concept: "Forms explode when they collide with life."[28] The neo-Kantian "philosophies of life" that then emerge are the best expression of this new paradigm of temporality, the "new historicism" (from which Roig took his fundamental concepts, such as those of "anthropological *a priori*" and "horizon of understanding") being its translation into the field of historical philosophy.

The point that matters here is that this bifurcation in the régime of knowledge that took place at the end of the nineteenth century brought about, in turn, the splitting of the concept of the subject between what Husserl called the "*thetic* subject" and the "*non-thetic* subject" (the "ontic" and the "ontological," for Heidegger). On the one hand, we would have the situated subject, which takes on a specific identity from within a given system of references. The "self" is recognized as a subject only insofar as it occupies a particular position within a relational whole. These positions would be the "situated subjects." On the other hand, there would be that transcendental "ego" from which all these subjective positions emanate, but would not be reducible to any of them, or any set of them, which always exceeds them. The latter is thus

---

[26] See Edmund Husserl, *Ideas Pertaining to a Pure Phenomenology and to a Phenomenological Philosophy. First Book: General Introduction to a Pure Phenomenology* (The Hague: Martinus Nijhoff Publishers, 1983).

[27] On this, see Elías Palti, "The Return of the Subject as a Historical-Conceptual Problem," *History and Theory* 43 (2004): 57–82; *An Archeology of the Political: Regimes of Power from the Seventeenth Century to the Present* (New York: Columbia University Press, 2017).

[28] György Lukács, "Das Zerschellen der Form am Leben," in *Die Seele und die Formen* (Berlin: Egon Fleischel, 1911), 61–90. I have slightly modified the English translation of the title, which reads: "The Foundering of Form Against Life." For an English translation, see György Lukács, "The Foundering of Form Against Life: Søren Kierkegaard and Regine Olsen," in *Soul and Form* (New York: Columbia University Press, 2010), 44–58.

LATIN AMERICAN PHILOSOPHY II   71

always elusive, ungraspable according to (generic, abstract) concepts, which already entail a system of categorical references (a profession, a nationality, a social position, and so on) allowing distinctions. The ego indicates that instance that gives rise to distinctions, to the different modes of "distribution of the sensible" (Rancière),[29] but predates them, the pre-categorical realm where all of them are still fused. We meet here the ultimate limit of reason. It can only know "something as something" (*etwas als etwas*); in it, therefore, meaning is always deferred, it can never penetrate and understand the being itself, in its immediacy, that is, without referring it to something different from it.

Going back to the epistemic rupture that occurred at the end of the nineteenth century, systems, or structures, are always contingent realities. Therefore, they presuppose a primitive institutional instance. Every conceptual order, like every legal-political order, is founded on a series of premises given to it and, consequently, (as, at that very same time, Kurt Gödel established in the field of mathematics) they cannot be demonstrated within that very system; the latter cannot account for that which constitutes the ground on which it rests.[30] Max Weber, in turn, translated this same concept into the socio-historical sphere. As he said, reason can tell us what means we should use to achieve certain ends, but it cannot tell us what ends we should pursue.[31] This refers us back to an ethical sphere, located beyond rationality, which is where sheer subjectivity emerges, where all normativity, all objectivity, is broken.

Now, this raises, in turn, the issue of where these very ethical frameworks emerge from. For phenomenology, it is precisely the transcendental egological realm where the premises on which a given order or system stands emerges, and it is also the one that eventually dislocates them, forcing their reconfiguration, producing its "rupture." In short, it is from there that a "horizon of understanding" displays, the *a priori* that Roig mentions. But it is not really a historical product. It refers us back to the subjective conditions of possibility of all historicity. In his later writings, Husserl referred to it in terms of "Lifeworld" (*Lebenswelt*).[32] This indicated a set of truths immediately given to consciousness, which, like the fundamental codes of our own

---

[29] See Jacques Rancière, *Key Concepts* (London: Acumen Publishing, 2010), 95–103.

[30] It is what Kurt Gödel called "the constitutive incompletitude of axiomatic systems." See S. G. Shanker, ed., *Gödel's Theorem in Focus* (London: Routledge, 1981).

[31] See Max Weber, *Economy and Society, Vol. I* (Berkeley: University of California Press, 1978).

[32] See Edmund Husserl, *The Crisis of European Sciences and Transcendental Phenomenology; an Introduction to Phenomenological Philosophy* (Evanston: Northwestern University Press, 1970).

72   THEORETICAL APPROACHES

culture, are given to us spontaneously, without any reflection, thus enabling our meaningful relation with our social and natural environment, and, lastly, setting the basis for a discursive, rational, kind of knowledge (the "symbolic horizon that structures the discourse," in Kusch's words).

It was Heidegger who made of the critique of reason a synonym for the critique of modernity at large (for Husserl, the point was not really putting modernity into question but rather recovering its original sense which had become "routinized"). As Heidegger stated in "The Age of World Picture," it was with modernity, with Descartes and his *ego cogito*, that the "forgetting of being" was produced (although in subsequent works he projected that moment back in time to Socrates). He associated it to the moment when the subject separated from the world, became placed in front of it as the one who gives meaning to it. In the premodern world, as for Kusch in native cultures, subject and things co-belonged to the world.[33] Everything in it was fused, beings and objects referred to each other, communicated with each other. In short, before the emergence of modernity, it was not the subject who rendered the world meaningful, who re-presented (etymologically, "to make present what is absent") the world; meaning was supposed to be already inscribed in things themselves, they showed themselves, made themselves present. It is with modernity, then, that this inversion of senses was produced by which man placed himself as the founding subject of meaning.[34]

Here we find that "ground" on which Kusch's discourse rests and from which he reads native cultures.[35] The conceptual procedure, characteristic of this phenomenological trend, consists in retranslating into Latin Americanist terms that set of antinomies that are typical of the twentieth-century régime of knowledge, or episteme (what I call the "Age of Forms"), which arose from the break of the evolutionist-teleological views of history, and, as we have

---

[33] See Martin Heidegger, "The Age of World Picture," in *The Question Concerning Technology and Other Essays* (New York: Harper & Row, 1977), 115–154.

[34] "Man becomes the relational center of that which is as such. But this is possible only when the comprehension of what is as a whole changes." Heidegger, *The Question Concerning Technology and Other Essays*, 128.

[35] It is necessary to remark here again the fundamental difference between the notion of "ground" and that of "influence." The "influences" can normally be found explicitly stated in the very texts, and their authors do not ignore them. The "ground" indicates, instead, the level of that unthinkable for them, and indeed for their very sources. None of them are really aware of how their views result from broader conceptual changes, from an epistemic mutation that established the particular régime of knowledge that rendered their own philosophies conceivable.

seen, was articulated around the opposition between self-regulating systems and transcendental subjectivity. The result can be summarized in the following table.

Self-regulated Systems ("Forms")	Transcendental Subjectivity ("Life")
Being	Being-there
Coast	*Sierra*
Europe	Latin America
Reason	Lifeworld
Science-philosophy	Popular wisdom
Abstraction	Intuition
Reification	Subjectivation
Acculturation	Phagocytation
Domination	Emancipation

It is in the Quechua and Aymara cultures that Kusch finds the substratum of original humanity, the realm of transcendental subjectivity from which senses emanate. Through them, he says, he could gain access to that pre-ontic field (ontological, for Heidegger) inaccessible to reason, conceptually elusive, and in which an emancipatory potential would be nested. From it derives that set of antinomies that organizes his discourse, which is not, however, intrinsic to what Foucault called the "modern episteme," as Castro-Gómez states, but inherent in the régime of knowledge that I call the "Age of Forms," which arises precisely from the break of the "modern" régime of knowledge, or episteme, and, more specifically, from the dislocation of the nineteenth-century evolutionary-teleological conceptions of history.

The Argumentative Circularity

At this point, we can see that, beyond their divergences, behind the arguments of the historicist and phenomenological trends underlies the same mechanism, the same logical circularity, by which the ought-to-be, the *a priori*, is projected onto Being, thereby constituting it as such a being, and then proceeds in an inverse manner, affirming that it is from that very being it has constructed that the *a priori*, the ought-to-be, arises. Hence the

74 THEORETICAL APPROACHES

coincidence between the two (being and ought-to-be), as it results from the very circularity of the argument. The very reasoning ensures their convergence, makes it inevitable as, at bottom, it is a tautological reasoning, a specular procedure.

However, the circularity of its logic does not occlude the ultimate infirmity of its conceptual foundations. To connect the two terms (the *a priori* and the *a posteriori*), it was necessary to find something that works as an absolute underlying them. What changes, in each case, is the realm in which these conceptual constructions of an *arkhē* is posited: in History and in Being, respectively. It is at this point that their respective arguments bifurcate. However, none of these trends will be able to hold the logic of their respective discourses in a consistent manner. In the previous chapter, we saw the aporias to which the Latin Americanist historicist concept led once the conceptual ground on which it was founded had become undermined; that is, that the teleological assumptions that were inherent in it had become theoretically untenable. Now we will see the kind of problems that the Latin Americanist phenomenological argument raised.

As we have seen, the perspective of the phenomenological trend claims to be based on an existential link with that transcendent, ontological realm of reality, which is not conceptually mediated, in which meaning would be given immediately to consciousness, without having to traverse the distorting element of rational discourse. However, in that very postulate we can observe the distance that separated it from its object, its strangeness, foreignness. The same thing that Vincent Crapanzano said of Clifford Geertz's Balinese can be said of Kusch's Aymara:

> We must not be carried away by Geertz's Grand Guignol sensibility. We must ask: On what grounds does he attribute "social embarrassment," "moral satisfaction," "aesthetic disgust" (whatever that means), and "cannibal joy" to the Balinese? To all Balinese men? To any Balinese man in particular? Clearly Geertz's aim, like Catlin's, is to render the moment vivid, but unlike Catlin, who makes no pretense of uncovering the subjective meaning—the experience—of the O-Kee-Pa ceremony for the Mandan, Geertz does make such a claim of the Balinese.[36]

---

[36] Vincent Crapanzano, *Hermes' Dilemma and Hamlet's Desire* (Cambridge, MA: Harvard University Press, 1992), 65.

In the same fashion, Kusch's discourse remains attached to the idea of "cultural totality." In his perspective, the native appears as a generic and abstract being. In fact, Kusch does not doubt that the sayings of his informant, Santa Cruz Pachacuti (which he conveniently retranslates according to his own categories), are valid and shared, not only by all members of his community, but also by others very distant from them, both in geographical and cultural terms, from the Tlaxtaltecas of the Central Valley of Mexico to the Mapuches of the South of Chile.

That supposed generic native "being," besides, would not only comprise, in an undifferentiated way, the populations of the entire continent, but it would also have remained identical to itself from before the Conquest to the present.[37] The sayings of his informant would refer to an ancestral knowledge ("the profound modality of pre-Columbian culture")[38] which refers back to a remote, mythical past, impossible to be located in time.

However, it is at this point that the discourse of the phenomenological trend falls into a "performative contradiction," which consists of the fact that, in the very act of saying something, one contradicts what is affirmed (as when one says "I am not speaking"). In this case, the very operation by which the subject of enunciation seeks to identify itself with its object is precisely what makes manifest its alienness with respect to it: what shines through such a generic view of the "natives" is the foreigner's view; as a matter of fact, Native Americans could never have identified themselves as such (in the terms popularized by Marvin Harris, it is an *etic* category, not an *emic* one).[39]

The point is that the reproduction of the same circular logic in the discourses of both currents—the historicist and the phenomenological—is not incidental. They are opposed to each other, but at the same time they are mutually inseparable, from the moment that both are erected on the basis of the same epistemic ground. Underlying their antagonism lies a common régime of knowledge, which ultimately explains the permanent oscillation of the Latin Americanist discourse between these two trends.

As we have seen, the Latin Americanist discourse is founded on a given conceptual ground, a certain régime of knowledge that results from the break of the evolutionary-teleological views of history. However, the bifurcation

---

[37] "Hence," says Kusch at the beginning of *América profunda*, "this book arises from the firm conviction of the continuity of the American past in the present." Kusch, *América profunda*, 19.

[38] Kusch, *América profunda*, 21.

[39] See Marvin Harris, *Cultural Materialism: The Struggle for a Science of Culture* (New York: Random House, 1980), 29–45.

76 THEORETICAL APPROACHES

then produced on this archaeological level of knowledge contained a paradox, which is also the one manifested in the Latin Americanist discourse. In this new conceptual universe torn by the opposition between "forms" and "life," between self-regulating systems and transcendental subjectivity, both poles oppose each other but at the same time they presuppose and refer back to each other permanently. In short, they are mutually contradictory, but one cannot be sustained without the other. The Latin Americanist discourse could not avoid replicating this paradoxical relationship at the bosom of its own discourse.

On the one hand, from the moment that the idea of history as a closed, self-contained system became untenable, the historicist trend could not avoid relapsing into the metaphysical terrain (the pure *a priori*, that is, the appellation to an instance in which meaning becomes immediately present to consciousness).[40] But, conversely, the phenomenological trend shows us why it will not be possible for it to stay in that terrain either, why the idea of an ultimate foundation (a transcendental being) cannot avoid occluding the historicity of its very institution; in short, being tainted by the stigma of the contingency of its foundations, which demolishes it as an *arkhē*.

In effect, the discourse of the phenomenological trend departs from the idea of history as a closed, self-contained, and self-generated totality. It thus seeks to transfer reflection to a plane prior to it, to the conditions of possibility of historicity,[41] that which the historicist discourse presupposes without being able to thematize; that is, without falling into argumentative circularity: the modes of constitution of the *a priori*. The transcendental being (or being-there, for Kusch), as the instance of subjectivity from which history emanates, would therefore be situated outside of it, constituting its *a priori*. Now, that *a priori*, that being, is no longer a generic human being, one that plunges its roots into nature itself, as in Kant, but it could no longer be itself a historical, contingent entity, either, without falling into circularity. Phenomenological essentialism thus represents an escape toward transcendence (a realm of timeless essences), an attempt to move beyond history,

---

[40] This is what Derrida, after Heidegger, denounced as the "metaphysic of presence." See Jacques Derrida, "Ousia and Grammē: Note on a Note from 'Being and Time,'" in *Margins of Philosophy* (Chicago: The University of Chicago Press, 1972), 29–67.

[41] According to Dussel, the essence is not a historical construction, but the other way around: history is the manifestation of the essence. As he says, "It is not that the essence is realized in history, but rather that it manifests its notes over the course of the history." Enrique Dussel, *Historia de la filosofía y filosofía de la liberación* (Bogota: Editorial Nueva América, 1994), 118.

beyond pure empiricity, never being able to achieve it. The only way to solve that contradiction, of making the *a priori* and the *a posteriori* converge, is, again, by resorting to the idea of a logic in history, a spontaneous identity between the realms of facts and the realm of values, a concept which, as we have seen, would no longer be available. It is actually that against which the phenomenological project reacted, which emerged, precisely, as a consequence of the break of the teleological views of history.

This realization would eventually force a redefinition within this phenomenological line of philosophical Latin Americanism. At this point, what would confer an identity on this Latin American being, the set of attributes that supposedly would define it, could not be sought on the level of the ancestral knowledge of the native culture, as Kusch intended, or in history, as Roig proposed, but in the present condition of that being; that is, as the result of the colonial situation to which it is subjected. It is this that, in the following years, will become placed at the center of the reflection of the phenomenological trend. The colonial condition will then become the core of its discourse, the axis around which all of it will subsequently revolve. It is that which will define the nature of the "Latin American" being, and not its presumed roots.

However, the reflection on the colonial condition will take place in that very metaphysical terrain in which all this form of discourse is situated, thus giving rise to a series of intellectual operations by which the concepts of the anti-colonial discourse will be retranslated in terms of the categories of phenomenology and post-phenomenology (in their different variants). In any case, while this new orientation clearly takes distance from Kusch's argument, it finds in it already designed the conceptual path to be followed. The pre-ontic realm, the *being-there* that Kusch spoke about, conveniently redefined, will then be reinterpreted as indicating the "outside" of the colonial order, where the latter finds it denied *Truth*.[42] In the work of the other fundamental representative of this trend, Enrique Dussel, we can see more clearly the series of conceptual operations to which this project gives rise.

---

[42] Hence, the phenomenological current of philosophical Latin Americanism will never abandon completely the reference to some archaic substratum of being allegedly still present and oppressed by the colonial system.

78 THEORETICAL APPROACHES

Enrique Dussel and the Analectical Method

Dussel is perhaps the last of the Latin American philosophers. In any case, he is the one who has assumed today its paternity and appropriates almost exclusively its legacy. In fact, he is the one who has breathed new life into this phenomenological trend of philosophical Latin Americanism, incorporating new conceptual references into it.

An important influence in his trajectory was Jesuit Juan Carlos Scannone (a teacher of the present Pope, Francis I), who introduced Dussel into Emmanuel Lévinas's thinking, especially his work *Totalité et Infini, Essai sur l'exteriorité* (1961).[43] He also let him know about the analectical method, which Scannone took up, in turn, from Bernhard Lakebrink.[44] He had applied it to scholastic thought to distinguish it from the modern dialectical method, but Dussel would reformulate it as indicating the characteristic method of Latin American thought, as opposed to the European dialectical method. For Dussel, it condenses Lévinas's idea of "otherness." Based on these new conceptual coordinates, Dussel reconfigures the logic of the Latin Americanist discourse, departing from the binary scheme that was inherent in it and rearticulating it according to a ternary structure, which, in the last instance, replicates the Christian Trinitarian pattern (a tradition in which both Scannone and Dussel are deeply imbued).

In effect, the structure of his thought breaks the binary schematism that we find in Kusch, which opposed two realms of reality: the ontic and the ontological or pre-ontic (*being* and *being-there*, in Kusch's terminology). From his reading of Lévinas, Dussel draws the presence of a third realm, which he calls trans-ontological.

As he points out, the ontic realm is that of pure objectuality, pure dispersion, it is in the ontological realm where a world is instituted, where the former is invested with meaning. Following the classical tenets of phenomenology, for Dussel it is in that ontological realm that the social and natural environment becomes meaningful. However, for Dussel this entails what he

---

[43] Emmanuel Lévinas, *Totalité et Infini, Essai sur 1 'exteriorité* (Paris: Kluwer Academic- Martinus Nijhoff, 1971).

[44] Juan Carlos Scannone, "Hacia una filosofía a partir de la filosofía popular," in *Para una filosofía desde Latinoamérica*, ed. Juan Carlos Scannone and Ignacio Ellacuría (Bogota: Universidad Javeriana, 1992), 134.

calls an "involution" to the whole, the reduction of plurality to a single generative principle (the "uniprinciple," as he calls it).

It is at the trans-ontological realm that the rupture of totality takes place as the result of the irruption of an "other." That "other," for Lévinas, was the one that does not lend itself to be reduced to a mere object, a "someone" who rebels against its objectification, its reduction to a "something," and thus opens the horizon to transcendence, to that which points out beyond the regulated order of the totality. Dussel takes up this Levinasian concept of the emergence of the "other" and identifies it with the "face of the poor," in general, and the oppressed Latin American people, in particular.[45]

The ontological field, that of totality, is presided by a system of identities and differences, which is what underlies the dialectical method. The trans-ontological, instead, is governed by a system of analogies and distinctions, the one on which the analectical method is founded. In the identity system, comparisons are established out of a single principle that allows the dissimilar to be equalized. On the contrary, in the analogical system, the encounter with the alien makes room for the creation of a common ground, a field of contact and mutual understanding, where an exchange can be produced without seeking to reduce the alien to the same, thereby opening the horizon to the heterogeneous, the irreducible to the totality which is, for Dussel, the one currently governed by the capitalistic order. It is this, the capitalist system, that today works as the articulator of a "world," the one in control of supplying mechanisms of meaning.

However, as we will see, at this point Dussel incurs a performative contradiction, different from Kusch's, but analogous in its structure. In his case, when trying to give a *political* translation to the Levinasian philosophy, to supplement it by developing a political project based on the analectical method—whose lack, according to Dussel, represents the fundamental shortcoming in Lévinas's system—he ends up offering the best example of what he himself calls the system of "totality," founded on a régime of identities and differences, articulated around an "uniprinciple."

---

[45] "Lévinas always speaks of the other as the 'absolutely other.' He then tends towards equivocation. On the other hand, he has never thought that the other could be an Indian, an African, or an Asian. The other, for us, is Latin America with respect to the whole of Europe, it is the poor and oppressed Latin American people with respect to the dominating and yet dependent oligarchies." Enrique Dussel, *Método para una filosofía de la liberación* (Buenos Aires: Ágora, 1974), 181–182.

80 THEORETICAL APPROACHES

Dialectics' Forking Paths

Let us first see the evolution of the dialectical method, according to Dussel. As he says, it followed two opposite directions. The first, the oldest, expressed by Aristotle, starts from the original fact, the *factum*, and moves toward the beyond, toward transcendence. This form of dialectics, he says, was critical, rejecting any claim of totality. The second form of dialectic, the modern, conversely, starts from the *factum* and moves toward the beneath, that is, it produces an "immanentist involution."

At this point, Dussel follows Heidegger's approach, identifying this "immanentist involution" with the emergence of the Cartesian *ego cogito*. It starts from facticity, he says, only to subsequently deny it and produce the involution toward the immanence of the subject. The substance then becomes consciousness; "Subjectivity now becomes a founding and fundamental subjectivity." "Facticity," he concludes, "becomes then irretrievable: *Lifeworld*, existential understanding, can unfold within the interiority of the *cogito* only under the form of ideas. The *cogito* becomes the point of departure and of arrival: it is everything."[46] Hegel is allegedly the one who completes the involution of dialectics. The *ego cogito* then becomes imperialistic reason. "The ontology of the identity of reason and divinity with being ends up founding the imperial wars of a Europe dominating all other peoples."[47]

It is to this immanentist involution of dialectics that the analectic evolution to transcendence comes to oppose. According to Dussel, the reaction against the "immanentist involution" begins with the so-called irrationalist philosophies, whose origin is in the "second" Schelling, a reaction that Lukács—wrongly, in Dussel's view—identified with the process that would eventually lead to the emergence of Nazism.[48] However, the key figure in this reaction is one alien to that irrationalist tradition of thought, but which, according to Dussel, converges with it in the process of dismantling of Hegelian dialectics: Ludwig Feuerbach. His importance, he says, resides in the fact he detaches anti-dialectics, the liberation process, from the purely ideal realm, and puts in its center the issue of incarnation:

---

[46] Dussel, *Método*, 36.

[47] Dussel, *Método*, 114.

[48] See Geörgy Lukács, *The Destruction of Reason* (Atlantic Highlands, NJ: Humanities Press Inc., 1981).

LATIN AMERICAN PHILOSOPHY II   81

In contrast with Schelling, who only shows the trans-ontological transcendence of eternal freedom (a creationism without incarnation), Feuerbach understands that Christianity, in a first moment (and it is what he properly understood), was the denial of fetishes and the affirmation of man as the transcendence of the "unjust current order" (fetish); Christianity is not only face-to-face with God, the creator, but "in-incarnation."[49]

This reference to the "first moment" of Christianity and its relationship with the question of the incarnation contains the key to understand Dussel's conceptual system. We find here its core, and its link with theology. With Feuerbach, he says, a new materialism arises, no longer alien to the spiritual; on the contrary, it expresses its empirical materialization. As Dussel says:

> The essence of Christianity is incarnation, but it is impossible in pure rationalism. Reality is discovered by the material or sensible conditions of knowledge because man is not only consciousness, nor is he only matter, since "in the human essence there is a qualitative change" in respect of animals.[50]

Feuerbach's concept is thus revealed here as the prehistory of Latin American philosophy, that which opened up the horizon to it. "The new philosophy, the Latin American, must also assume this prehistoric moment of its constitution: the sensitive face of the other man, who is hungry and bloody, lays beyond the system where being is [merely, EP] thinking."[51]

The key concept here is that of incarnation. For Dussel, the "other," the Latin American poor, is not a merely empirical subject. In it, something of the order of the sacred becomes manifest in the world. The face of the humiliated is the epiphany of God, the material incarnation of Him. Ultimately, Dussel's God is not the Father who is in Heaven, but the one who descended to Earth and died on the Cross. This is not that of Christianity, the ecclesiastical institution, which participates in the system of totality, situated on the ontological realm, but that of primitive Christianism, which supposes its rupture, takes us to the trans-ontological realm.[52] For him the issue of incarnation constitutes the core of Christianism.

[49] Dussel, *Método*, 130.
[50] Dussel, *Método*, 131.
[51] Dussek, *Método*, 136.
[52] As a matter of fact, Dussel's project aims to fuse theology and anthropology, to create something like an "anthropological theology." "We want to show," he says, "that faith can be an anthropological

82   THEORETICAL APPROACHES

For Dussel, the struggle between Western reason and the Latin American oppressed being is no longer, properly speaking, a struggle between historical forces, or between empirical subjects. They are the embodiments of two transcendent principles, of two eternal substances. It is a struggle between gods, the *ego cogito* being the god of evil against whom the liberation philosophy will engage in an existential battle. Ultimately, the *ego cogito* is not a historical-conceptual formation, but the name of an eternal principle. Whenever there was domination, it is the *ego cogito* that stuck its tail in. As Dussel points out:

> From the "I conquer" Aztec and Inca worlds, all of America; from the "I enslave" to the blacks in Africa sold for the gold and silver obtained through the death of the Indians at the bottom of the mines; from the "I win" in the wars in India and China and the shameful "opium war;" from that "I," it is always the Cartesian thinking of the *ego cogito* that appears.[53]

Of course, there is no way of discovering the existence of some empirically verifiable link between Descartes's philosophy and the events he refers to. In any case, it does not make any sense to analyze what Descartes postulated in his *Discourse on Method* to establish it, because, in Dussel's perspective, the concept of *ego cogito* is not a historical entity but that of a figure, upon which values, assumptions, situations, dilemmas, problems, that far exceed it, were projected. Dussel's narrative is not, properly speaking, a historical-conceptual reconstruction (nor does it claim to be so, in fact), but the relation of a theodicy, of the march of God in the world, of the different modes and moments of its manifestation on Earth.

The Ethical Turn

For Dussel, the reaction against immanentist involution is completed by Heidegger. "Now the dialectical movement will start, not towards the

---

position (in the face-to-face of the man–woman, parents–children, brother–sister) and that is why there is philosophy in revelation and anthropological faith." Enrique Dussel, "El método analéctico y la filosofía latinoamericana," in *Hacia una filosofía de la liberación latinoamericana*, ed. Oswaldo Ardiles et al. (Buenos Aires: Bonum, 1973), 118, n.1.

[53] Enrique Dussel, *Filosofía de la liberación* (Bogota: Editorial Nueva América, 1977), 19–20.

involutive immanence of subjectivity, but towards the transcendence of the world whose last onto-logical horizon is the being that manifests itself."[54] However, for him, it is still inscribed within the horizon of the totality. Beyond the process of the ontological reduction of chaos to world, Dussel introduces a third term, which he calls "cosmos." The cosmos contains the world but exceeds it. In it is inscribed all of that which the world cannot comprehend:

> The world, my world, that opens up from the ontological horizon of being, is only a small space of "meaning" superimposed within the much larger space of the cosmos. . . . The non-identity between reality and being, between cosmos and world, between real constitution and meaning, is the very negation of the last Hegelian claim and the implantation of Heideggerian thinking on bases that surpass it.[55]

We are ready now to "take the essential step,"[56] the step to *analectics*. For this, it is necessary to abandon the realm of science, the ontic realm, but also the realm of dialectics, that of ontology, and move to the ethical plane. The "openness towards the other" is, in essence, an ethical invocation:

> The characteristic of the analectic method is that it is intrinsically ethical and not merely theoretical, as is the ontic discourse of the sciences or the ontological discourse of dialectics. That is to say, the acceptance of the other as an Other already means an ethical choice, a choice and a moral commitment . . . "Every morning my ear awakens so that I can hear as a disciple" (Is 50, 4).[57]

It is in this ethical turn—which, as he says, lies at the core of the analectic method—that the aforementioned performative contradiction becomes more clearly manifest. It entails a relapse into the kind of dualisms proper to the kind of ontology that Dussel claimed to have overcome. Dussel's account of "analectics" is actually founded on a series of binary oppositions, which rest, in turn, on what he calls the "system of identities." Ultimately, for Dussel, history is nothing more than the deployment of an essential antagonism

[54] Dussel, *Método*, 159.
[55] Dussel, *Método*, 170.
[56] Dussel, *Método*, 175.
[57] Dussel, *Método*, 182.

84   THEORETICAL APPROACHES

between two transcendent ethical principles embodied, respectively, in two traditions, the Indo-European and the Judeo-Semitic. According to him, the latter is characterized by an ethical and dialogical drive, which would already be present in Hammurabi's Code:

> [Unlike the Indo-European] the Semitic man is born and grows not in the "logic of totality" (man-nature), but in the "logic of otherness" (man's face before the other's face, free). The sacred, the divine is never the *fysis*, the totality, but "the other," the nameless, the exteriority, the nothingness as the unconditional freedom of the "person" (*propsopon*, which means "face").[58]

This binarism is intrinsic to his ethical predicament, which demands clearly established oppositions, whose respective axiological contents were immediately graspable. And it is also at the basis of his definitively ahistorical perspective, given the transcendent nature of the values here at stake, which leads us to the question of the "Other."

The Levinasian Other is that which does not lend itself to become reduced to a mere object, that rebels itself against being caught within the categorical web projected upon it by the "One." Now, Dussel's "Other," the "Latin American poor," is not really an "Other" but actually a projection of the "One" of the Latin Americanist philosopher. The former is just telling of the anxieties of the latter, who needs that figure of the "Other" because it is a fundamental category within the economy of its own discourse. Ultimately, the figure of the "Other" is just a node within a given discursive network. It fills a hole within a conceptual grid. In any case, what matters here is that this discursive network is no longer that of Kusch's; although it derives from the latter's, the logic of its articulation differs. It is in this sense that the figure of the "Other" in Dussel becomes relevant because it is revealing of the changes that political-philosophical language underwent in the last quarter of the

---

[58] Dussel, *Método*, 211. Dussel considers that the inheritors of that tradition of thinking alternative to "Indoeuropean rationalism" are not the "philosophers of suspicion," as Roig stated, but Jewish thinkers, particularly, Emannuel Lévinas, Martin Buber, and Franz Rosenzweig. See Enrique Dussel, *El humanismo semita. Estructuras radicales del pueblo de Israel y otros semitas* (Buenos Aires: Eudeba, 1969). Other authors, such as Walter Mignolo, although they prefer to limit the search for the genealogy of their own thought to the local context, share the same vision of the forms of thinking as timeless entities that cross through the centuries without break in continuity. Mignolo may thus believe that he has found the "decolonial" idea that he endorses already perfectly articulated in the work of Guaman Poma de Ayala. "I place my theory," he asserts, "in the context of the decolonial paradigm that we already find in Guaman Poma de Ayala." Walter Mignolo, *La idea de América Latina. La herida colonial y la opción decolonial* (Barcelona: Gedisa, 2005), 16–17.

twentieth century. Lastly, it illustrates how what we call the "Age of Forms" then also began to dissolve and a new epistemic ground started to take shape.

In effect, the transition from phenomenology to post-phenomenology witnessed the process of dissolution of the idea of a transcendental subject. If it was not left aside, it indeed became deprived of any positive content, any attribute, and turned merely into the outward manifestation of a fissure located within systems themselves, their ontological void. The ontological (pre-ontic) realm, as the place where sense was immediately given to transcendental consciousness (that of popular *wisdom* that precedes *knowledge*), loses then its former transparency and becomes a problem. It ceases to be that which explains everything, the *arkhē*, and turns into something which needs itself to be explained.

Political-philosophical reflection then moved from the question on the subject to that on the intra-systemic conditions for the emergence of subjectivity; more precisely, to what prevents politico-juridical and conceptual orders from reaching their vocation to constitute themselves as self-integrated, closed systems, logically and rationally founded.[59] The axis of reflection thus shifted from the transcendent subject to structural indeterminacy, to the inner fissures in systems that open up the field to the irruption of contingency, which thus becomes an immanent dimension in systems, the result of their own dynamics, and not something that comes to them from without (from intentional action). In short, the subject is no longer transcendent to systems, but neither merely a "structural effect," as Althusser affirmed, but a kind of *effect of dis-structure*.[60]

The best expression of this conceptual turn is the emergence of post-foundational philosophies.[61] Dussel's system cannot be properly inscribed within this post-foundational current, but his thinking participated of that broader process of conceptual transformations that took place in the last quarter of the twentieth century. The ground on which Kusch stood had already started shaking, opening a latitude to a conceptual constellation that was not its own. If many ideas remain, the logic of their articulation had then changed. Its expression is the ternary logic that articulates Dussel's thought,

---

[59] On the epistemic mutation then produced, see Elías Palti, *New Directions in Political-Intellectual History* (Cambridge: Cambridge University Press, forthcoming).

[60] I have elaborated on this in *Intellectual History and the Problem of Conceptual Change*.

[61] See Oliver Marchart, *Post-foundational Political Thought in Nancy, Lefort, Badiou and Laclau* (Edimburgh: Edimburgh University Press, 2007); Elías Palti, *Verdades y saberes del marxismo. Reacciones de una tradición política ante su "crisis"* (Buenos Aires: FCE, 2007) [French edition: *Vérités et savoirs du marxisme. Réactions d'une tradition politique à sa crise* (Paris: Editions Delga, 2018)].

86   THEORETICAL APPROACHES

which underlies the play of antinomies on the superficial level of the semantic contents of his discourse, the realm of "ideas."

As we have seen, Dussel breaks the binary scheme proper to phenomenology (the opposition between the ontic and the ontological) introducing a third realm of reality: the trans-ontological. Now, the same ternary scheme is reproduced within his own discourse. And it is here that Dussel's discourse connects with the Christian Trinitarian pattern. We have already seen that the core of Dussel's philosophy lies in the issue of incarnation, the way in which the sacred makes itself present in the world. Now, in the Christian trinitarian scheme, the transubstantiation of the Father into the Son demands the intercession of a third term; otherwise, without mediation, in the "face-to-face with God," one could not properly speak of incarnation, there would be an immediate communion between the substance and its manifestation, a pure identity. It is the introduction of this third term, the Holy Spirit, which allows the three terms to become fused into a single substance, thereby solving the paradox of God being three and one at the same time. However, the fundamental point here is that, in the Christian eschatological pattern, the Fall, the split between the transcendent and the immanent realms, between the sacred and the profane, in short, the alienation of man from the divine essence (which is what makes the intervention of a third factor necessary), is not merely an incident, it is the very condition of possibility for the plan of salvation, that which opens up the horizon for it. And this brings us back to Scannone.

We have already said that Scannone played a key role in the development of Dussel's philosophy, introducing him to Lévinas's thought, as well as to the concept of the analectic method. But there is something even more important that Dussel does not point out which imbues his discourse even more deeply: the concept of the "third," that is, the figure of the mediator, the subject that has overcome his situation of alienation and gained insight into its "inner, authentic being," thus opening the horizon for transcendence.

For Scannone, the "mediator" would be the very oppressed people who have become aware of their situation (or, eventually, also the oppressor who rejects his condition as such). However, the idea of a "mediator" supposes that the transition to self-awareness of one's own being necessarily requires an external intervention (otherwise, as we have seen, it would not be a "mediation," but a spontaneous communion, a plain identity between the divine essence and its worldly manifestation). This is also the basic assumption of the "phenomenological" ("populist") trend of Latin American philosophy.

Dussel's reasoning is as follows. The "irruption of the other" already presupposes the "openness towards the other," a certain ethical disposition. Ultimately, the face of the other is not what produces the dislocation of the system of the totality, but the other way around, the former is the consequence of the latter: it is first necessary for the system of totality to become dislocated for that which cannot be reducible to it, to the régime of identities and differences, to become present; that is, for the face of the other to appear as such (otherwise, nothing would prevent the other from being reduced to the same). And this then raises the question of how this "openness to the other" is produced, in short, how it is that the "world" (in Dussel's sense) is dislocated, and "chaos" is introduced in it, that which exceeds and is unassimilable into it.

Ultimately, the subjective decision to embrace that Truth embodied in that which is strange to us has the form of a "conversion," of a sudden enlightenment. It presupposes, in turn, an ethical disposition (God only speaks to those who are willing to listen to Him). But for such a conversion to occur, something or someone is required to ignite the spark, someone to produce that shock in the subject that leads it to abandon its merely mundane existence and redirect its sight toward the transcendent. It is here, in sum, that we find the place for the Latin American philosopher.[62] It thus emerges as an "evanescent mediator," the third term, neither *a priori* nor *a posteriori*, that serves as a catalyst to articulate these two incompatible realms (immanence and transcendence).

Now we can complete the basic structure of Dussel's argument, his version of the Sacred Trinity. To the One (Totality) Dussel opposes the Two (Scission). Yet, the Two, in turn, presupposes the Three (Mediation), which produces the "rupture" of the One. Therefore, at this point, we must revise our previous statement. In his later writings, the core category that articulates Dussel's discourse moves from that of "incarnation," the mundane expression of the divine essence, to that of "rupture," the scission between the sacred and its mundane manifestation. Incarnation, conceived as an immediate identity between the substance and its mundane manifestation, would be a mere monologue of God with Himself (ontology, dialectical involution).

---

[62] In Thomistic theology, there are two ways in which God operates in the world. The immediate modes can be recognized because they are inscribed in the very nature of things; they are part of their very definitions. This is not the case with God's indirect ways of operating, in which there is room for latitude, that is, things can be in one way, but also in another. In these cases, the action of mediating agents is needed to connect the phenomenon with its ultimate cause, which is God, and thus produce specific effects.

88 THEORETICAL APPROACHES

Only the rupture, the scission, the alienation of the subject with respect to its sacred essence opens up the field to a dialogical relation (trans-ontology, analectics).

Hence, what the figure of the Third produces is not the reunion of the split elements into the Totality (the dialectical synthesis of the opposites), but its rupture, the revelation of the dominating, oppressive nature of Totality. Lastly, only the introduction of this figure of the "mediator" renders Dussel's discourse coherent, and, at the same time, paradoxically, it is what installs a fissure in it. In Chapter 2, we saw how the bankruptcy of the evolutionary-teleological view of history made it impossible to entrust the constitution of the (Latin American) subject to the spontaneous development of history, manifesting the fact that it is only constituted as such in the very discourse that invokes it; that is, within a given horizon of understanding, to which the constitution of the subject thus presupposes. Even though the idea of History (with a capital 'H') is not abandoned, what we discover then is that it does not speak for itself, that someone must speak in its name, to force it to tell its Truth. It is this, in fact, what is expressed in Roig's discourse in its indecisive oscillation between the *a priori* and the *a posteriori*, between *being* and what *ought-to-be*, between the given and the sought-for, and which ends up locking it in an argumentative loop.

Now, what is expressed behind the idea of the "third" in Dussel is the fact that, just as History never speaks for itself, neither does the "people," that it is necessary for someone to speak on its behalf, someone who assumes its expression.[63] This is what leads to the introduction of the figure of the mediator. And it is also here that the problematic core in the discourse of this phenomenological trend resides, from which Dussel's perspective takes distance without really breaking away from it and the metaphysical assumptions implicit in it. The figure of the mediator introduces the presence of a subject alien to the people and that constitutes a fundamental factor in its constitution.

---

[63] As we saw in the previous chapter, the problem of mediation is also fundamental for the historicist line. As Roig said in his criticism of the concept of "ideology": "The doctrine of the ideology, according to which this would be a 'reflection' of the social relations considered in their pure facticity, has led to ignoring the phenomenon of mediation, creating the illusion that extralinguistic reality and its expression in language can be immediately confronted, since access to the former would be direct. But this is not the case, since, in order to establish the desired confrontation, that reality must also be expressed at a discursive level. There are no raw economic or social facts without the mediation of discursive forms. The confrontation does not occur, therefore, between a naked reality and the theories or doctrines, scientific or not, but among discursive forms." Roig, *Teoría y crítica del pensamiento latinoamericano*, 19.

Whether this is the Latin Americanist philosopher, as Dussel postulates, or someone who emerges from the people itself, as Scannone affirms, is irrelevant here. The point is that, in any case, the idea of a self-manifestation of (Latin American) being, the self-expression of those contents immediately given to intentional consciousness, is revealed as unviable. And this ends up locking this discourse within a logical circularity, different from that of the historicist trend, although closely associated with it.

What we find this time is an indecisive oscillation between expression and transformation, which is, in actual fact, what underlies that between the *a priori* and *a posteriori*. The phenomenological trend, as we have seen, splits the body of the subject, distinguishing between the empirical, material people, and its immaterial, transcendent substance. It posits the presence of an insubstantial essence behind the former. And its explanation must be found in the very economy of its discourse. It is not a mere corroboration of a reality that exists independently.

As we have seen, the Latin American philosopher, or the one who assumes the role of the mediator, addresses an alienated society which does not know its true being. It has been a central point in Dussel's work since his seminal presentation at the First National Congress of Philosophy (1971), in which he stated that:

> Philosophy is a thinking that clarifies to a people their own situation. And if the sciences of the spirit and, especially, philosophy are alienated, our people stop having teachers.[64]

It thus places itself in a position of transcendence with respect to that society. And *it is this* what leads to invoking the existence of a subject behind that subject, to building that figure of a transcendent being, of which, in turn, the philosopher claims to be its spokesperson and expression. This does not have an empirical reference, it is a purely discursive construction, it does not indicate anything whose identity and nature could be determined. It is not a

---

[64] Enrique Dussel, "Metafísica del sujeto y liberación," in *Temas de Filosofía contemporánea*, ed. Alberto Caturelli (Buenos Aires: Sudamericana, 1971), 32. In a posterior version of that work, Dussel insisted on the missional character of the philosopher's work: "Philosophy must discover in Latin America its liberating, prophetic function; It must anticipate the project of a people [. . .]. It is not so much a question of passive Socratic maieutics, but rather of active participation in fertilization, by fecundity, in the procreation of the new child, the liberated Other." Dussel, *Para un ética de la liberación latinoamericana* (Buenos Aires: S.XXI, 1973), 155.

90 THEORETICAL APPROACHES

sociological reality but a metaphysical, immaterial substance, whose entity is always elusive, ungraspable.

We have here the fundamental point, that which is at the basis of this form of discourse, the point where its deep nature is revealed. Ultimately, *the transcendent nature of the being it invokes is just the projection of the transcendent character of the very discourse that invokes it*. The postulate of the existence of a being situated beyond the empirical realm is the inverted reflection of the transcendent position in which the one who enunciates its existence places itself. And the elusive character that this being assumes is a reflection of the difficulties the thinker comes up against when defining its own role in society.

In the last instance, what is made manifest is the philosopher's impossibility to assume the radical contingency of the foundations of his own knowledge. The result is a kind of fetishist unconscious mechanism. The anxieties and expectations deposited in its product then appear as if they were inherent attributes in it. Thus, what the thinker has built (in this case, the "Latin American being") suddenly appears as acquiring a life of its own and thereby able to determine the orientations, to impose itself upon its own creator.

More precisely, it is the internal split within that very discourse, its double nature, immanent and transcendent at the same time, its oscillation between expression and transformation, what produces the diffraction of its vision of the Latin American subject. The invocation of that Latin American "being" different from the "really existing" people is, ultimately, only the symptomatic, manifest expression of a hidden *pathos* inherent in this régime of discourse.

Now, the split that Latin American philosophy introduces in the body of the people inevitably ends up reverting and replicating itself in the very discourse on it. That foreclosed aspect in it that the philosopher tried to expel from its own being by projecting it outside, by extrojecting it onto a transcendent realm, where it subsequently affirms to find its own foundation, comes back to it in a phantasmatic way. The problem of the "people's two bodies" (its immaterial, transcendental being and its actual, alienated existence) finds its counterpart in that of the "philosopher's two bodies." This gives rise, in turn, to that inconsistent mixture, to that other indefinite oscillation, typical of this type of discourse, between intellectualism and populism.

As these authors themselves assert, the Latin American philosopher does not escape the mesh of ideology either; on the contrary, he is more prone to become trapped in his web because ideology is placed at its very origin. "Philosophy," said Carlos Cullen, "is also a historical product of the imperial project and, therefore, our philosophy is dependent, because it is philosophy, and not because it is made by members of dependent peoples."[65] Thus, the claim to the role of philosophy and the philosopher as mediator will always coexist with its mistrust. Both contradictory expressions are, however, inextricably linked. The creation of a Latin American philosophy entails the articulation of a body of knowledge that must at once deny itself as a body of knowledge, it must remain blind to its very conceptual foundations (the well into which the Milesian fell).[66] Ultimately, it represents the paradox of a knowledge in permanent struggle against itself, which has made of itself its true object, but only on the condition that it ignored itself as such (projecting itself on an outward reality placed beyond the empirical realm).

We meet again that syndrome characteristic of Latin Americanist thought as a whole. What unifies all its different trends is the circular logic of its field of reflection. They can escape from it only by reifying, projecting their own conceptual categories onto an ontological plane. While, as we have seen in Chapter 2, the historicist current claims to be the end term in the genealogy it itself has constructed, the phenomenological current claims to be the ultimate expression of that being that it itself has constructed. In fact, both that being and its genealogy are kinds of mirror for the Latin Americanist philosophers to see their own image and elaborate on their condition, as is self-perceived and experienced. In actual fact, as we have seen, they are the true object of their narratives, all of them only talk about themselves.

This specular logic that presides over this form of discourse, derives, in turn, from the régime of knowledge on which it is founded. Yet, what Dussel's work illustrates is how this epistemic ground was then becoming eroded, rendering the idea of a transcendental, a "Latin American being," a problem. It was still at the center of his discourse, yet it had lost it former aura of transparency, its self-evident character, rendering his discourse more complex and, at the same time, more unstable. In the last instance, once the epistemic foundations on which this kind of discourse rested, once not only the teleological concept of history, but also the essentialist assumptions behind the concept of an inner being have lost the ground on which they stood, the Latin American discourse cannot help but becoming self-referential. It gets thus locked within the endless circle of its own narrative self-construction,

---

[65] Carlos Cullen, "El descubrimiento de la nación y la liberación de la filosofía," in *Hacia una filosofía de la liberación latinoamericana*, ed. Ardiles et al., 93.

[66] See the Prologue of this book.

92 THEORETICAL APPROACHES

spinning in a void, lacking now any external reference from which to postulate itself to be its expression, from the moment when all of which has already
revealed its ultimately mythical character.

The Phenomenology's Epistemic Ground Eroded

In effect, the assumption of the immediacy of the ideal contents of consciousness was then rendered problematic, which led Dussel to introduce the concept
of a third dimension of reality (the trans-ontological). Yet, far from making its
discourse more consistent, it introduces a number of new problems which will
not find any possible solution. Lastly, it merely reproduces, on a different plane,
the circular logic that articulates the whole discourse of Latin American philosophy, in its different versions. As we have seen, the introduction by Dussel
of that third dimension of reality led to shifting the axis of his reflection from
the issue of "incarnation" to that of "rupture." The implicit assumption here is
that the former entails the latter; that is, that the rupture of the system of identity is the condition for the overcoming of alienation, the reunion of the empirical subject with its sacred essence. Conversely, the rupture of totality already
demands and entails incarnation; that is, the presence of a subject (the evanescent mediator) placed beyond the system of identity, in which its sacred nature
and worldly manifestation are *immediately* one.

In the last instance, the idea of "rupture" is just the name designating a
paradox: that incarnation at the same time demands and excludes mediation, the idea of a Third. For the logic of mediation to work, it is necessary at
least one to be placed outside that logic, one who allegedly is in an immediate
communion with the essence of its being, and that is thereby instituted as
the place of Truth, the one that will work as the *arkhē*. In this case, the one
that fulfills that role is the Latin Americanist philosopher itself. It gathers
now the attributes that were formerly detached from the people, the Latin
American poor. It would thereby have a double nature, at once sacred and
profane. In it, the immanent and the transcendent would be immediately
fused, which, however, contradicts the very logic of mediation. Actually,
Dussel's attempt to escape from the metaphysical terrain (the metaphysics
of presence) through the introduction of the figure of the Third inevitably
reemerges on this other figure. It simply translates the problem into another
plane without really solving it. As Lacan said, while the Other, the sight of the
Other, is the one that constitutes the subject, there is no Other of the Other;

that is, the founding instance is itself unfounded.[67] Similarly, while in Dussel the rupture effect demands a Third which sparks it, there is no possible Third of the Third, it is thus simply assumed to be self-constituted, *causa sui*, that uncaused cause that sets into motion the emancipation dynamics from alienation, the rupture effect, at the price of placing itself outside it, which sends this discourse back to that metaphysical terrain (the metaphysic of presence) from which it intended to escape.

The concept of thirdness, of an unmediated mediator, reveals thus itself as ultimately inconsistent, at once necessary and impossible. What founds it is also what frustrates it, marking a point of fissure in that logic: for it to be possible, it is necessary to postulate the existence of one which escapes that logic of mediation (otherwise, that logic would inevitably lead to an infinite regress). In sum, the problematization of Kusch's binary logic led Dussel to redefine the phenomenological discourse, rearticulating it according to a ternary structure. However, as we can see, the concept of thirdness still hinges on the basis of that binary system, of a metaphysics of the subject that assumes the immediacy of the ideal contents of consciousness in the inner being. In conclusion, while the historicist trend must cling to a teleological concept of History that, nevertheless, had by then already lost its conceptual ground, the phenomenological trend still cannot avoid clinging to a metaphysics of the subject, an essentialist concept of being, that had by then become theoretically untenable, as well.

This leads us to our own project of an archeological approach to philosophical Latin Americanism. At this point, I hope I have been clear about the aim of this essay to move beyond the surface level of "ideas," beyond what the authors themselves affirm in their texts and, eventually, the filiation of the ideas contained in them, which is the proper object of the history of ideas. It seeks to gain access and reconstruct that epistemic ground lying at its basis, and from there to recreate the series of conceptual operations through which, in each case, the different possible lines of thinking unfold, that is, the different directions in which said epistemic ground opens up. More precisely stated, what the present study intends is to unravel the mechanisms

---

[67] This actually means, for Lacan, that the Other does not exist. There is only the barred Other, as there is no Other of the Other. While the Other guarantees the subject's discourse's coherence, this is a false guarantee since there is no Other that guarantees the coherence of the Other's discourse. You can never step out of the frameworks of language. There is no outside to the Symbolic order (not even the *Real* is outside the it, but indicates and inner fissure in it, thus remaining unassimilable to it, simultaneously inside and outside the Symbolic, its constitutive external). See Jacques Lacan, *The Object Relation: Seminar of Jacques Lacan. Book IV* (New York: Polity Press, 2021).

94 THEORETICAL APPROACHES

by which a place of *Truth* is instituted as such within a given régime of discourse, that which will be posited, in each case, as an *arkhē*, the presumed point from where sense emanates, where it becomes fully revealed to us and the social whole becomes transparent to itself. But also, and above all, what prevents it, that is, identifying the lines of fissure that run through that particular form of discursivity in its various variants, the blind spots inherent in it. Ultimately, this is what we understand by an "archaeological" approach to discourses, which is also that to which Gómez-Castro appeals, even though, as we have seen, his own approach requires some clarification in historical-conceptual terms.

This same historical-conceptual (archaeological) perspective is also the one from which, in the next part, we will approach the historical reconstructions of a series of particular events and specific issues in nineteenth-century Latin American history. But, first, we will consider, in Chapter 4, the theoretical perspective of another author who also analyzed the problems entailed by intellectual production in peripheral regions to Western culture, albeit from a very different perspective from that of Latin American philosophy: the Brazilian sociologist and literary critic Roberto Schwarz. In his writings on the topic of "misplaced ideas," Schwarz takes up the tenets of the so-called dependency theories to apply them to the field of cultural theory, and, although these tenets were not at all alien to Latin American philosophy, the result, in his case, is a opposite perspective, which may well be considered as a reaction against the essentialism that the former exuded.

4

Revisiting the Topic of "Misplaced Ideas"

Dependency Theory and Ideological Production in the Periphery

The transition from the "history of ideas" to "Latin American philosophy" chronologically coincided—and was somehow associated—with the development in the region of the so-called dependency theory. They shared some premises. The two sought to approach the problem of the colonial or semi-colonial condition of the region, its consequences, and, lastly, to propose a way out from it. However, in their common concerns they follow opposite directions. Contrary to Latin Americanist philosophy, the dependency theory sought to counter the nationalistic and essentialist views that considered the "center" and the "periphery" as two distinct entities, emphasizing instead their fundamental unity, constituting together a single (capitalistic) world-system.[1] And the same occurred in the realm of culture. Rather than an "alternative" to Western culture, Latin American culture was considered to be an integral part of it. Ultimately, Latin American philosophy and dependency theory established, in the 1960s and 1970s, the fundamental coordinates articulating the terrain for the debate in the field of intellectual history and cultural theory in the region.

In fact, dependency theorists were not originally concerned with the cultural and philosophical aspects connected to the peripheral condition of the

---

[1] This perspective triggered a work of historiographical revision that profoundly altered our images of nineteenth-century Brazil. The most important studies undertaken by this group of thinkers revolved around the attempt to demonstrate that slavery in Brazil played a functional role in capitalism. The key works on the subject are Celso Furtado, *Formação econômica do Brasil* (Río de Janeiro: Editora Fundo de Cultura, 1959) and Fernando H. Cardoso, *Capitalismo e escravidão no Brasil Meridional. O Negro na sociedade escravocrata do Rio Grande do Sul* (Río de Janeiro: Paz e Terra, 1977) (originally published in 1962). A good summary of dependency theory can be found in Ruy Mauro Marini and Márgara Millán, eds., *La teoría social latinoamericana. Textos escogidos. Tomo II: La teoría de la dependencia* (Mexico: UNAM, 1994) and Cristobal Kay, *Latin American Theories of Development and Underdevelopment* (London: Routledge, 1989). For a critical review of that theory, see Stuart B. Schwartz, "La conceptualización del Brasil pos-*dependentista*: la historiografía colonial y la búsqueda de nuevos paradigmas," in *Historiografía latinoamericana contemporánea*, ed. Ignacio Sosa and Brian Connaughton (Mexico City: CCYDEL-UNAM, 1999), 181–208.

Misplaced Ideas?. Elías J. Palti, Oxford University Press. © Oxford University Press 2024.
DOI: 10.1093/oso/9780197556641.003.0004

96   THEORETICAL APPROACHES

region, but they concentrated their focus on social and economic aspects. Basically, they tried to oppose the "developmentalist" or "dualistic" theory that had spread over the region in the 1950s. The latter affirmed the co-existence in Latin America of two opposite means of production, a modern-capitalistic means and a traditional-pre-capitalistic means. From this perspective, the solution for underdevelopment consisted of expanding the former (the modern capitalistic system) to encompass the whole economy and, in this fashion, reproduce the central countries' pattern of development.

The dependency theory, instead, stated that underdevelopment was not the consequence of the limited expansion of the capitalistic system in the region, but quite the opposite: it was the result of its very expansion. For dependency theory, the world system is one and the same on a global scale that, however, operates in a differential manner in the two areas. The very same logic—that of the optimization of the benefit—has thus contradictory consequences. While in the center it produces modern régimes of production and social relationships, in the periphery it reproduces the traditional, pre-capitalistic ones, immersing the region in backwardness and underdevelopment.

Now, beyond its immediate target—the "developmentalist" idea—the dependency theory had another implicit aim. It intended to counter the "nationalistic deviation" of the Brazilian Communist Party, which, at that moment, adhered to Stalin's "stages theory," which affirmed that the communists in the colonial and semi-colonial worlds had first to support the national bourgeoisie in its struggle against imperialism and only subsequently seek to impose a socialist system. It led the leftist discourse to adopt many of the classical motifs of the nationalists.

Roberto Schwarz participated in the "Marx seminar," formed in 1962 by students at São Paulo University, where the core of the dependency theory emerged, and from which, after the exile of most of its members, it spread to the rest of the region. He was the one who proposed to translate that very same concept, formerly applied to the fields of economy and society, to that of cultural production, and thus to try to understand the contradictory dynamics of the processes of ideological exchange in the marginal regions vis-à-vis the centers of cultural production.

Schwarz's proposal was condensed in a paper, published in 1973, that profoundly marked a generation of thinkers in Latin America: "As idéias fora do lugar" ("Misplaced Ideas").[2] As we have said, it was originally intended

---

[2] Roberto Schwarz, "As idéias fora do lugar," *Estudos Cebrap* 3 (1973), reprinted in *Misplaced Ideas* (London: Verso, 1992), 19–32. For an account of the article's reception and the debates it generated,

REVISITING THE TOPIC OF "MISPLACED IDEAS" 97

to provide a theoretical framework for "progressivist" authors to counter the nationalistic tendencies that had then become very influential among leftist forces.[3] Yet, his concept of "misplaced ideas" soon proved especially productive for theorizing the problematic development of ideas in Latin American history. Schwarz's text thus became the fundamental point of reference in the field for those who intended to question the hitherto predominant paradigms in cultural and literary critique, which were mostly inspired by the romantic-nationalistic tradition.

Notwithstanding, Schwarz's original contribution also triggered a number of controversies. In fact, it contained several issues that remained unsolved. And, as we will see, the shortcomings in Schwarz's theory have conceptual roots. In the last instance, they spring from a crude linguistic view, which is inherent in the "history of ideas," that reduces language exclusively to its referential function. A more precise distinction of levels of language will help us to reveal aspects and problems that Schwarz's perspective obliterates. In any case, Schwarz's original intellectual project may be disentangled from its linguistic premises and recovered for cultural critique. As we will see, only in this fashion would it be possible to rescue the core of his project, which consisted of providing a theoretical framework to comprehend the intricacies of the processes of cultural exchange in peripheral areas without relapsing into essentialist views, and, lastly, without appealing to metaphysical entities like a Latin American "inner being."

On Places and Non-Places of Ideas

As we have said, Schwarz's specific contribution lies in having perceived the potential contained in the postulates of the dependency theory, hitherto applied exclusively to the realm of economic and social history, for the ambit of literary criticism and cultural theory. Following its postulates, he was convinced that the paradoxical consequences of cultural modernization in the region ultimately made manifest contradictions that, rather than being "local anomalies" were intrinsic to the very world system. "From this perspective,"

see José Murilo de Carvalho, "História intelectual no Brasil: a retórica como chave de leitura," *Topoí* 1 (2000): 123–152.

[3] See Schwarz, *Misplaced Ideas*, 126–159.

98   THEORETICAL APPROACHES

Schwarz stated, the "Brazilian scene sheds a revealing light on the canonical, metropolitan notions of civilization, progress, culture, liberalism, et cetera."[4]

Schwarz's ultimate goal was to refute the nationalist (and Latin Americanist) belief that it was enough for Latin Americans to get rid of their "foreign garments," a set of categories and ideas imported from Europe and submissively replicated by the local, European-minded elite, to find their "true, inner essence."[5] Following the tenets of dependency theory, Schwarz maintains that there is no such thing as a "Brazilian national culture" preceding Western culture. The former not only is the result of the expansion of the latter, but also constitutes an integral part of it: "in aesthetics, like in politics," he stated, "the Third World is an organic part of the contemporary scene."[6] In the realm of culture, a complex dialectic operates between the "alien" and the "native," just as it does in politics and society. Ultimately, referring to liberal ideas in Latin America, the ones at the heart of this debate, he asserted that "it does not help to insist on their obvious falsehood"; our object should rather be "to understand their dynamics, of which this falsehood is a true component."[7]

If it is true that the adoption of foreign concepts generates serious distortions, the point, for Schwarz, is that conceptually distorting their reality is not something that Latin Americans can avoid. On the contrary, it is precisely in these distortions, in always designating local reality with improper names, that the specificity of Brazilian (and Latin American) culture resides. "They [Brazilians] are recognizably Brazilian," he stated, "in their particular distortions."[8]

This concept actually maintains an ambiguous relationship with the postulates of the dependency theory. Although it is perfectly compatible with them, the former does not necessarily follow from the latter. The dependency theory's translation from the realm of politics and economy to that of culture inevitably demanded reformulations that introduced some torsions

[4] Roberto Schwarz, "A nota específica (1998)," in Seqüências brasileiras. Ensaios (São Paulo: Companhia das Letras, 1999), 153.
[5] "In 1964," he asserted later, "the two nationalist tendencies [the right-wing and the left-wing] were alike in hoping to get their goal by eliminating anything that was not indigenous. The residue would be the essence of Brazil." Schwarz, Misplaced Ideas, 4.
[6] Roberto Schwarz, "Existe uma estética do terceiro mundo? (1980)," in Que horas são? Ensaios (São Paulo: Companhia das Letras, 1997), 28.
[7] Schwarz, Misplaced Ideas, 28. "To know Brazil," he continues, "was to know these displacements, experienced and practiced by everyone as a sort of fate, for which, however, there was no proper name, since the improper use of names was part of its nature." Schwarz, "Existe uma estética do terceiro mundo?," in Que horas são? (São Paulo: Companhia das Letras, 1997), 28.
[8] Schwarz, Misplaced Ideas, 25.

REVISITING THE TOPIC OF "MISPLACED IDEAS"   99

in that theory. In Schwarz's case, his fundamentally anti-essentialist stance hinged on the argument that representations always entail a given theoretical framework. And, in Latin America, such a framework is provided by systems of thinking originally alien to the native reality (in fact, as we have seen in previous chapters, the concepts with which Latin American thinkers tried to think about the peculiarity of local culture were all taken from European thinkers). Hence, for Schwarz, Latin Americans are condemned to "copy"; that is, to think equivocally, using categories inevitably ill-suited to the reality they intend to represent.

This last affirmation, however, would not be equally evident indeed for many of the holders of the dependency theory. Shortly after the publication of "Misplaced Ideas," the journal *Cadernos de Debate* published a work by Maria Sylvia de Carvalho Franco—a well-known student of the slavery system in Brazil—whose very title is illustrative of its content: "As idéias estão no lugar" ("Ideas are in place").[9] Drawing also from the premises of dependency theory, Carvalho Franco systematically refused not only the idea that slavery was incompatible with capitalistic expansion, but also that liberal ideas were "ill-adjusted" to nineteenth-century Brazil.[10] To Carvalho Franco, liberal ideas were neither more nor less alien than the pro-slavery ones. Both constituted integral parts of the complex reality of Brazil. It cannot even be said that they were mutually incompatible: like capitalistic profit-seeking and slavocrat forms of production, individualistic bourgeois attitudes and clientelism (paternalistic relationships) were so intimately imbricated in Brazil that they became barely distinguishable.[11] As she states, with the concept of "misplaced ideas," Schwarz in fact wound up by relapsing into the kind of dualism he intended to counter; that is, the postulate of the existence of "two Brazils." To the "artificial" Brazil of ideas and politics (which was liberal), Schwarz would oppose a "true," social, Brazil (which was slavocrat):

> We would have, on the one hand, the bourgeois, European reason obsequiously adopted for nothing, and, on the other hand, Brazilian favor and slavery incompatible with them. Holding this position is, *ipso facto*, to

---

[9] Maria Sylvia de Carvalho Franco, "As idéias estão no lugar," *Cadernos de Debate* 1 (1976): 61–64.

[10] Maria Sylvia de Carvalho Franco, *Homes livres na ordem escravocrata* (São Paulo: USP, 1997), originally published in 1969.

[11] "In my brief remarks on the genesis and practical meaning of *favor*," she said in connection with her above-mentioned work, "I tried to show how bourgeois ideas were one of their pillars—formal equality. *Favor* does not 'enter' Brazil, as it were, from outside, but it *emerges* in the process of the constitution of market relations, in which it is inherent." Carvalho Franco, "As idéias estão no lugar," 63.

100   THEORETICAL APPROACHES

separate their terms abstractly, in the indicated fashion, thus losing sight of the actual processes of ideological production in Brazil.[12]

Ultimately, Carvalho Franco's contention raised a broader methodological issue. Ideas, for her, were never "misplaced" due to the very fact that, if they can socially circulate in a given milieu, it is because they serve some purpose in it, that is, because there are conditions in it for their reception. The opposition between "ideas" and "realities" on which Schwarz's theory rests would thus be false; the two terms are never completely alien to each other.

Carvalho Franco's criticism, therefore, points to the core of Schwarz's argument, as she takes her premises from Schwarz's own postulates while reaching opposite conclusions. This criticism would haunt Schwarz throughout his subsequent career, determining the successive reformulations of his theory. As Paulo Arantes remarks, the accusations against Schwarz of remaining within a "dualistic" frame would be repeated until the present.[13] And although his biographer rejects this accusation, he admits that the consistency of the criticism in this regard cannot be due to a mere misunderstanding.

At this point, we must consider the fact that Schwarz's formulation of the issue contains something of a paradox: the expression "misplaced ideas" is actually not completely consistent with the argument it intends to describe. Schwarz's original objective was, precisely, to reject that topic. Indeed, as he demonstrated, the accusation of "political unrealism," that certain ideas were "misplaced" in Latin America, was an easy means of disqualifying his adversaries' arguments. Taken literally, it is untenable: obviously, nobody could have ever ignored the fact that, for example, constitutions are not all equally viable at any time or place. That there are ideas that are misplaced in a given social context is, actually, commonplace; almost nobody could have denied it. The contested point emerged when determining what they were in each case, and in which sense they were so. And as can be predicted, the misplaced ideas will be, in all the cases, *those of the others*. Furthermore, as he remarks, these attributions of alterity of ideas also have reactionary implications: typically, the "unrealistic" people have always been those who have held the most *progressivist* ideas of their time. As Schwarz states, "in 1964 the right-wing nationalists branded Marxism as an alien influence,

---

[12] Carvalho Franco, "As idéias estão no lugar," 62.
[13] Paulo Eduardo Arantes, *Sentimento da dialética na experiencia intelectual brasileira. Dialética e dualidade segundo Antonio Candido e Roberto Schwarz* (São Paulo: Paz e Terra, 1992).

REVISITING THE TOPIC OF "MISPLACED IDEAS" 101

perhaps imagining that fascism was a Brazilian invention."[14] The spread of the topic is, ultimately, incomprehensible if detached from the ideological functions it performed.

This also explains Carvalho Franco's reaction: with his formula, Schwarz would lend credibility to the affirmations that Marxists ideas (like liberal ones in the nineteenth century) were alien to Brazilian reality, exotic imports; in sum, that they were "misplaced" in Brazil. In this fashion, Schwarz would plainly relapse into that very topic he allegedly intended to set into question, with the potentially reactionary consequences it has always implied. For Carvalho Franco, the very attempt to determine which ideas are "misplaced" and which are not is absurd. For her, both liberal and pro-slavery, Marxist and fascist ideas, were, in that country, "in place"; that is, they were integral parts of Brazilian reality because, otherwise, having no conditions of reception in local reality, they could have not have circulated there, they would have remained invisible. In this regard, as we will see, Carvalho Franco's view is much more consistent than Schwarz's. However, although her criticism is certainly justified, it misses the core of the latter's argument.

For Schwarz, it was not a matter of debating which ideas were "misplaced" and which were not because, as he stated, all of them were misplaced. Both fascist and Marxist ideas, liberal and pro-slavery ones, were "imported" and alien to Brazilian reality. The core of his criticism of Silvio Romero—whom he considered to be the best representative of the romantic-nationalist views in literature—lay, precisely, in his denunciation of the illusion that ideological maladjustments were avoidable in the region. Romero, he said, believed that it was simply a matter of no longer copying; then "all the effects of 'exoticism' ... would vanish, as if by magic."[15] Thus, "by suggesting that imitation is avoidable," Romero "locks the reader into a false problem."[16]

Carvalho Franco's and Schwarz's proposals ultimately represent two opposite ways of escaping from the topic. The former, by means of emphasizing the reality of ideas (their actual conditions of possibility); the latter, by stressing not the maladjustments between ideas and realities, as Carvalho Franco interprets, but those maladjustments in Brazilian reality itself. For Schwarz, it was not that "two Brazils" existed in mutual opposition (a fictive one: that of ideas, and a real one: that of society), but that the most specific feature of

[14] Schwarz, *Misplaced Ideas*, 4.
[15] Schwarz, *Misplaced Ideas*, 11.
[16] Schwarz, *Misplaced Ideas*, 15.

102 THEORETICAL APPROACHES

Brazilian society (and, by extension, its culture) is to be permanently maladjusted with respect to itself, precisely because of its peripheral-capitalistic character.

For Carvalho Franco, this concept of Schwarz's merely renames the old dualistic opposition between two logics of development, two conflicting modes of production: one properly capitalistic, the other "peripheral-capitalistic" (i.e., not properly capitalistic). For Schwarz, instead, it is not a matter of two diverse logics, but of one and the same logic that operates, nevertheless, in different ways in diverse regions. Schwarz's view is thus more sensitive to the peculiarities resulting from the peripheral character of local culture, which in Carvalho Franco's perspective seems to become dissolved in the idea of the unity of Western culture. Yet, it does not resolve the original question about the alleged maladjustments of Marxist ideas in Brazil—the fact that the fascist ones are no less maladjusted seems merely a poor consolation.[17] In principle, Schwarz's position leads to skepticism regarding the viability of any emancipatory project in the region. The problems that such an issue poses to him can be observed in his "Respostas a *Movimento*" (1976).

Prompted by an interviewer's question whether "a naïve reading of your essay 'As idéias fora de lugar' could lead to the conclusion that any ideology, even an emancipatory one, would be out of place in peripheral countries," Schwarz replied:

> Ideas are in place when they represent abstractions of the process they refer to, and it is a fatal consequence of our cultural dependency that we interpret our reality with conceptual systems created somewhere else, whose basis lies in other social processes. In this sense, emancipatory ideas themselves are often ideas out of place, and they only stop being so when they are reconstructed on the basis of local contradictions.[18]

Both the question and the answer are deeply significant. In fact, with his inquiry the interviewer points out the above-mentioned paradoxical consequence in Schwarz's concept: its affinities with the nationalist view which, in principle, leads to condemning the Marxist ideas of this author as "alien" to local reality. His answer clarifies the point but raises a new aporia. As we

---

[17] Here we can hear the echoes of the 1905 debates in Russia regarding the possibilities of socialism in the periphery of capitalism.

[18] Schwarz, *Misplaced Ideas*, 39.

REVISITING THE TOPIC OF "MISPLACED IDEAS" 103

can imply from it, not *all* ideas in Latin America are, always and irremediably, out of place, as he affirmed in his criticism of Romero. On the contrary, he affirms that they could eventually be rearticulated and made to fit local reality. Such an answer, besides marking a new—and always problematic—confluence with the Nationalists, who had seldom refused the need to "adapt" foreign ideas to local realities, leads him back—this time, without escape—to search for the distinction between ideas that are (or become) well-adjusted to Brazilian reality and those that are (or do) not. And, predictably, the maladjusted ones *will always be the those of the others*. In any case, thus posed (in its "weak" formulation, shall we say) Schwarz's concept only updates the old *anthropophagic* dilemma (or, in Kusch's terms, of phagocytation); it does not provide any original contribution to cultural theory in the region.[19]

Regardless, the point is that this affirmation is not really consistent with Schwarz's own concept. It actually dislocates all of his previous argument. If formulated thus, there is no way of approaching the question of "misplaced ideas" without assuming the existence of some kind of "inner essence," which "foreign" ideas would fail to represent appropriately. Even more seriously, and this is the point in which Carvalho Franco's perspective looks more consistent than Schwarz's; this presupposes, besides, the possession of a description of that inner reality that is not mediated by concepts, and eventually allows us to identify and evaluate the respective degrees of distortion in the diverse intellectual frameworks. The opposition between "ideas" and "realities" thereby becomes a mere rhetorical device to hide the fact that what are opposed to are always different "ideas," alternative descriptions of "reality."

We finally find here what constitutes the ultimate limit in Schwarz's concept. The formula of "misplaced ideas" leads necessarily to the projection of a definite place as the place of *truth* (and reduces all the rest to the level of mere ideologies). Carvalho Franco's interpretation, although it tends to dissolve the problem of the peripheral nature of local culture, makes manifest the eminently *political* character of the attributions of alterity to some given ideas.

---

[19] It refers to Oswald de Andrade's "Anthropophagic Manifesto," which asserted that the mission of Brazilians was to eat European culture and assimilate it to its own organism. De Andrade referred there to the native inhabitants of Brazil, the Tupi, who practiced anthropophagy. His moto was "Tupi or not tupi, that is the question." Oswald de Andrade, "Manifesto Antropófago," *Revista de Antropofagia* 1, no. 1 (1928): 1–5.

104   THEORETICAL APPROACHES

As a matter of fact, this is also the point toward which Schwarz's original elaboration converged, given that, for him, all ideas were equally, and inevitably, out of place in the region, which is the basic tenet of the "strong version" of his theory; but it is a point that the formula of "misplaced ideas" fails to express accurately. It would thus pave the way to a simplistic interpretation of his view as a plain denunciation of the "unreality" of ideas, and, more specifically, of the liberal ideas in the region during the nineteenth century. Nonetheless, such an interpretation, although hardly subtle, is not completely unfair. Schwarz's relapse into the topic, catalyzed in part by the ambiguity of his formula, finds grounds in his own original concept (even though, it is true, it does not necessarily follow from it). Lastly, this relapse into the topic only makes manifest the ultimate limit of his theory, which Carvalho Franco's criticism lays bare. It confronts Schwarz at that point to which all his own argumentation leads but he cannot thematize without at once dislocating the entire categorical apparatus on which it rests. In the end, Carvalho Franco exposes the blind spot on which Schwarz's concept is founded, the premise on which that concept rests but is unapproachable from within; that is, the fact that one can never determine which ideas are out of place, and which are not, except from within a given, particular conceptual framework.

What matters here is to analyze the limitations in Schwarz's concept, defined not merely in ideological but, fundamentally, in epistemological terms; the *conceptual* limitations preventing him from effectively attaining critical distance from the topic, and avoiding his relapse into it. As we will see, Schwarz's decisive contribution lies not so much in the solutions he provides, which, as we have observed, are not really adequate, but in the very formulation of the problem he originally posed: how to tackle the issue of the peripheral nature of local culture, approaching the peculiar dynamics that such a condition imposes on ideas in the region, without relapsing into dualistic schemes, and, lastly, into the essentialist views proper to the nationalistic and Latin Americanist currents. However, before discussing this, we must briefly review another debate in which Schwarz participated. The polemics we have hitherto discussed referred to the field of culture at large, that is, following Paulo Arantes's terms, to the dialectic between ideas and society. The controversy we will now examine relates, instead, to a specifically artistic matter, and involves a second kind of dialectic—which is, more precisely, the one that would eventually yield the critical model that made Schwarz one of the most prominent literary critics in the region: the dialectic between aesthetic form and social content.

REVISITING THE TOPIC OF "MISPLACED IDEAS"   105

On Places, Non-Places, and "In-Between" Places

Schwarz's fundamental point of reference in this regard is Antonio Candido's work.[20] For Schwarz, Candido's fundamental contribution lies in having succeeded in developing a sociological approach to literature without obscuring the specifically aesthetic dimension inherent in any work of art. Schwarz's Marxist critical method was intended as an elaboration of that model, which we may summarily define, according to Lucien Goldmann's terms, as "genetic structuralist."[21] Basically, it tried to combine aesthetic and socio-historical analyses, an oscillation which, according to Schwarz, characterized a "leftist" approach. This entailed a double rejection: of "content-centered" views, which produced a de-differentiation of spheres and thereby annulled the richness of literary works, on the one hand, and of formalist approaches that detached artistic products from the material conditions of their production, on the other. The key for such a conjunction between two different levels of analysis is the concept of *form*. As he states, it allows one to grasp the social background out of which a work was born, accounting, at once, for the productivity of its specifically linguistic and literary dimensions. It is not in the materials an artist uses, but in the constructive procedures of the narration that its surrounding world is represented, or, better said, reenacted in a specifically literary manner. Yet, this is so because the social is not merely a neutral content upon which the literary form comes to be impressed. Lastly, the critic can transcend the antinomy between *literary form* and *social content* by conceiving the latter not merely as a material to be elaborated by linguistic means, but as already structured wholes, *objective* forms "able to organize either a romance or a deprecatory formula, a political movement as well as a theoretical reflection, *which can be confronted with that mediating practical condition.*"[22] Hence, we can find functional homologies between both textual and extra-textual levels of reality. The "social content" not only *has* a form; it *is* a form. As he says:

> [The social idea of *form*] is a practical scheme, containing a specific logic . . . . It can be translated into an economical-political interest, an ideology, a verbal game, a narrative approach. Regarding its affinities,

[20] See Antonio Candido, *O discurso e a cidade* (São Paulo: Duas Cidades, 1993).
[21] See Lucien Goldmann, *Cultural Creation* (Saint Louis: Telos Press, 1976).
[22] Schwarz, *Seqüências*, 30.

106 THEORETICAL APPROACHES

we are here within the Marxist universe, according to which the material constraints of the reproduction of society are the basis which impresses itself, well or badly, upon the different areas of spiritual life, in which they circulate reelaborated in more or less sublimated or distorted versions; in short, a form working forms. Ultimately, the forms we find in literary works are the repetition or transformation, with variable results, of preexisting, artistic or extra-artistic, forms.[23]

Actually, at the time Schwarz began his critical *oeuvre*, this concept formed part of the conventional wisdom in the profession. "The combination of structure and history"—he would later remember—"was at the center of the theoretical debate of the period." Sartre's *Critique of Dialectical Reason*, he continues, "made that combination the cornerstone of the leftist comprehension of the world."[24] Candido's contribution consisted in relating the dialectic between content and form, structure and history, literary analysis and social reflection with the one between "center" and "periphery." In this fashion, he tried to understand how the Latin American reality—which defines the particular conditions of reception of artistic genres and forms (as we should recall, always inevitably "foreign," given the marginal position of the region in the systems of cultural production)—eventually alters them. As he remarks, in peripheral areas the result of the juxtaposition of these two kinds of dialectic would be both inevitable and problematic.

José de Alencar's work is particularly illustrative of the shortcuts and contradictions generated by the transfer to Brazil of a literary form (the realist novel, as developed in France by Balzac) that was typically bourgeois and, therefore, hardly suitable to represent the Brazilian social reality of slavery, paternalism, and personal dependency. Schwarz's memorable discussion of *Senhora*, Alencar's last novel, discloses how the above-mentioned dialectic between falsity and truth operates at the literary level. Here, the *false* form, the parodical effect generated by the transposition to the Brazilian context of situations that are specific to the bourgeois, realist fiction, exposes the *true* content of that social reality, namely, a system where the individual striving for wealth and social prestige is cast into and mediated by paternalistic relations.

---

[23] Schwarz, *Seqüências*, 30–31.
[24] Schwarz, *Seqüências*, 50.

REVISITING THE TOPIC OF "MISPLACED IDEAS" 107

As Schwarz indicates, Joaquim Maria Machado de Assis's genius consisted in having turned that parodic effect into a constructive principle of narration. Parody thus converts into self-parody and becomes the *form* of narration, whose mode of articulation is *digression*. It replicates in its very writing the paradoxical logic of Brazilian history: a form of movement forward with no advancement, progression, or development. With this concept, Schwarz marks a milestone in Machadean studies, providing the fundamental clue to understanding the rupture that Machado de Assis introduced in Latin American literature. By means of *digression*, he transcended the effect of verisimilitude, making parodical the very mimetic impulse of realist fiction. Reworked "from the periphery," the genre thus makes manifest the discursive devices it must hide to constitute itself as such (a situation which leads Schwarz to compare Machado de Assis's work with that of his Russian contemporary writers: "there is in Machado," he states, "something of Gogol, Dostoyevsky, Goncharov, and Chekhov").[25]

Here again we observe the same dialectic between truth and falsehood that Schwarz discussed in connection with Alencar, but this time it takes a particular twist, it takes an inverse direction. In this case, the "false" content of Brazilian reality discloses the truth of the European *form*, which is its inherent falsehood. In this fashion, "our national oddities," he states, "became world-historical." Hence the link between Machado de Assis and his Russian contemporaries:

> Perhaps this is comparable to what happened in Russian literature. Faced with the latter, even the greatest novels of French realism seem naïve. And why? In spite of their claims to universality, the physiology of rational egoism and the ethics of Enlightenment appeared in the Russian Empire as a "foreign" ideology, and (were/became) therefore, localized and relative. Sustained by its historical backwardness, Russia forced the bourgeois novel to face a more complex reality.[26]

Schwarz thus reveals the secret of the universality of Machado de Assis's work. Two dialectics converged in his work: the problems regarding how to achieve a specifically literary productivity while being socially representative here becomes associated with the issue of how to be universal in the

---

[25] Schwarz, *Misplaced Ideas*, 29.
[26] Schwarz, *Misplaced Ideas*, 29.

108 THEORETICAL APPROACHES

periphery, not by denying its marginality but rather by exploiting it. Yet, it is also at this point that Schwarz's interpretive scheme becomes complicated.

First, it is evident—and Schwarz was by no means unaware of it—that parody, and even self-parody, of the genre is not really of Brazilian origin, or a feature exclusive to the literary production in peripheral areas. As a matter of fact, Machado de Assis took his model from a European author, Laurence Sterne. This renders problematic the second dialectic Schwarz discusses, namely, that between "center" and "periphery": even to "subvert" European models, local authors must always appeal to foreign models. At this point, not only does the idea (which only a simplistic reading of Schwarz's essay may appear to endorse) of an opposition between the "false" and the "true" as correlative to the "local" and the "imported," respectively, start to crumble. As he remarked, the "true" in this context is no less "foreign" than the "false," and vice versa. Pursuing this argument to its logical consequences, what we find, in all the cases (i.e., both in the center and the periphery), are constellations of contradictory elements, *whose logic of agglutination is not attributable to given contexts*. In sum, this situation would inevitably frustrate all attempts to discover the presumed features that distinguish Latin American culture and identify its "peripheral" condition.

In effect, the observation of "local distortions" generated by the transposition to the region of discursive forms, ideas, and institutions originally alien to local reality does not allow one to draw the conclusion that ideas are always well placed in Europe and always out of place in Latin America, as Schwarz's definition of the concept of "misplaced ideas" may suggest. This is evidently not true. "Distorting" ideas and improperly naming realities is certainly not a Brazilian or Latin American peculiarity.[27] We may still accept that the kind of dialectic Schwarz observes in Machado de Assis's work indicates a particular type of distortion, specific to peripheral areas. This affirmation saves Schwarz's theory regarding its object; however, it confronts him with a more serious dilemma. The most disturbing aspect implicit in this attempt to perceive the textual vestiges of the peripheral condition of local culture actually

---

[27] The case of the novel illustrates this. Authors like Friedrich Hebbel, to set an example, questioned whether, as a literary form, the realistic novel was suited to German reality. Hebbel, like Schwarz for the Brazilian case, considered that this was because German history did not have an "organic" evolution. As he said, "It is true that we Germans do not maintain any link with the history of our people . . . But, what is the cause? The cause is that our history had no results, that we cannot consider ourselves the product of its organic development, like the French and the British." Quoted by Georg Lukács, *La novela histórica* (Mexico: Era, 1971), 75.

REVISITING THE TOPIC OF "MISPLACED IDEAS" 109

resides in the fact that it ends up leading Schwarz's theory dangerously close to that of one of his fundamental intellectual opponents: Silviano Santiago.

As early as 1970, in "The In-Between Place in Latin American Discourse,"[28] the Brazilian critic Silviano Santiago introduced a number of concepts taken from the most recent French critical theories (reception theory, deconstructionism, poststructuralism, etc.) with the object of developing a concept also implicit in Schwarz's analyses. Like Schwarz, Santiago considered Machado de Assis to be the paradigmatic figure of the particular condition of "Latin American discourse." This condition finds its specific ambit in the "in-between" place, which is that of the deviation from the norm, the mark of the difference inscribed in the very original text that destroys its *purity* and *unity*. The readings in the periphery of capitalism are, then, never innocent. They are not a merely passive assimilation of foreign models, nor are they the means to make manifest an inner being that preexists them. They aim at inscribing themselves as the *other* within the *unity* of Western culture, of which they form part, thus exposing its inherent inconsistencies.

In Santiago's reinterpretation of Candido's (and also Schwarz's) analytical model, the proper mode of conceiving patterns of interaction between local and Western cultures should transcend the concept of "influence" and put in its place that of "writing," understood as a *work* over a tradition. Peripheral areas participate in this tradition and, at the same time, dislocate it by revealing their local maladjustments as constitutive of its very concept. Santiago's idea of the "in-between" place thus questions the definition of the relationships between "center" and "periphery" in terms of "original" and "copy." Neither Santiago nor Schwarz saw Machado de Assis's work as a degraded version of some original European model (presumably superior and self-contained). Machado de Assis's peripheral condition somehow allowed him to overcome his French model, revealing its intrinsic limitations. In fact, this view is perfectly consistent with Schwarz's recent reading (or rather rereading) of the postulates of dependency theory, when he remarks that the contradiction in capitalistic development in the periphery, "sheds some revealing light on the canonical, metropolitan notions of civilization, progress, culture, liberalism, etc."[29]

Nevertheless, having reached this point, Schwarz raises some reservations regarding his own conclusions. For him, the concept implicit in this view

[28] See Silviano Santiago, *Uma Literatura nos trópicos* (São Paulo: Editora Perspectiva, 1978).
[29] Schwarz, *Seqüências*, 153.

110 THEORETICAL APPROACHES

of the "advantages of backwardness" (an echo, again, of the discussions in 1905 in Russia) runs the risk of turning into a kind of celebration of underdevelopment and backwardness.[30] This poses a dilemma, namely: how to explain the universality of Machado de Assis's work without denying its definite connections with its peripheral condition, which, after all, defines its particular context of emergence and thereby converts it into an authentically representative work, and, at the same time, without ending up diluting its marginal position in Western culture. It is significant here that the theories that Santiago applies to the Latin American context are also originally European. Thus, in the face of Santiago, against the naïve perception of the peripheral condition as providing superior epistemic conditions, Schwarz would insist on the need to pose the peripheral condition as a *deficiency*, without relapsing, along the way, into the similarly naïve perception of it as indicating a mere *lack* (a misrecognition of an inner self). In sum, this was a complicated dilemma, whose very formulation represented a fundamental contribution to cultural theory in Latin America, insofar as it delineated a horizon of inquiry definitively multifarious and absolutely relevant. Yet, Schwarz himself could not find any solution to that dilemma consistent with his own concept.

This can be observed in the lecture he delivered in Buenos Aires in April 2001. There, Schwarz summarized his proposal in this regard in terms of a double "disentangling." As he remarked, Candido's contribution consisted in having "disentangled" the opposition between "center" and "periphery" from the opposition between "superior" and "inferior." As Machado de Assis's example first showed, the peripheral character of local literary production does not condemn it to a situation of inferiority vis-à-vis the European one. However, he still rejected the "poststructuralist" attempt to "disentangle" that opposition between center and periphery from the one between the "model" and the "copy." Schwarz went back here to an issue he had raised in "Nationalism by Elimination" (1986), when he discussed what he called the new theories of the "French philosophers" (Foucault and Derrida). According to these theories, stated Schwarz, "it would be more accurate and unbiased to think in terms of an infinite sequence of transformations, with no beginning or end, no first or last, no better or worse."[31] By annulling the notion of the copy, he said, such theories "would enhance the self-esteem and relieve the anxiety of the underdeveloped world" without, however, solving

[30] Cf. Haroldo de Campos, *De la razón antropofágica y otros ensayos* (Mexico: Siglo XXI, 2000).
[31] Schwarz, *Misplaced Ideas*, 6.

REVISITING THE TOPIC OF "MISPLACED IDEAS" 111

the problems that have sunk the region into underdevelopment.[32] These theories would thus simply ignore the actual asymmetries among the different regions both in terms of material and symbolic resources.

Ultimately, Schwarz thinks that poststructuralist theories represent merely a kind of intellectual adjustment to the process of commoditization of artistic production, nowadays projected on a global scale. In the context of economic globalization, the old formalism acquired a new sense. In the transition from structuralism to poststructuralism, he states, "its aesthetic pseudo-radicalism, an abstract cultural subversion, especially in language, became the general literary ideology."[33] The postmodern symbolic dislocation of hierarchies is, in the last instance, only its back side and the complement of their reinforcement in actual practice. The permanent revolution at a formal level would thus be a functional adjunct of the material counterrevolution allegedly nowadays in process.

What we have seen explains the paradox observed in the previous section: Schwarz's resorting to a formula like that of "misplaced ideas" which is, in actual fact, barely appropriate to its goal of rendering problematic the nationalist postulate that European ideas are out of place in Latin America. This paradox is clarified when we place it in the particular context of debate in which Schwarz elaborated his concept. By the early 1970s, the issue of "periphery" and the criticism of "nationalist" deviations within the Left had actually started to lose their former centrality, ceding their place to the question of the consequences for artistic and critical production of the development of an advanced-capitalistic market of cultural goods, with its apparent capacity to absorb all attempts of transgression, to assimilate them to its logic, and to turn them into instruments for its own reproduction.[34] Schwarz was therefore writing in a context that was increasingly hostile to the postulates of dependency theory. He thus clung to the formula of "misplaced ideas," even though it tended to smooth over the intricacies of his thinking, because at least it permitted him to preserve the notion of the presence of asymmetries between center and periphery, between European "model" and local "copy."

As we have seen, Schwarz framed his criticism of postmodern theories in an ethical-political perspective. And this allowed him to refute them on the basis of pragmatical considerations; that is, their inability to generate actions

[32] Schwarz, *Misplaced Ideas*, 6.
[33] Schwarz, *Seqüências*, 85.
[34] See the series of essays compiled by Florencia Garramuño and Adriana Amante, eds., *Absurdo Brasil* (Buenos Aires: Biblos, 2001).

112 THEORETICAL APPROACHES

conducive to overcoming the region's cultural dependency. Lastly, he thought that postmodern theories were merely forms of symbolic compensation for actual contradictions which they thus helped to perpetuate. Yet the issue at stake here was not really ethical or political, but one of an eminently epistemological nature. More concretely: Is the opposition between "model" and "copy" really an appropriate description of the kind of cultural asymmetries he intended to underline and analyze?

Going back to his scheme of "disentanglings," even though the dilemma formulated by Schwarz is highly significant, we must say that the solution he offers—to accept the first disentangling produced by Candido, but not the second put forward by Santiago—is clearly fragile. One may argue that the former disentangling already presupposes the latter. In effect, the dissolution of the opposition between the "superior" and the "inferior" as a parallel to that between the "center" and the "periphery" also demolishes its parallel with a third opposition: if a "peripheral" production stops being "inferior" we must assume that it is because it has somehow overcome its condition as a merely degraded "copy" vis-à-vis some assumed "model" and gained certain "originality" of its own.[35] At any rate, following Schwarz's own argument, Candido's disentangling makes Santiago's disentangling redundant insofar as Candido demolishes the opposition between center and periphery far more decisively than Santiago does. Weighing the two perspectives according to the yardstick of their practical effects, which is the context in which Schwarz himself intends to frame the discussion, it is no longer clear why one should accept Candido's disentangling and not Santiago's.

In any case, Schwarz's insistence on preserving the scheme of "models" and "deviations," although hardly effective in theoretical terms, has important (and mostly regrettable) consequences in historiographical practice. His proposal ultimately reinforces problems which, as we saw in Chapter 1, are inherent in the tradition of the history of "ideas" in Latin America.

---

[35] The ultimate question that Schwarz's definition raises is: How can we draw, in practice, the line separating the context in which ideas are well-located from that where they are "misplaced"? To give an example taken from literature, *Noches tristes y día alegre* (1818–1819) by Fernández de Lizardi, is an "imitation" of *Noches lúgubres* (1771) by José Cadalso, which is, in turn, an "imitation" of Edward Young's *Night Thoughts* (1742–1745), which is probably an "imitation" of previous works, and so on. Furthermore, the "imitators" of Fernández de Lizardi in Mexico have been numerous. Now, how can we distinguish, in the series of its displacements, the "original" (or "originals") from the "copy" (or "copies")?

The Inherent Limitations in the "History of Ideas"

We must observe here the presence of tension between his critical method in literature and its historiographic and intellectual implications. During its translation into the ambit of conceptual discourses, the subtleties of his insights as a literary critic are missed, laying bare the heuristic strictures of the scheme of "models" and "deviations" as a grid for understanding the erratic evolution of ideas in Latin America. In effect, while, as we have seen, in his works as a literary critic his focus is on the *formal* dimension of discourses, when he addresses political and cultural discourse, he goes back to a more traditional approach exclusively concentrated on their ideological contents, the "ideas" contained in them (the semantic level of language). As a consequence, his theory ends up replicating the kind of problems that are proper to the traditional approaches of the history of ideas. As we saw in Chapter 1, the historiography of ideas in Latin America has been organized, since its very inception, around the goal of identifying the "distortions" produced by the transposition to the region of liberal ideas that were allegedly incompatible with the region's inherited traditions and culture. Historians of local ideas thus converged toward postulating that the result of the nineteenth century collision of an atavistic native culture and the universalistic principles of liberalism was a kind of compromised ideology which Romero termed "liberal-conservative."[36] When confronted with an environment which was strange and hostile to them, "modern" liberal ideas acquired a conservative and centralist bent.

Such a scheme tends to reduce all problematic aspects in local intellectual history to what in legal language is called *adjudicatio*, the application of a norm to a specific case. In this sense, it impedes historians from critically interrogating the putative "models," foreclosing the possibility of their problematization, which is, precisely, as Schwarz showed, the most interesting aspect in Machado de Assis's work: *how it made manifest, from within the genre, problems which were inherent in it* (and not the expression of merely local "pathologies"). From the perspective of "misplaced ideas," the fact that the ideas of a given author departed from the postulated "ideal type" of liberalism (the *logos*) can only be interpreted as symptomatic of a hidden *pathos* (conservative prejudices, economic backwardness, an atavistic culture, and so on). Models are simply assumed as perfectly consistent and their meaning

---

[36] José Luis Romero, *Las ideas políticas en Argentina* (Buenos Aires: FCE, 1985), chapter 5.

114   THEORETICAL APPROACHES

transparent. Textbook definitions are simply taken as valid; the only problem that the "history of ideas" apparently raises in Latin America is something actually external to ideas: whether or not they are "applicable" to the specific local context.

From a methodological perspective, the main consequence of the previous point is, as Schwarz lucidly observed, that the approaches to the "history of ideas" systematically and necessarily fail in their attempt to find anything particular to Latin America. To postulate the finding of a "Latin American peculiarity," whatever it may be, these approaches must necessarily simplify the history of European ideas, smoothing over the intricacies of its actual course. Even so, they can hardly find a way of describing the postulated "idiosyncrasies" with "non-European categories." As Schwarz remarks, it is clear that terms such as "conservatism," and indeed the ideological mixture expressed in Romero's formula ("liberal-conservatism") are no less "abstract" and "European" categories than their opposite "liberalism." Notwithstanding, it is still true that, within the framework of these approaches, the only thing which may justify the study of Latin American ideas and make them relevant is the expectation of finding "distortions," how ideas "deviated" from the presumed pattern. This leads us back to the basic contradiction in the approaches focused on "ideas" that we observed in chapter one: *these approaches generate an anxiety about peculiarity that they themselves can never lessen*; in short, *the "history of ideas" leads to a dead end.*

Hence, having to postulate a goal that is unattainable for the history of "ideas" undermines its own foundations. Schwarz is particularly aware of this situation—the simultaneous necessity-impossibility of distortions in the local history of ideas—but he takes as a characteristic of Latin American intellectual history that which is, in fact, a problem inherent in its very approach. If historians of ideas fail to find the presumed features that particularize ideas in the local context, it is ultimately because of the kind of approaches they use to prevent it: seen from the perspective of their ideological contents, every system of thought necessarily falls within a limited range of alternatives, none of which may aspire to appear as exclusive to Latin America. Within this scheme, the ideas of a given author can be either more conservative than liberal, or vice versa, or lie in some middle point between these two extremes (and the same applies to the rest of the topics around which traditional histories of ideas are normally organized). Ultimately, when we approach the texts exclusively at the level of their semantic contents, the spectrum of

REVISITING THE TOPIC OF "MISPLACED IDEAS" 115

possible results can be perfectly established *a priori*; eventual historiographical controversies are thus limited merely to how to categorize them.

The problems found in historicizing ideas (discovering their distinguishing marks) spring from the fact that "ideas" are ahistorical by definition; the conditions for their eventual emergence in specific contexts denote circumstances which are external to them. Hence, the tendency among the historians of ideas is to complement their descriptions of intellectual contents with quasi-historical explanations; that is, to refer them to their social, "external" context, and, in sum, to take the presumed "deviations" as indicative of a "social malaise." But, as Pocock remarked, this form of "contextual reductionism" cannot "rescue the historian [of ideas] from the circumstance that the intellectual constructs he was trying to control were not historical phenomena at all, to the extent they had been constructed by non-historical modes of inquiry."[37]

Here we find the fundamental limitation with which Schwarz's concept collides. If it cannot account for the epistemological reasons for that necessity-impossibility of "distortions," it is because his concept still hinges on the same premises determining that impossibility-necessity. The last root of this lies in a crude linguistic view, which is inherent to the "histories of ideas," which reduces language to merely its referential dimension. This provides the grounds for the opposition between "ideas" and "reality" on which the problem of "misplaced ideas" rests, and this is only so within the framework of the former opposition: as soon as we undermine it, the whole problem of "copying" becomes meaningless.

Representation and Use of Ideas

The true paradox implicit in Schwarz's theory is that it begins as an attempt to counter the essentialist views of nationalist (and Latin Americanist) thought, yet he cannot avoid replicating in his own discourse what he questioned in them. In fact, from the moment that we understand ideas as merely "representations" of reality, there is no way of approaching the issue of "misplaced ideas" without appealing to the existence of some inner Latin American being to which "foreign ideas" are allegedly unable to capture.

---

[37] J. G. A. Pocock, *Politics, Language, and Time: Essays on Political Thought and History* (Chicago: The University of Chicago Press, 1989), 10.

116   THEORETICAL APPROACHES

Now, the irony is that exactly the same thing happens with that other, more radical, "deconstructive" perspective developed by Santiago. Positing that Latin American discourse produces a rupture effect in European models of ideas entails a similarly essentialist perspective regarding the maladjustment between foreign categories and Latin American "inner being," an *intrinsic nature* that makes it unassimilable to European reason, thus revealing its inherent shortcomings. In the end, Santiago's proposal does not look very different from the proposal of Latin Americanist philosophers. At this point it becomes clear that approaching the issue of the particular dynamics of ideological processes in the periphery without relapsing into a metaphysical terrain demands the complete reformulation of the issue. And Schwarz himself provides some clues for it.

As we have seen, far from endorsing the topic of "misplaced ideas," he initially intended to render it problematic. In his retrospective review of the fate of his original text, forty years later, Schwarz complained about the kind of misunderstandings it had generated. As he said:

> The problem to which the title of the essay alluded ironically, as a dramatization, was another: it was to clarify the historical reasons, the reasons why the ideas indispensable for the modernization of the country, however, caused an undeniable sense of strangeness and artificiality even among admirers and followers.[38]

Lastly, the title of the article was misleading, because, as he said, it "focused the discussion on a false problem, or rather, on the problem I sought to overcome."[39] In fact, as the previous quote remarks, he did not intend to establish which ideas are misplaced and which are not in Latin America, but, more precisely, which ideas were, at every given context, *perceived* as misplaced, by whom, why, etc. This means rendering those very perceptions symptomatic; something that must be interpreted rather than taken as merely expressing an actual fact.

It thus opens the doors to a radical reformulation of the issue, its translation to a second-order level of discourse: it is the very *perceptions* of the

---

[38] Roberto Schwarz, "Las ideas fuera de lugar: algunas aclaraciones," *Políticas de la Memoria* 10/11/12 (2011–2012): 26. This article is preceded by an introduction by Maria Elisa Cevasco, "El significado de 'las ideas fuera de lugar,'" *Políticas de la Memoria* 10/11/12 (2011–2012): 21–24.
[39] Schwarz, "Las ideas fuera de lugar: algunas aclaraciones," 25.

REVISITING THE TOPIC OF "MISPLACED IDEAS" 117

alterity of ideas, and how they changed, that provides fundamental clues for the understanding of intellectual history. However, Schwarz's answer to the question he poses is disappointing. "The paradox," he says, "was clamorous in Brazil, where the slave labour and slave trade were not only not abolished but prospered during the first half of the nineteenth century." This calls to mind what I call "Fabio Zerpa's syndrome."

Fabio Zerpa was, in the 1960s and 1970s, a famous ufologist. As far as I remember, at that time everybody was seeing UFOs. It was a set topic at the dinner table. Today, instead, almost nobody sees them. And these changing perceptions, why fifty years ago everybody saw UFOs but not today, is very telling of the cultural changes that occurred in the intervening years. Now, if we ask Zerpa, he would say that it is because in the 1960s and 1970s more UFOs came to the Earth than they do today. In this fashion, all that the topic has of interest for cultural history fades away. It would be simply a matter of an empirical verification, the corroboration of an actual fact. There is nothing more to say about it.

The same thing happens with Schwarz's last statement. According to it, the reason why liberal ideas were perceived as misplaced in Latin America is simple: they were, in effect, misplaced. The perceptions of alterity of ideas are taken as mere reflections of an actual reality, which is, besides, evident ("clamorous," as he says). It does not leave any room for any further analysis, concluding it at the very same point where it should have started. All that the issue had of interest for intellectual history becomes obliterated.

We can also see here why the kind of misunderstandings that Schwarz regretted were not merely incidental. They have some ground in his own text. We have seen it in connection with the definition of the status of Marxist ideas in Brazil, when he assured that, although they were originally misplaced, they could eventually become adjusted to local reality, a statement which, actually, demolished the premises of his own theory. However, beyond the, let us say, practical problem he faces here (how to justify the relevance of his ideological stance within the framework of his theory) there underlie deeper problems of a conceptual nature. In the last instance, they are associated, as we have said, with a poor linguistic perspective. An expression by Pocock is, again, particularly enlightening in this regard: "the point here," he says, "is rather that, under the pressure of the idealist-materialist dichotomy, we have been giving all our attention to thought as conditioned by social facts outside itself, and not enough attention to thought as denoting, referring, assuming, alluding, implying, and

118   THEORETICAL APPROACHES

performing a variety of functions of which the simplest is that of containing and conveying information."[40]

In effect, Schwarz's identification of the fact that ideas in Latin America are "misplaced" for being inadequate descriptions (distorted representations) of local reality indicates that his perspective still hinges on the basis of that traditional concept of the "history of ideas" which reduces language to its merely referential function (which is, precisely, what he rejects in his works as a literary critic). However, the issues he intends to thematize far exceed the strictly semantic ambit of language. In fact, if understood in this sense, Schwarz's formula is simply a *contradictio in adjectio*. The definition of a given discourse as out of place involves a reference to its *pragmatic* dimension, the conditions of its utterance. Some conceptual distinctions will allow us to clarify the problems raised by Schwarz's erratic formulations of the issue of "misplaced ideas."

If this formula represents a terminological contradiction, it is because Schwarz collapses two very different linguistic instances in it; he introduces a *pragmatic* factor into the *semantic* level of language, which necessarily engenders a conceptual discrepancy: it leads him to describe ideas in terms of propositions and their meaning, while attributing to them functions that are proper to their use. "Ideas" (the semantic level) involve *statements* (affirmations or denials regarding the state of the world). These are context-free: the semantic content of a proposition ("what is said") can be established independent of the specific context and mode of its enunciation. Contextual considerations relate, instead, to the proposition's *pragmatics*. Its unit is the *utterance*, not the *statement*. What matters in an utterance is not the *meaning*, but the *significance*. The latter, unlike the former, cannot be established except in connection with the context and mode of its enunciation. It refers not only to "what is said" (the semantic content of ideas), but also to *how* it is said, *who* says it, *where*, to *whom*, etc.[41] The understanding of its *significance* entails the comprehension of its *meaning*; yet these two instances are of a very different nature. The latter belongs to the order of *langue*, it describes events or situations; the former belongs to the order of *parole*, it implies the realization of an action. What we have seen so far can be represented as follows:[42]

---

[40] Pocock, *Politics, Language, and Time*, 37.

[41] To set an example, if I say that "Iran is the empire of evil," it is not the same as if the US president says that at an United Nations conference. The meaning of the words is the same, but the significance of the utterance is not.

[42] See Oswald Ducrot, *El decir y lo dicho* (Buenos Aires: Hachette, 1984), 31.

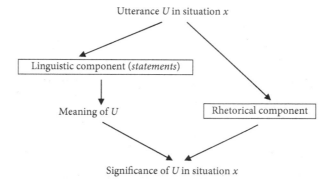

In the context of the present discussion, the critical point is that *statements* ("ideas") are *true* or *false* (right or wrong representations of reality), but they are never "misplaced;" only *utterances* can be. Being "misplaced" is necessarily a pragmatic condition; it indicates that something was said in a wrong way, or by the wrong person, or at the wrong moment, etc. Conversely, utterances, as such, can be "misplaced," but they cannot be *true* or *wrong* (i.e., "distorted representations"). Only statements can. An utterance may eventually contain a false statement ("distorted representations"), but it is still "true" (real) as such. Utterances actually undercut the distinction between "ideas" and "realities": they are always "real" *speech-acts*, to put it in John Austin's words.[43] This explains the paradox commented on by Schwarz: that an utterance containing wrong statements (distorted representations of reality) is still "true" as such. Yet this does not relate to a Brazilian or Latin American peculiarity, but to a property inherent in language.

To summarize what we have seen so far: the definition of a model which could account for the problematic dynamic of ideas in Latin America, insofar as it entails the consideration of the pragmatic dimension of language, cannot be achieved with the kind of conceptual tools Schwarz handles (which are the traditional ones in the "history of ideas"). Only the simultaneous consideration of the different levels of language permits tracing significant relationships between texts and their particular contexts of enunciation, finding a link which connects the two channels of the "stereoscopic vision" (textual analysis and social reflection) proposed by Schwarz,[44] thus rendering intellectual history a truly hermeneutical undertaking.[45] By focusing

---

[43] See John Austin, *How to do Things with Words* (Cambridge, MA: Harvard University Press, 1975).
[44] Schwarz, *Seqüências*, 28.
[45] See Pocock, *Politics, Language, and Time*, 105.

120   THEORETICAL APPROACHES

exclusively on the referential level of discourse, there is no way of tracing in them the vestiges of the contextual conditions of their utterance because they do not reside at that level. Hence, following the habitual procedures of the history of "ideas," students cannot find in Latin American discourse any trait that singularizes it: only the consideration of their pragmatic dimension permits their comprehension as *events* ("speech acts"). Ultimately, the search for the contextual determinations conditioning the modes of appropriation, circulation, and articulation of public discourses leads us beyond the reach of the history of "ideas."

Rethinking the kind of question that Schwarz intended to thematize and thus rescuing it for cultural critique involves, at the same time, the revision of the tenets on which it is founded. An example may help to clarify this point. The model elaborated by Iuri Lotman is particularly relevant in this regard.[46] The application of Lotman's concept of "semiosphere" to the analysis of the issue raised by Schwarz allows us to observe in which sense an approach centered on "languages" may provide a more refined set of categories to carry out Schwarz's own project, enlightening the nature of the limitations resulting from its inscription within the frameworks of the traditional history of "ideas."

As is well known, semiotics is the discipline which has come to occupy, in part, the place left vacant by the decline of classical rhetoric, systematically trying to analyze the processes of communicative exchange. Its cornerstone was the definition of the basic communicative unit represented by the scheme "emitter → message → receptor." However, for Lotman, this monolingual scheme results in an abstract, highly stylized, and static model of the processes of meaning-generation and transmission of ideas. As he observes, no "code," "language," or "text" exists in an isolated fashion; every communicative process, he says, entails the presence of at least two codes and a translating operator. The concept of "semiosphere" indicates precisely the coexistence and juxtaposition of a large number of codes in the given semiotic space, which determines its dynamics. This concept may help us to rearticulate Schwarz's theoretical proposal and simultaneously preserve the core of his original insights.

First, Lotman's model clarifies an aspect that is only partially articulated in the texts of the Brazilian critic. As the Russian-Estonian semiologist

---

[46] See Iuri M. Lotman, *La semiosfera I: Semiótica de la cultura y del texto* (Barcelona: Cátedra/Universitat de València, 1996), and Iuri M. Lotman, *La semiosfera II: Semiótica de la cultura, del texto, de la conducta y del espacio* (Barcelona: Cátedra/Universitat de València, 1998).

affirms, although every code (e.g., a national culture, a disciplinary tradition, an artistic school, or a political ideology) permanently interacts with those elements which form its semiotic environment, it always tends to its own closure to preserve its internal balance or homeostasis. Thus, it generates a self-description or metalanguage by which it legitimizes its particular discursive régime, demarcating its sphere of action and internally delimiting and confining the possible uses of the symbolic materials available within its boundaries. In this fashion, it also establishes the conditions of appropriation of the "extra-systemic" symbolic elements: an idea pertaining to a given code cannot be introduced in a different one unless it has previously undergone a process of assimilation to the latter. Lastly, this shows that semiotic "cannibalism" is not a Brazilian peculiarity, much less Tupi's cultural legacy, as Oswald de Andrade imagined.[47]

This model helps to clarify Schwarz's first criticism of the nationalists' rejection of "imitation" of "foreign" models: his insistence that imitation is not self-explanatory, that we must look at Brazilian reality to find the conditions for its tendency to adopt alien concepts to (always inappropriately) describe local reality. Ultimately, he said, in the very process of "imitating," Brazilian culture made manifest its intrinsic nature. But this also shows that, as Carvalho Franco remarked, "ideas" are actually never "misplaced"; that is, communicative exchanges never involve merely passive receptions of "alien" elements. To be assimilated, they must be (or become) legible by the culture that is to incorporate them. Otherwise, they would be irrelevant for the latter, invisible from that culture's particular horizon. This observation confronts Schwarz's proposal with a problem: How may ideas be assimilable as proper and still be alien? Apparently, the only alternative left is to postulate a divorce between culture and nation; that is, the existence of a more authentic substratum, a hidden essence of nationality which its own "superficial" culture fails to express or represent—which is precisely what the nationalists (and the Latin Americanists) assert. Here again we come to the two horns of the dilemma: either to dissolve the question of the peripheral condition of local culture, or to go back to the dualistic framework of the nationalist (essentialist) perspective. There is, however, a third variant, which Schwarz outlines, but does not consistently elaborate.

---

[47] On this topic, see E. J. Palti, "The Nation as a Problem: Historians and the 'National Question,'" *History and Theory* 40 (2001): 324–346.

122   THEORETICAL APPROACHES

The touchstone of Schwarz's concept is a fundamental shift in the way he approaches the topic. As we have seen, his inquiry actually does not refer to the presumed "alienness" of ideas in Brazilian culture but, rather, to how they eventually came to be perceived as such by certain sectors of the local population. Yet, as we have also seen, he cannot elaborate the point, relapsing into the very topic he said he intended to refute, that of "misplaced ideas": as we have seen, that perception would be explained, for him, because they are actually misplaced; in the end, there is nothing there that demands an explanation. We can now try to provide that project with a more consistent formulation, and the reference to Lotman's ideas is particularly helpful also in this regard.

As Lotman remarks, even though the processes of cultural exchange do not involve a merely passive reception of "alien" elements, indeed precisely for that reason, semiotic ambivalence is intrinsic to them. This has two origins. Firstly, the equivocation springing from the fact that codes, like the semiosphere at large, are not internally homogeneous: they contain a plurality of subcodes which coexist and intercross and tend, in turn, to their own closure, often rendering impossible their mutual translatability. Secondly, the very openness of the codes to their semiotic environment, which also permanently produces new internal unbalances. To make an external element assimilable, a system must eventually adjust its internal structure, reorganize its components, and thus destabilize its present configuration. This is linked to what Jean Piaget studied under the name of the processes of *assimilation* and *accommodation*, the two fundamental mechanisms, for him, for the equilibration–disequilibration of cognitive structures.[48] Following this concept, it must be said that ambivalences are simultaneously the cause and effect of unbalances. Uneven developments necessarily result in asymmetries among codes and subcodes (hierarchies and differences in power-relations). Thus, in every exchange process some semiotic *violence* is present, operating in both the mechanisms of systems stability and the dynamic impulses that dislocate them, along with insufficient compensations that result from it.[49]

What Schwarz perceives as the determinant of "Latin American peculiarity" (the problematic interaction between the "center" and the "periphery")

---

[48] See Jean Piaget, *Biology and Knowledge: An Essay on the Relations Between Organic Regulations and Cognitive Processes* (Chicago: The University of Chicago Press, 1971).

[49] The notion of symbolic compensations as the procedure that permits the reversibility of cognitive structures (without which there is no true knowledge) was developed by Piaget in the above-mentioned work, *Biology and Knowledge*.

REVISITING THE TOPIC OF "MISPLACED IDEAS" 123

should be interpreted as an expression of the above-mentioned uneven developments and asymmetrical exchanges in the field of culture, resulting in a double phenomenon. On the one hand, codes in the periphery of a system would always be more unstable than in the center, and their capacities to assimilate alien elements are relatively more limited. On the other hand, the semiotic distance separating them from the center would make the pressures for accommodation more powerful in them. From this perspective, Carvalho Franco's and Schwarz's views lose their antagonistic aspect. The two would emphasize, respectively, two different aspects, equally intrinsic in every phenomenon of cultural exchange. While Carvalho Franco's concept focuses on the mechanisms of *assimilation*, Schwarz's concentrates on the processes of *accommodation* to which the former mechanisms, in turn, generate (and the inevitable tensions they involve).

This reformulation condenses the core of Schwarz's theoretical program.[50] Yet, at the same time, it implies a revision of his concept in three fundamental aspects. Firstly, in this linguistic perspective, "centers" and "peripheries" are not stable and fixed; they move in time and space. Determining them is not, therefore, a simple task. They are not only historically changeable, but also relative at every given moment (what is a "center" in one regard, may be a "periphery" in another; both centers and peripheries contain, in turn, their own centers and peripheries, etc.).[51] In sum, it is simplistic and misleading to speak about "centers" and "peripheries" as if they were homogeneous, fixed entities—a habit that necessarily leads to abstract and generic views of "Europe," "Latin America," and their mutual relationships—that is, as if they were objects whose nature and defining characteristics could be established *a priori*.

Secondly, semiotic dislocations are not placed on the level of the semantic component. It is not that ideas are "distorted representations of reality." Unbalances here do not refer to the relationship between "ideas" and "realities" (a concept that always has implicit—at least, as a counterfactual— the ideal of a fully organic society, in which "ideas" and "realities" would converge), but to that of ideas with respect to themselves. And these kinds of dislocations are, in effect, inevitable. As we have seen, they spring from the coexistence and superposition of heterogeneous codes in one single system.

[50] In "Discutindo com Alfredo Bosi" (1993), he comes the closest to this formulation. In this text, he discusses Bosi's idea of "cultural filter." Alfredo Bosi, *Dialéctica da colonização* (São Paulo: Companhia de Letras, 1992).

[51] Cfr. Haroldo de Campos, *De la razón antropofágica*.

124 THEORETICAL APPROACHES

This means that, whereas ideas are never "misplaced," because the meaning of a given idea does not preexist its own conditions of intelligibility, they are simultaneously always "misplaced" due to the fact that every system shelters mutually contradictory reading protocols. More specifically stated, they are "always partially dislocated."

This is so not because alien ideas and institutions cannot become adjusted to local reality (in fact, they are always, in some sense, well adjusted, *in place*), but because that process of assimilation is always contradictory due to the presence, in the interior of every culture, of a plurality of agents and modes of appropriation ("a complex, plural society," states Pocock, "will speak a complex, plural language; or rather, a plurality of specialized languages, each carrying its own biases as to the definition and distribution of authority").[52] Thinking that they could be completely dislocated would imply postulating a state of total *anomia* (the dissolution of every system), which is never empirically possible, as even a situation of civil war entails some rules. Conversely, imagining a state in which ideas were perfectly adjusted would amount to supposing the existence of a fully organic system, a completely regimented order, which has managed to erase every contradiction and to fill its internal fissures, in brief, to fix its metalanguage—which is not really feasible in relatively complex societies.

Social perceptions regarding the "alienness" of Brazilian culture observed by Schwarz can thus be explained as an expression of the dislocations produced by this complex dynamic within the processes of cultural acquisition. Such an "alienness" is not merely a fact that "popular opinion" records, as nationalists think, but, as Schwarz eventually suggests, the product of contradictions and ambivalences generated by the very processes of production, transmission, and appropriation of discourses. We can no longer speak of "misplaced ideas"; that is, categories or notions which are, by their very nature, maladjusted to local reality and thereby the source of distorted descriptions. Maladjustments are rather an expression of the fact that *every assimilation is, in itself, contradictory*. What is important is to understand the very process of *misplacing* ideas. And this leads us to the third, and the truly problematic, point because it definitively escapes the reach of Schwarz's categorical horizon.

The third aspect that the introduction of the consideration of the pragmatic dimension of language obliges us to revise in Schwarz's concept lies

---

[52] Pocock, *Politics, Language, and Time*, 22.

in the fact that, as a consequence of the preceding considerations, not only are ideas never completely "misplaced" because if the appropriate conditions of reception by a given system were lacking, they would be irrelevant—invisible, as Carvalho Franco states—but also the sense of their mis-location cannot be defined except in connection with a given, particular code. That is, the determination of ambivalences for a specific system is itself equivocal, a function of the particular pragmatic context of enunciation. There is not *one* "place of reality" where one could determine which ideas are "misplaced" and which are not. Lastly, the definition of what is "misplaced" and what is "properly placed" is already a part of the game of equivocations, where, as we have seen, the "unrealistic" ones are always *others' ideas*.

Recognition of this completely redefines the object of intellectual history. Its aim now becomes trying to comprehend what is "misplaced" in each particular discursive context: how certain ideas or models and not others come to appear as "misplaced;" how, for some people, some ideas or models are "misplaced," while, for others, they are well adjusted to local reality; finally, how some ideas or models that appeared in certain circumstances, to certain people, to be well placed eventually came to be seen, by these same people, as "misplaced" (and vice versa).

Schwarz's classical example of Brazil's 1824 constitution is enlightening on this point. The drafters of that Constitution reproduced the formula in the French Declaration of the Rights of Man and of the Citizen affirming that all citizens were free and equal before the law. As Schwarz observes, this was obviously a misrepresentation of reality: at that time, about one-third of the Brazilian population was in slavery. In sum, it would be another example of the series of maladjustments produced by the transposition of liberal ideas to a social context where the conditions that had created them no longer existed. However, the Declaration was not necessarily contradictory with the existence of slavery. This was so only under the assumption that *slaves were subjects of right*, which was precisely what the slavery discourse denied. The fact that it seems "misplaced" to us is revealing only of our own current beliefs (i.e., that we assume that *all* men, including slaves, are subjects of law; in sum, that we no longer share the slavery discourse), which is not relevant in the framework of a historiographical work.

Yet, Schwarz was correct when he said, against Carvalho Franco, that the Declaration was "misplaced." It does not matter what *we* think; the point here is that, in effect, it seemed misplaced for the *very actors* (or, at least, for some of them); and, in the nineteenth century, especially in the second half, this

126   THEORETICAL APPROACHES

perception spread rapidly. This was not a confrontation between "ideas" and "realities," but between two opposing discourses (as Lotman asserts, the generation of contradictions or semiotic ambivalences entails the presence of at least two mutually heterogeneous codes), which, in specific circumstances, came into contact and collided. At any rate, the fact is that the "mis-location" of the constitutional charter is not something "natural" or "fixed," nor is it something which becomes immediately apparent as soon as we read its text and contrast it with the "social reality" of its time. It is, rather, a historical result, the contingent product of a series of uneven developments which determined the particular conditions for the public articulation of discourses in that country at that specific moment. Contrary to Schwarz's assertion, its being "misplaced" cannot be understood if we detach that circumstance from the decomposition process that the institution of slavery was then undergoing in a country whose economy, however, depended fundamentally on that institution. It ultimately reflects how the premises of the slavery discourse were becoming undermined.

This makes us move back to a definition centered on the semantic contents of discourse ("ideas"), but now within a perspective that incorporates the consideration of their pragmatic dimension. This shows us why the question of whether liberal ideas were misplaced in Brazil cannot be answered with a "yes" or "no." It leads us to situate our approach on a different level of analysis (a movement which Schwarz initiates but does not complete). A history of the "always partially disjointed ideas" must be defined as a kind of history of "the ideas about misplaced ideas," a history of a second-order ideas; that is, a history of political languages and the modes of their social articulation, circulation, and appropriation.

In sum, we may say that Schwarz's concept of "misplaced ideas," thus reformulated—reinterpreted in terms of the "always partially disjointed ideas"—is highly enlightening of the processes of symbolic exchange, in general, and of the uneven dynamics of cultural developments in Latin America, in particular. It supplies a more refined conceptual tool to comprehend them than that provided by the scheme of "models" and "deviations" within which Schwarz inscribed his theory, which led him to analyze "ideas" in terms of meanings and propositions, while attributing to them functions that are proper to their use. As we have seen, an appeal to more complex linguistic models allows us to recover the core of his original proposal: how to account for the maladjustments generated by asymmetrical exchanges from a non-dualistic perspective of cultural developments in peripheral areas, while reformulating it in such a way as to prevent a relapse into the topic. Indeed, the point is to gain critical distance with respect to the topic, to de-familiarize and de-naturalize it, thereby turning it into an object susceptible of critical scrutiny.

Ultimately, such a revision of Schwarz's interpretive framework is not only one of the possible directions in which it can be developed, but it also turns out to be more compatible with the anti-essentialist assumptions implicit in Schwarz's own contention. Yet, the price we must pay for this greater sophistication is the renunciation of all expectations of finding any generic trait, describable in simple terms, that would identify local intellectual history; that is, of discovering some particular feature perceivable in the cultural dynamics of the region that would reveal the commonality of all types of discourse throughout the respective countries and historical periods and, simultaneously, distinguish this cultural dynamic from that of the discourses from all other regions. In short, we must renounce the aspiration to define which ideas are "misplaced" and in which sense they are so in Latin America as a whole, independently from their particular context of utterance. In the last instance, the basic tenet of this argument has been perfectly condensed by Schwarz himself in his criticism of Tropicalism: "the generality of this blueprint [tropicalism]," he said, "is such that it embraces all the countries of the continent, at every stage in their history—which might seem to be a defect. What can a formula say about Brazil in 1964 which is equally applicable, say, to nineteenth-century Argentina?"[53]

---

[53] Schwarz, *Misplaced Ideas*, 143–144.

PART II
HISTORIOGRAPHICAL APPROACHES

The Syndrome of Alphonse the Wise: Teleologism and Normativism in the History of Ideas

In this second Part, we will critically analyze the approaches to specific historical processes and events from the perspective of the history of ideas. We will focus more particularly on the debates around the revolutions of independence and the emergence of new national states, the different lines of interpretations and perspectives of what led to the break of colonial ties and the problems for the consolidation of the newly emerged political systems founded on a new, republican principle of legitimacy. As we will see, despite their profound differences, most of them revolved around the topic "from tradition to modernity" (ultimately, a version of the teleological scheme "from *mythos* to *logos*"). It provided the basic framework to comprehend the meaning of the break of the colonial tie. Even those who question the pertinence of the topic to the Latin American case assume it to be the yardstick against which all political-conceptual developments in the region would be assessed. Yet, we can also find some exceptions to this rule, perspectives that provide a more complex and nuanced view of the process that culminated in the revolutionary event.

The most prominent of these exceptions is the perspective elaborated by Tulio Halperin Donghi in *Tradición política española e ideología revolucionaria de Mayo*, which we will study in Chapter 5. As we will see, Halperin Donghi radically reformulates the topic of the "ideological origins of the revolutions of independence," and, in the process, provides an

130 HISTORIOGRAPHICAL APPROACHES

approach that effectively departs from the teleological frameworks inherent in the tradition of the history of ideas. In this fashion, Halperin provides a means of comprehending complex ideological processes, which cannot be reduced to the scheme of "models" and "deviations," thus revealing the limitations of that scheme and the series of antinomies deriving from it; more specifically, in this case, those between "tradition" and "modernity," and between "continuity" and "change."

In the second and final chapter of this Part (Chapter 6 of the book), we analyze the more recent "revisionist" approaches to the revolutions of independence and Latin America's nineteenth-century political history.[1] As we will see, following the "revisionist" perspective, which we observed at the beginning of this book in connection with Charles Hale's and the "culturalist" school's" work, the more recent "revisionist" currents also emphasize—in opposition to the "epic views" of Latin American independence—the permanence of a traditionalist culture that prevented the establishment of modern, democratic, régimes of governments. Yet, in this fashion, far from breaking with the teleological assumptions underlying the "epic" views, as the revisionists assert to have done, their approaches remain within the very teleological frameworks they intended to dislocate. Thus, from these perspectives, Latin American political experience appears as a kind of failed modernization.

What underlies all the different versions of historical teleologism is a normative drive that leads one to observe past realizations retrospectively from the perspective of a presumedly untimely ideal of modern democracy, as each one conceives of it. This ideal type is assumed as the final goal to which the political process under consideration led—or should have led. Previous political formations are thus retrospectively reconstructed, either as an advance or as a deviation in the march toward that ideal. We find here what I call the "syndrome of Alphonse the wise," which is implicit in the topic of "from tradition to modernity."

Like Thales of Mileto in the story told by Plato, the Medieval King Alfonse of Castile was fascinated with the contemplation of the sky. He was convinced that by observing it, the comprehension of its structure could reveal its meaning and destiny. However, he was critical of it, as he perceived a fault

---

[1] For an early criticism of the literature on the topic from a historical-conceptual perspective, see Pierre Chaunu, *La independencia de América Latina* (Buenos Aires: Nueva Visión, 1972).

in its structure. And this led him to assert that "if God had consulted him at the moment of the Creation of the Universe, the result would have been much better than it is." Now, the same can be said of historians of ideas. They believe that, if the founding fathers of Latin American nations had consulted them at the moment of their creation, the result would have been much better.

5

On the "Ideological Origins" of the Revolutions of Independence

The revolutions of independence have been a central topic in Latin American historiography from its beginning.[1] The reason is rather predictable, as they take place in the very origins of the newly emerged nations. And, within the framework of the "genealogical" concept of the nation, which was that of the nineteenth-century historicism that informed the first national narratives, this fact was crucial, insofar as the origins contained the key that explained and made sense of all subsequent historical developments. In this context, the issue of the "ideological origins" of the revolutions gained a particular relevance. The definition of the conceptual framework of the revolutionary discourse would allow us to understand the foundations on which these nations were built, the set of principles and values that allegedly presided over its historical evolution.

According to what we will call the "epic view," which was dominant at the moment of independence, the origins of the new nations must be sought in the influence of the Enlightenment's ideas. Rousseau's concept of the social contract would have provided the basis on which the entire revolutionary discourse rested.[2] As Juan Bautista Alberdi stated:

> We have had two existences in the world, a colonial and a republican. The former was given to us by Spain; the second, by France. The day we stopped being a colony, our family ties with Spain ended: as a republic, we are children of France.[3]

---

[1] As Ana Carolina Ibarra asserts, the interpretation of this event "has structured national politics and history." Ana Carolina Ibarra, "Autonomía e independencia en la crisis del orden virreinal," in *Mito y realidad en la cultura política latinoamericana*, ed. Elías Palti (Buenos Aires: Prometeo, 2010), 120.

[2] On the reception of Rousseau's ideas in Latin America, see Noemí Goldman, *El discurso como objeto de la historia* (Buenos Aires: Hachette, 1989) and Gabriel Entin, ed., *Rousseau en Iberoamérica. Lecturas e interpretaciones entre monarquía y revolución* (Buenos Aires: SB Editores, 2018).

[3] Juan B. Alberdi, *Fragmento preliminar al estudio del derecho* (Buenos Aires: Biblos, 1984), 153.

Misplaced Ideas?. Elías J. Palti, Oxford University Press. © Oxford University Press 2024.
DOI: 10.1093/oso/9780197556641.003.0005

134   HISTORIOGRAPHICAL APPROACHES

The desire to break with the colonial past led to that view as a logical conclusion. It blocked the possibility of trying to find links connecting the new reality and the pre-revolutionary one. As Tulio Halperin Donghi states, revolutionary forces thus appeared to themselves as "only the armed wing of a system of ideas whose strength derives exclusively from the timeless truth of its contents."[4]

The contestation to this epic view came mainly from the Catholic, pro-Hispanic historiography. It insisted that the mental framework that paved the way to revolutions of independence, far from being provided by the Enlightenment, had its roots in the Spanish political tradition itself. One of the most prominent proponents of that view was Jesuit Guillermo Furlong, who asserted that the idea of a social contract to which revolutionaries appealed to justify the rupture from the metropolis was not that formulated by Rousseau. For Furlong, that concept refers back to the Spanish Neo-Scholastic thinking of the seventeenth century. Certainly, the so-called second generation of Neo-Scholastics, whose main representative was Jesuit Francisco Suárez (1548–1617), elaborated on the idea that sovereignty did not come to the king directly from God but through the intercession of the people, which conferred it upon the monarch.[5]

This Catholic historical current remained marginal in the region; however, its postulates permeated other ambits in the historical profession. In part, this was because, in the early twentieth century, the antagonism with Spain receded and paved the way for a more nuanced perspective of the colonial past. A good example is the so-called New School in Argentina,[6] whose members were then believed to have found the local roots for independence in Spanish juridical tradition. It allegedly contained the germs of self-government and local autonomy. As Ricardo Levene showed, in strictly

---

[4] Tulio Halperin Donghi, *Tradición política española e ideología revolucionaria de Mayo* (Buenos Aires: Prometeo Libros, 2009), 25.

[5] This concept was developed by Suárez in his work *Defensio Fidei*, which was intended to counter the doctrine of the king's divine right formulated by James I of England. Francisco Suárez, *Defensa de la Fe Catolica y Apostólica contra los Errores del Anglicanismo (Defensio Fidei)* (Madrid: Instituto de Estudios Politicos, 1971). On this topic see Elías Palti, *An Archaeology of the Political: Regimes of Power from the Seventeenth Century to the Present* (New York: Columbia University Press, 2017), ch. 1.

[6] The "New School" was a group of historians, presided by Ricardo Levene and Emilio Ravignani, who intended to professionalize historical research in Argentina in the 1920s and 1930s. See Fernando Devoto and Nora Pagano, *Historia de la historiografía argentina* (Buenos Aires: Sudamericana, 2009) and Fernando Devoto and Nora Pagano, eds., *La historiografía académica y la historiografía militante en Argentina y Uruguay* (Buenos Aires: Biblos, 2017).

ON THE "IDEOLOGICAL ORIGINS" 135

legal terms, the ultramarine possessions of Spain were not considered colonies but autonomous kingdoms under one common crown.[7]

In fact, the Hispanic legal tradition contained not only the aforementioned principle, but also a rich collection of institutions, some of which, such as the practices of communal self-government, could well be seen retrospectively as more or less imperfect antecedents of the future Republican political systems. However, for this to be possible, it was necessary to avoid any detailed exploration of that past that could illuminate the extent to which these institutions formed an integral part of the Hispanic monarchical structure and had their roots in a political culture far removed from the Enlightenment's ideals which the revolutionaries would later embrace.[8] In any case, it did not yet seem to be possible to posit colonial ideas and institutions as the foundations of the post-revolutionary reality without losing sight of all that was novel in it. Hence, liberal-nationalist narratives tended to cling to the topic of the "ideological origins" of the revolutions of independence. Only ideas coming from outside could bear such a demiurgic power intrinsic to the ideal of a new beginning, an ideal that was implicit in every revolutionary event, and that the "epic view" would later adopt as its own. The ideological factors will thus continue to appear as the independent variable from which other transformations of political order unfold and to which certain historical circumstances (such as the real vacancy produced in 1808) simply serve as an occasion to become manifest.[9]

The exploration of the ties between the social contract ideas that served as the ideological foundation of the revolution and the Hispanic political tradition will thus remain a task reserved, almost by definition, for the Catholic, pro-Hispanic historiographical currents. These would not have deserved more detailed attention were it not for the fact that such a vision would be

[7] Ricardo Levene, *Las Indias no eran colonias* (Madrid: Espasa Calpe, 1973).

[8] On the "republican" institutions in the colonial régime, see Ambrosio Velasco Gómez, *La persistencia del humanismo republicano en la formación del estado y la nación en México* (Mexico: UNAM, 2009) and Francisco Quijano Velasco, *Las repúblicas de la Monarquía: pensamiento constitucionalista y republicano en Nueva España 1550–1610* (Mexico: UNAM, 2017). Yet, the latter author also warns us about possible retrospective projections of that concept. As he says, "it is not the goal of this study to show that we can find in sixteenth-century New Spain a true republicanism or a true constitutionalism" (Quijano, *Las repúblicas de la Monarquía*, 63).

[9] As José María Samper said in his *Ensayo sobre las revoluciones políticas* (1861): "As soon as any episode arises, perhaps totally insignificant in its form, it is capable of evidencing the deep antagonism between dominant Spaniards and dominated Creoles." José María Samper, *Ensayo sobre las revoluciones políticas* (Paris: Imprenta de Thumot, 1861), 148–149; quoted by Carlos Altamirano, *La Invención de Nuestra América. Obsesiones, narrativas y debates sobre la identidad de América Latina* (Buenos Aires: Siglo XXI, 2021), 94–95.

136 HISTORIOGRAPHICAL APPROACHES

based on a very rich—albeit largely ignored in Latin America—specialized literature that, already in the times of the *Generalísimo* Francisco Franco, had established in Spanish universities the foundations for a field of historical studies on political thought that would reach levels of development never matched on the other side of the Atlantic (and at the top of which were authors of the stature of Miguel Artola and José Antonio Maravall). The naïveté of liberal Latin American historiography in uncritically endorsing the views of the actors of the revolutionary event themselves could only be explained because it paralleled their ignorance of that Hispanic political tradition, which would lead them to lose sight of the extent to which the eagerness by the emancipatory discourse for denying the preceding history had its foundations in that very same past from which it intended to break away, foundations it would have to deny but would not cease to exist for that reason.

This labor of disclosing the Hispanic roots of the revolutionary discourse would eventually enable a more accurate historical reconstruction of the ideological process leading to the breaking of the colonial tie. However, it would not be these Spanish historiographical currents themselves that made such a discovery that would do it. They could only understand this task in terms of the search for the antecedents of revolutionary ideas and motives, which necessarily entailed inflicting systematic violence upon the traditional conceptual matrices. Only in this way could these currents find connections between these two clearly heterogeneous universes of thought, which would not keep any substantive identity at the level of their contents. The tracing of complex ideological processes, the understanding of the paradox of how an intellectual horizon can open the field to a type of discourse whose logic of articulation is, however, completely strange to it, demanded other strategies, other heuristic procedures very different from the mere search for analogies among ideas pertaining to different moments, and the tracing, on that basis, of presumed genealogies of thought.

It was this context in which Halperin Donghi's intervention took place. In *Tradición política española e ideología revolucionaria de Mayo* (*Spanish Political Tradition and Revolutionary Ideology of May*) (1961), he symmetrically takes distance from the two opposite views (the liberal-nationalist and the pro-Hispanic, the former emphasizing the Enlightened foundations of the revolutionary discourse, the latter, its Neo-Scholastic premises).[10]

---

[10] For other studies on that work, see Gabriel Entin, "Tulio Halperin Donghi y la revolución como exploración," *Prismas. Revista de Historia Intelectual* 15 (2011): 185–188; Fabio Wasserman,

ON THE "IDEOLOGICAL ORIGINS" 137

Ultimately, Halperin Donghi reveals why the whole debate about the presumed "ideological origins" of independence is misleading. The very project of defining the nature of revolutionary processes by seeking their ideological origins, the presumed models that each one followed is, for him, simplistic and fruitless. Actually, there is no way of establishing whether the idea of social contract that the revolutionaries endorsed was taken from the Enlightenment or Neo-Scholasticism.[11] And, more importantly, in the case of that being possible, it would be irrelevant for the comprehension of the nature of the revolutionary discourse and how revolutions took place.

Halperin Donghi then reframed the whole question. According to him, the point is not to establish where these motifs and ideas came from or what their origins were, but what the revolutionaries of the end of the eighteenth century and the beginning of the nineteenth century did with them; that is, how those motifs or ideas then became re-arranged and re-signified, giving rise to the peculiar conceptual universe within which revolutions took place.[12] Lastly, whatever their origins were, it is clear that they then served new purposes and were addressed to new, specific, problems and questions, which were absolutely different from those to which they had been addressed in their origins. At that point, even though ideas did not change, the logic of their articulation did, thus giving rise to a new ideological constellation. This is actually the premise for Halperin Donghi's historical perspective. As he says:

"Intelectuales, sociedad y política en los siglos XVIII y XIX: la historia intelectual en el espejo de Halperin Donghi," *Boletín del Instituto de Historia Argentina y Americana "Dr. Emilio Ravignani"* Número Especial (2018): 59–74; Marcela Ternavasio, "Los enigmas de Halperin Comentario al artículo de Fabio Wasserman," *Boletín del Instituto de Historia Argentina y Americana "Dr. Emilio Ravignani"* Número Especial (2018): 86–98 and Segio Serulnikov, "Tulio Halperin Donghi y la independencia hispanomaericana," *Boletín del Instituto de Historia Argentina y Americana "Dr. Emilio Ravignani"* Número Especial (2018): 132–154.

[11] "We can accept that some of Suárez's ideas (including that of the consensual character of political power), were re-discovered in an ideological framework, as well as historical, totally different from the original one [...]. Thus considered, the search for the ideological influences becomes highly difficult. Perhaps in no history of ideas are tradition and originality so closely intertwined as in political thinking. Let us examine any other system of modern political thought: Suárez's, Locke's, Rousseau's. Do any of them contain any ideas of Suárez, of Locke, of Rousseau? However, the originality of the whole is out of the question: it is given by the way ideas are used, by the structures created with them, by the consequences drawn from them, by the trends expressed in a neatly rationalist language." Halperin Donghi, *Tradición política española*, 34.

[12] The studies on the conceptual history of the period of independence have proliferated in recent years under the aegis of Javier Fernández Sebastián's editorial and intellectual production. A major synthesis of it is Javier Fenández Sebastián, ed., — *Diccionario político y social del mundo iberoamericano. Conceptos políticos fundamentales, 1770–1870*, 10 vols. (Madrid: Centro de Estudios Políticos y Constitucionales—Universidad del País Vasco, 2014).

138   HISTORIOGRAPHICAL APPROACHES

If, as we have seen, the originality of a thinking resides only exceptionally in each one of the ideas that are coordinated in it, seeking the source of each one of them seems to be the less fruitful (as well as less secure) in tracing the history of thinking.[13]

This leads us back to the limitations inherent in the old "history of ideas" that we discussed in previous chapters, and of which, as we can see, Halperin Donghi was clearly aware. The history of ideas is, in fact, radically incapable of understanding what changed at that moment, as the kind of conceptual shift produced by the emergence of a revolutionary discourse cannot be perceived on the level of the ideas that it gathered but in the ways it re-articulated them. Nor can these transformations be defined in terms of variations of models without smoothing over all the intricacies and problematic edges intrinsic to this kind of complex historical-conceptual processes. And this explains, in turn, why, beyond their differences, all the currents participating in the debate regarding the "ideological origins" of independence have remained locked within the frameworks of the trans-historical antinomies of the history of ideas.

In the next chapter we will analyze, in greater detail, the historiography of the revolutions of independence in light of the problem of "continuity" and "change." We will review the different interpretations regarding whether they marked a rupture vis-à-vis the colonial patterns, highlighting the kind of both theoretical and historiographical problems that this dichotomy raises for the comprehension of the phenomenon there at stake. Let us say now that they are connected, in large measure, with the fact that all the participants of that debate premise on the basis of a rather static and homogeneous view of the colonial period, as if it had been a homogenous whole that remained unchanged for three centuries, a kind of quasi-eternal ("organicist") essence, opposed to another or quasi-eternal ("individualistic") essence (the Anglo-Saxon). In both cases, whether emphasizing the continuities between the colonial past (its organicist imaginary and institutions) and the independent period or asserting the radical rupture introduced by the revolutions of independence, the so-called Spanish political tradition is retrospectively reconstructed as incarnating a definite and fixed set of principles. There is no room in those approaches for suspecting that that tradition could have undergone a series of fundamental redefinitions over the centuries that

---

[13] Halperin Donghi, *Tradición política española*, 35.

ON THE "IDEOLOGICAL ORIGINS" 139

preceded independence; that it does not refer to any definite set of ideas but to a complex political-conceptual process which entailed a series of fundamental successive reformulations. And this leads us to the topic of the present chapter.

As we will see, Halperin Donghi's fundamental contribution consists in dismantling that static perspective of the colonial past. From the traditional perspectives founded on "models" of thinking or "ideal types," it is necessary to fix the political tradition and identify it with a fixed set of ideas so that it can be subsequently compared with another fixed set of ideas conceived as the properly "modern" ones. In opposition to these static, schematic perspectives, Halperin Donghi shows that the Spanish political tradition was very complex and changing over time, and, more importantly, that we cannot understand how the revolutions of independence came about if we do not observe the series of conceptual and political transformations that preceded them. Hence his aim is not to discover the putative "models," but to recreate political and ideological *processes*, and make manifest the complexities intrinsic to them. In this fashion, he unlocks a way of approaching the political-conceptual process that led to the independence revolutions in Latin America that is very different from the traditional ones, definitely alien to the concern of their "ideological origins," and that we can define, adopting an expression by Hans Blumenberg, as a "history of effects" (*Wirkungsgeschichte*).[14]

His point of departure is the definition of what he considers the basic paradox that the revolutionary discourse raised, and which challenges simplistic, dichotomic approaches: that the very revolutionary vocation for a radical rupture from the past had its roots in that very past from which it wanted so violently to break away. As he shows, paradoxically, "the ideas in whose name the pre-revolutionary reality was condemned were born out of that same reality."[15]

Yet, this corroboration may pave the way to endorsing the view of a linear continuity between the pre- and the post-revolutionary ideas, thus missing the fundamental issue, for him: the fact that those very traditional ideas eventually served as the basis for a revolutionary discourse. The "continuist" approach, although it makes a fundamental contribution revealing the

---

[14] See Hans Blumenberg, *The Genesis of the Copernican World* (Cambridge: MIT Press, 1987). In this book, Blumenberg describes the series of torsions that Aristotle's physics and its fundamental concepts underwent as a result of the very efforts to save it from the anomalies that it presented in the course of the centuries immediately preceding the astronomical revolution initiated by Copernicus.

[15] Halperin Donghi, *Tradición política española*, 25.

140 HISTORIOGRAPHICAL APPROACHES

conceptual ground in local political culture of revolutionary discourse—
how most of the ideas it gathered were already present in Spanish political
tradition—obliterates the series of conceptual torsions that these traditional
ideas underwent in the course of the preceding centuries to produce that paradoxical result, one which was exactly the opposite to what these ideas were
originally intended to produce. As Halperin Donghi says:

> [By looking for the origins of ideas, these interpretations] run the risk of
> underlining the affinity between the world of revolutionary ideas and that
> existing before the revolution, overlooking a fact which is much more es-
> sential than that very affinity: that—as we already have remarked—those
> ideas now structured a revolutionary ideology, an ideological tool to deny
> and condemn all that past.[16]

Lastly, for him, the true point in question here, that which a conceptual history of the revolutions of independence should be aimed at, is to recreate the
series of semantic displacements through which the very traditional ideas
ended up giving rise to a revolutionary ideology that was alien to (and indeed contradictory with) the conceptual frameworks within which those
very ideas were initially conceived. Tracing the origin of the ideas and motifs
that the revolutionary discourse gathered thus appears irrelevant. The point,
for Halperin Donghi, is not that, but is how these ideas became re-signified
once they became inscribed into a new discursive field, which was organized
around new kinds of problems and issues.

Ideological Change and the Reconfiguration of
the Discursive Field

For Halperin Donghi, the line of interpretation that emphasizes the traditional roots of the idea of the social contract that the revolutionaries endorsed
made a fundamental contribution insofar as it allowed one to take critical
distance from the self-interpretations of the agents, who perceived the moment of revolution as a kind of virginal aurora of liberty. This self-perception,
he thinks, cannot be taken at face value but itself must be explained. The
incapacity of the revolutionary discourse to come to terms with its own

---

[16] Halperin Donghi, *Tradición política española*, 28.

ON THE "IDEOLOGICAL ORIGINS" 141

conditions of possibility is, to him, symptomatic, it makes manifest an inherent blind spot that is constitutive of it.

Yet, challenging the image that the revolutionaries forged of themselves and revealing how much their views were indebted to past traditions may lead us, in turn, to miss the critical point: how traditional ideas became, in the process of their appropriation, reformulated, gaining a completely different meaning from the established one. Although the ideas remained, the language in which they were then articulated had mutated.

In fact, the conceptual ground on which the Neo-Scholastic idea of social contract was based underwent a number of transformations over the course of the centuries that preceded the revolutions of independence. Halperin Donghi starts by underlining a first fundamental aspect in which the conceptual universe of the sixteenth and the seventeenth centuries differed from that of the Enlightenment in the late eighteenth century. For the former, it was impossible to think of the idea of the self-constitution of the community, which made the revolutionary concept inconceivable. Imagining that a political community could exist on the margins of any center of power around which it could coalesce and from which it could take its consistency was simply absurd. As Francisco Suárez stated, "a body without a head is mutilated and monstrous."[17] The constitution of a political community necessarily entailed relations of command and obedience. Prior to the institution of a political power, we just have a plurality of dispersed individuals, not a community properly speaking. As Halperin Donghi remarks:

[For Suárez] the multitude can be considered from two different points of view: as a mere aggregation, with no order or physical and moral union, or as a political body. Now—and here we find again a postulate derived from an authoritarian concept of political relationships—the political body demands, as one of its essential conditions, the presence of political power.[18]

Royal authority was thought to belong to the realm of the natural right, the need for it was inscribed in nature itself. Political power and the community were mutually and simultaneously constituted ("it is only thanks to the king that the political body exists")[19] and, in consequence, the latter cannot

---

[17] Francisco Suárez, *De Legibus: De natura legis Book I* (Madrid: CSIC, 1971), ch. 8, §9.
[18] Halperin Donghi, *Tradición política española*, 54.
[19] Halperin Donghi, *Tradición política española*, 78.

be detached from the former. Thus, even though it is certainly true that the revolutionaries took the idea of the social pact from the Neo-Scholastics, it would be absurd to see it as a precursory idea of revolution. We must keep in mind that the Neo-Scholastic thinking, even though it made reference to the idea of the legitimacy of tyrannicide, was a discourse of power, not of revolution.[20]

The aforementioned explains the difficulties in thinking of a *pactum societatis* detached from the *pactum subjectionis* and why the former would remain as a necessary postulate to explain the second, but which, nevertheless, itself will never be explained. The postulate that sovereignty had been transferred to the monarch from an original pact with the people carried already implicit a first question: how, in turn, had that people emerged that was to transfer it? It is this question that would eventually give rise to the idea of the existence of a second covenant. However, the invocation of this second pact solved the question of how the people that will transfer sovereignty to the monarch is constituted only at the price of raising questions even more serious than the one it had come to resolve: could this second pact (the *pactum societatis*) be revoked? Under what circumstances? What would the resulting situation be? Ultimately, what it gave rise to was the definitely heretical idea of the possible existence of a pre-social state of nature.

If it was possible to avoid at that moment addressing these questions, it was because the medieval ideal of a universal Christian monarchy ("the republic of the whole world," as Francisco de Vitoria defined it, embodied in the figure of Charles V), which was still in force in Vitoria's time, made these questions irrelevant for all practical purposes. Only the crisis of this ideal would eventually force Neo-Scholastic authors to consider these questions.

However, there was a second fundamental difference between the Neo-Scholastic's and the Enlightenment's concept of social contract that Halperin Donghi points out, and that provides a clue to understand how the process of conceptual transformation of this political tradition was set into motion. Although both the Neo-Scholastic's and the Enlightenment's concept of the social contract imposed limitations on power, the kind of limitations that the former postulated were not associated to the idea that the monarch should follow or obey popular will. The social contract idea initially did not aim to suggest the voluntaristic origins of political power. The people here at stake was merely the transmitting agent of a sovereignty that, in the last instance,

---

[20] Halperin Donghi, *Tradición política española*, 60.

emanated from God. As a matter of fact, popular will had no normative force in the old régime's political system: the fact that people wanted something did not make it right or just; the idea of justice, which was the articulating principle of societies, designated a set of objective norms that were established by God himself and were imprinted in the very nature of things. Limitations to royal power were given, instead, by the ends to which the royal investiture was attached. The social contract at that time worked as the reminder to the sovereign that power should be exercised for the benefit of the welfare of the community and not for its own. Yet here we find the point where the first torsion would be produced in this traditional discourse that would eventually lead to the revolutionary discourse, the first conceptual displacement in this history of effects.

The First Conceptual Displacement:
The Secularization of the Ends

For Halperin Donghi, the figure of Juan de Solórzano (1575–1655) expresses a first series of torsions that occurred within traditional political discourse. As he says:

> Solórzano shares another fundamental feature of the Spanish political thinking in the Baroque period: the exalted and never solved contradiction between the ideals and the historical-political reality.[21]

The Neo-Scholastic thinking of the "second generation" must be inscribed within the context of the disintegration of the universalist ideals of the old Empires, which resulted in a fundamental reconfiguration of the political discourse regarding the Medieval Christian tradition. Let us take note of the fact that Halperin Donghi does not say that Solórzano affirmed that, but his writings reveal an objective transformation in the political discourse of the time, which has to do with changes in the kind of problems at stake at that time and not the subject's "ideas." At that point, the ends with which the social contract concept was hitherto associated were re-interpreted in increasingly secular terms. They were no longer transcendent (the realization of the

---

[21] Halperin Donghi, *Tradición política española*, 81.

144 HISTORIOGRAPHICAL APPROACHES

kingdom of God on Earth) but profane: "the common wealth was now defined as the *felicitas civitatis* as well as that of the citizens as such."[22]

In fact, the development of the Enlightenment ideas in the eighteenth century, far from contesting the absolutist concept of power, served to reinforce its authoritarian character, as well as that of the arcane associated to it. With it, the kind of knowledge associated with the exercise of power lost the self-evident nature that the traditional idea of Justice possessed, thereby escaping from the doxological realm, and becoming a specialized knowledge.[23] Yet, it produced a more radical departure from the seventeenth-century rationalism and imbued political discourse with a more marked empiricism: "the essential change resided in the revalorization of the data of experience."[24] Although this first redefinition was perfectly suited to the absolutist ideal (it actually reinforced its authoritarian nature), it would eventually pave the way to a second twist in the traditional political discourse that would bring about far-reaching political consequences.

The Second Conceptual Displacement: The Detachment of Nation and Power

As we have seen, the break with the universalist ideal of the old Empires did not change the concept that the kind of limitations the social contract imposed over political authority was associated with the ends to which this authority was conferred by the people. These ends became increasingly secularized. Now, this process in Spain accompanied, in turn, a profound feeling for the rapid decline of the Empire, which would lead to digging into the past in search of the roots of the present crisis. This fact already entailed a fundamental change in the ways society and power were conceived because it implied the emergence of the concept of a new subject: the nation, which

---

[22] Halperin Donghi, *Tradición política española*, 57.

[23] Insofar as the principles of Justice were eternal, they were self-evident, as the opposite contradicted its very definition. Consequently, they were immediately graspable by the subjects. The concept of *synderesis* expressed the idea of the natural capacity for the intelligence of the eternal principles of Justice. And this made it possible for the subjects to eventually assess the justice of the action of authority, with which the problem of the legitimacy of tyrannicide was always posed. This radically changed with the Enlightenment, from the moment that the values on which the community rested were now assumed as conventional, thus losing their self-evident nature. Thus, they were no longer publicly graspable and demanded a kind of specialized knowledge. On this topic, see Elías Palti, "El absolutismo monárquico y la génesis de las 'soberanía nacional,'" in *Conceitos e linguagens: construções identitárias*, ed. Márcia Naxara and Virginia Camilotti (São Paulo: Intermeios, 2014), 33–50.

[24] Halperin Donghi, *Tradición política española*, 69.

then became distinguished from the monarchical state and gaining an entity by itself.

This phenomenon resulted from a historical-conceptual displacement that was then taking place. In the eighteenth century, the Spaniards started to think of (ministerial) despotism as the fundamental cause of the decline of the Empire, whose expression was the abandonment of the "traditional constitution" of the kingdom. This view was prompted by the emergence of the school of "historical constitutionalism." Its origin is normally found in the inaugural discourse by Melchor Gaspar de Jovellanos at the Spanish Academy of History in 1778. Its main goal was to explore the national past in search of the Spanish traditional constitution that despotism had allegedly dislocated, and this school intended to recover. At that point, a new type of treatise emerged, organized around a new object of inquiry: the nation and its past, which thereby made its appearance on the level of political discourse. And this rearticulated the entire terms of the debate. As Halperin Donghi remarks, from then on, "the figure of the King is no longer identified with the entire nation; the latter now becomes placed on a higher and broader sphere."[25]

Here we find the second displacement in the traditional political discourse. At that moment, the nation became a substantive presence. It would find the means for its articulation on the margins of political power, which broke the logic of the absolutist state. Fatherland and nation—says Halperin Donghi— are notions that represent a radical innovation in the traditional political thinking, insofar as they are seen, increasingly emphasized, as entities that are able to subsist on the margins of the state apparatus.[26]

As a matter of fact, the series of uprisings that took place, both in the peninsula and in the colonies, in the second half of the eighteenth century, all ended in the same fashion. Authorities signed agreements with the insurgents and, as soon as they disarmed, their leaders were killed. And the argument for that seemed perfectly consistent. As the officers said, they signed the agreement in the name of the people, but what conferred upon them such representation? As the officers alleged, the agreements were invalid because the insurgent leaders were merely private agents who did not have the right to speak on behalf of the whole nation. Only the king could do that. Only he incarnated the *corpus mysticum* of the republic. Lastly, this was what the monarchical

---

[25] Halperin Donghi, *Tradición política española*, 131.
[26] Halperin Donghi, *Tradición política española*, 136.

146   HISTORIOGRAPHICAL APPROACHES

system could never accept because it dislocated its very foundations: the presence of some other instance, located outside the monarchical state apparatus, that could invoke the representation of the nation.

Summarizing, the first displacement in the traditional political discourse that Halperin Donghi traces had to do with the redefinition of the ends of political power, which became increasingly interpreted in secular terms. The second torsion was even more radical because it involved the emergence of a new subject on the political arena: the nation, which possessed a will of its own and, presumably, the power to impose itself even against the will and the action of the political authority. In any case, it was now assumed to pre-exist the monarchy and, in consequence, to eventually subsist after its fall. Lastly, it amounted to erecting two sovereignties on the same level of reality: monarchical and national sovereignties. At that point, if the revolution was not necessarily fated to take place, the horizon on which it became eventually conceivable had been opened.

This new concept of the nation introduced an element that was heterogeneous within the frameworks of the absolutist political discourse, within which the supreme power of the monarch could not accept the presence of an authority (the nation) placed above his own. The notion of national sovereignty (which was no longer that of "popular sovereignty" of the Neo-Scholastics) was contradictory with its logic.[27]

It was the result, in turn, of the efforts of the local oligarchies to control the advance of the state intervention by the Bourbons, especially on the local finances and the administration of justice at the first instance (the two faculties traditionally reserved to the local authorities). In the context of this struggle, the urban bodies invoked the people and the will of the people on behalf of which they started to speak. This process was similar to the one described by Edmund Morgan, on the case of seventeenth-century England, in his classical work, *The Invention of the People*.[28] We can call it "the invention of the people," or, more precisely, "the invention of the nation" in the Spanish world, which then became detached of political power and, more importantly, found its own organs of expression on the margins of the state apparatus.

The paradox here is that the very absolutist state also invoked "the people," or indeed "the nation," and its will to justify its action against local

---

[27] See Palti, *An Archaeology of the Political*, ch. 3.
[28] Edmund Morgan, *The Invention of the People: The Right of Popular Sovereignty in England and America* (New York: W. W. Norton, 1988), 49–50.

ON THE "IDEOLOGICAL ORIGINS" 147

oligarchies.[29] Public officials argued that their actions were addressed to liberate the communities from the oppression by the local powers. In any case, this nation, which had now been detached from the state apparatus and politicized by the very action of the monarchical state, would eventually come to confront that same state, which would then be declared as artificial. Against it, that other entity would be opposed, which now would supposedly be the only "natural" one that existed: the nation.[30] And this paved the way to a third torsion in political discourse.

The Third Conceptual Displacement: The Emergence of the Constituent Power

The second half of the eighteenth century thus witnessed a general trend to explore the national past in search of that "traditional constitution" from which it allegedly had departed by the action of despotism. Certainly, historical constitutionalism did not simply seek to recover past institutions; at that moment, the national tradition was actually re-invented. And, more importantly, this fact became evident indeed for its very agents and speakers as soon as the debate around that "traditional constitution" broke out. We cross here a further threshold, a third step in this *history of effects*.

According to Halperin Donghi, a further displacement within the traditional thinking would be produced as a result of the royal vacancy after the abdications in Bayonne which were forced by Napoleon, who then designated his own brother as governor of Spain. This triggered the so-called *Guerra de Independencia*, a general uprising by the Spanish population. At this juncture, the Cortes at Cádiz was summoned (which had not held

---

[29] Pablo Fernández Albaladejo shows how the Spanish patriotic discourse was used by the Bourbons in an attempt to legitimize the new dynasty. The 1740s were key years in the articulation of this patriotic nationalist discourse in the context of the conflict with England. See Pablo Fernández Albaladejo, *Materia de España. Cultura política e identidad de la España noderna* (Madrid: Marcial Pons, 2007), 197–244.

[30] At that point, Francisco Martínez Marina could say, "Paternal authority and the patriarchal government, without a doubt the first and for many centuries the only government amongst men, does not have any similarities nor connection with political authority, nor with absolute monarchy, nor with any of the legitimate forms of government adopted by nations in different times and eras [. . .]. Under the first consideration, parental authority comes from nature, precedes all convention; is independent of any pact, invariable, incommunicable, and legal: circumstances that are in no way applicable to political authority, and even less so to absolute monarchy. This genre of government has introduced time, necessity, and freedom of consent to men: it is variable in its shape and subject to thousands of vicissitudes." Francisco Martínez Marina, *Discurso sobre el origen de la monarquía y sobre la naturaleza del gobierno español* (Madrid: Centro de Estudios Constitucionales, 1988), 92–93.

148   HISTORIOGRAPHICAL APPROACHES

assemblies since the sixteenth century). Its first measure was to assume the sovereignty that was left vacant after the abdications. This meant the institution of a completely new figure: a constituent power. It no longer had anything to do with the traditional Cortes, other than its name. As deputy Francisco López Lisperguer remarked in the session of January 25, 1811:

> We must understand that this Congress is very different from other Cortes; its object is another one. None of the precedent ones have had absolute sovereignty; never have the people had so much authority. This Congress is not Cortes, it is something new, I do not know what name can be given to it.[31]

The deputies then assumed the representation of the nation on behalf of which they spoke and from which their prerogatives were supposed to emanate. The mission of the Congress was to restore the traditional constitution of the nation. Yet, it soon became clear that there was no agreement on what that traditional constitution was. Every party had a very different view of it. In any case, there was no doubt on one point: whether they had to create a new constitution or restore the traditional one, and, in this latter case, what it was, it was the Cortes themselves that had to decide. Only they were entitled to do that. And this represented a fundamental political-conceptual innovation.

The very formation of the Cortes at Cádiz meant breaking with the premises on which the ancient régime was founded. The institution of a constituent power was produced in the name of past traditions, but it was heterogeneous with the traditional order. As Guerra remarked, quoting Tocqueville (who, in turn, took up an expression by Loménie de Brienne in reference to the *États Généraux*): from the very moment that the constitution of the nation had become a matter of controversy, the ancient régime had crumbled.[32] We find here a fundamental paradox: the Spaniards then looked back to the national past *only to find in it the power to cancel that past* (that is, the Cortes, which were entitled to create a wholly new constitution, provided it wanted to do so). Yet, at that point, we also meet the limit-point of the so-called Spanish First Liberalism.

---

[31] *Diario de Sesiones de las Cortes*, January 25, 1811, quoted by María Cruz Seoane, *El primer lenguaje constitucional español* (Madrid: Moneda y Crédito, 1968), 92. On this, see Elías Palti, *El tiempo de la política. El siglo XIX reconsiderado* (Buenos Aires: Siglo XXI, 2007).
[32] See Chapter 1 of this book.

The Fourth Conceptual Displacement:
The Self-Constitution of the Nation as a Problem

The constituent power that emerged at Cádiz actually had a limited goal. The mission of the Congress (the *Cortes*) was to provide a constitution to institute a new political régime. In fact, it did not eliminate the monarchical system, but transformed it into a constitutional monarchy. However, the last limit of the first liberalism did not lie there (a constitution not necessarily had to be democratic) but elsewhere. The constitution of the state entailed the existence of the subject which could institute it. In effect, even though there was no agreement regarding the nature of the traditional constitution of the nation, the revolutionary process initiated in Spain after the royal abdications already presupposed the presence of that nation. And the spontaneous uprising against the foreign occupant seemed to prove its actual existence. The entire discourse of the first Spanish liberalism was premised on that assumption. Only in the colonies would this assumption become challenged. In them, a new problem emerged, which was not perceived as such in the Spanish peninsula: how to constitute the nation itself.

In effect, the invocation of a constituent power adopted in the colonies a sense of radical foundation that was absent in the peninsula. Beyond the character of the ideas, the actual conditions in the colonies imposed a Jacobin logic on the revolutionary process. As Halperin Donghi remarks, the revolutionary ideal there would become much more than an ideology, it would turn into the founding myth of the new nation, the one which would now be located in place of that past from which the revolution intended so brutally to break away.

Revolutionaries in the colonies thus faced a much radical challenge than their Spanish counterparts. Initially, the former, like the latter, claimed that, after the fall of the monarchy, sovereignty relapsed into the nation. But they would not take long to discover that, in Spain's American possessions there were no such nations that preexisted the monarchy and could assume sovereignty. After independence, the subcontinent appeared, to Bolívar, as a small world in a state similar to that at the moment of Creation.[33] According

---

[33] "This situation," said Bolívar, "differed from North America's in that those members proceeded to reestablish their former association. We, on the contrary, do not even retain the vestiges of our original being. We are not Europeans; we are not Indians; we are but a mixed species of aborigines and Spaniards. Americans by birth, Europeans by law, we find ourselves engaged in a dual conflict: we are disputing with the natives for the titles of ownership and at the same time we are struggling to maintain ourselves in the country that gave us birth against the opposition of the invaders. Thus,

150 HISTORIOGRAPHICAL APPROACHES

to *porteño* leader Mariano Moreno, at the origin of the colonial societies there was not any social contract but an act of sheer violence. As a consequence, there were no preexisting nations there which could be invoked.[34] The process of territorial disintegration that followed independence cast that problem to the forefront of political debate. Eventually, above all in the nuclear areas of the Hispanic American colonies, we can find invocations to an ancient "Peruvian nation," or a "Mexican nation."[35] However, at that juncture there was no means of discerning how they were constituted, what their boundaries and composition were; more specifically, what collective subjects were entitled to claim for themselves the possession of sovereign rights, an autonomous will: the inhabitants of the viceroyalties? of the *Intendencias*? indeed those of each city? or, as the *peninsulares* affirmed, only the population of the entire realm as a whole? Those vague invocations to the nations did not solve the bottom-line question: who should decide it, what already presupposed a definition in this regard; that is, the presence of that collective subject (the people or the nation) whose entity was, precisely, at stake.

This gave rise to a process of territorial disintegration that soon seemed to become unstoppable. Every province, and indeed every city, claimed to possess sovereign rights to constitute itself and an autonomous, national entity. The best example of this was Mexico. After the fall of the First Empire, produced only nine months after independence, Guatemala decided to break with the newly emerged power in Mexico to form a new nation, the Central American republic. The argument then invoked was reasonable: how can you, Mexicans, deny us the very same right to self-determination that you yourselves invoked against Spain? Now, this same principle was invoked against Guatemala by the cities subordinated to it. And, in turn, the same argument was invoked by the subordinated cities against the capitals of the new states that emerged after the dissolution of the Central American republic.

---

our position is the most extraordinary and complicated." Simón Bolívar, "Address Delivery at the Inauguration of the Second National Congress in Venezuela at Angostura (1819)," in *Selected Writings by Simón Bolívar*, ed. Vicente Lecuna and Lewis Bertrand, vol. 1 (New York: Colonial Press Inc., 1951), 175–176.

[34] See Mariano Moreno, "Sobre la misión del Congreso convocado en virtud de la resolución plebiscitaria del 25 de Mayo," in *Escritos políticos y económicos* (Buenos Aires: La Cultura Argentina, 1915), 269–300.

[35] See Mark Thurner, *History's Peru: The Poetics of Colonial and Postcolonial Historiography* (Gainesville: University Press of Florida, 2011).

ON THE "IDEOLOGICAL ORIGINS" 151

At that juncture, the subject of the sovereign imputation had become indiscernible, thus turning into the center of a properly *political* dispute (in Carl Schmitt's sense of the term).[36] Actually, the social contract discourse had no answer for it. It presupposed a demarcation criterion (how to delimitate who could freely contract with each other and legitimately constitute a nation of their own; what social groups were entitled to claim the possession of a sovereign right) but was radically incapable to establish it, given the generic nature of its subject. This issue marked the last limit of the revolutionary discourse, the point where it started dissolving, paving the way to a new, radical reconfiguration of political language.

In effect, the entire discourse of emancipation rested on the premise of the opposition between a *natural nation* and an *artificial state*. The Spanish First Liberalism (that dominated in the Cortes summoned at Cádiz) hinged on the basis of that assumption. As we have seen, for it, the constitution of the political power already presupposed the existence of the entity that should constitute it. Now, in the colonies, the revolutionary discourse would be confronted with the paradox that the revolution should constitute, along with a new political power, the very subject that should constitute that power.

Lastly, the issue that then emerged was how the very constituent power was, it itself, constituted. Here we come to the fourth and last torsion in the traditional conceptual universe, the point at which the revolutionary discourse took its final form, and, paradoxically, also where it started to dissolve, eventually paving the way to a new reconfiguration of political language. Finding an answer to that paradox was the mission of the nineteenth century, of what Foucault called, in *The Order of Things*, "The Age of History."[37] It would then transfer the burden of the constitution of the nation from the subjective realm to the objective realm. It would be the task of History itself, the new entity that then emerged.[38] At that point, the entire set of antinomies that the absolutist state had established (and eventually led to its own dislocation) would finally collapse to make room for a new conceptual constellation.

---

[36] See Carl Schmitt, *The Concept of the Political* (Chicago: University of Chicago Press, 2007).

[37] Michel Foucault, *The Order of Things: An Archeology of Human Sciences* (New York: Vintage, 1970).

[38] This conceptual transformation was analyzed by Reinhart Koselleck under the label of *Sattelzeit*. See Reinhart Koselleck, *Future Past: On the Semantics of Historical Time* (Cambridge, MA: MIT Press, 1985).

152 HISTORIOGRAPHICAL APPROACHES

Conclusion: From the History of Ideas to the History of Discourses

The way in which Halperin Donghi describes the series of conceptual twists produced during the colonial period recalls a certain paradoxical dialectic observed by Reinhart Koselleck in his doctoral thesis, *Critique and Crisis* (completed in 1954 and published in 1959). "Absolutism," says Koselleck, "necessitated the genesis of the Enlightenment and the Enlightenment conditioned the genesis of the French Revolution. It is around these two theses that the action of this book takes place."[39] This formulation synthesizes a perspective whose complexity, however, it fails to express fully. The truth is that it was the very absolutist discourse—in its desire to affirm its own foundations by accentuating the gap between the political sphere and the social sphere, the nature of political power and the spontaneous systems of hierarchies and subordinations present in society itself (the feudal powers)—which would open the field to the emergence of a concept that would undermine the premises on which it was based. It would finally enable the conception of the existence of a political community organized independently from what until then was the articulating center from which it necessarily emanated: the royal authority.

In other words, this would open the doors to detach the *pactum societatis* from the *pactum subjectionis*, the former thereby gaining autonomy as a proper object of reflection. This does not mean, however, that the problems it raised could finally be solved. On the contrary: it would be then that they would truly appear as such. As a consequence, the thought of emancipation will no longer be able to avoid its confrontation. But this would be an unforeseen drift, something that occurred as a result of the revolutionary irruption itself, and not its starting point. As we have seen, in its origin, the revolutionary discourse rested on the very same premise established by absolutist thought. It clung to the dichotomy between the "natural" nation and the "artificial" political power, to invoke the former and challenge the latter on its behalf. The nation, once converted into the only natural entity that existed, would come to confront a state apparatus that would eventually be declared not only alien to it, but also hostile to it. In any case, from the moment that it

---

[39] Reinhart Koselleck, *Critique and Crisis: Enlightenment and the Pathogenesis of Modern Society* (Oxford: Berg, 1988), 8.

ON THE "IDEOLOGICAL ORIGINS" 153

constituted a conventionally established creation, it could also be modified by a contrary will.

Yet, as Halperin Donghi points out, eighteenth-century historical constitutionalism, once transferred to the colonies, would reveal new problematic edges. That dichotomy between nature and artifice, referring to nation and political power, respectively, would be rendered problematic. In the colonies, the search in the past for the germs of local freedoms that supposedly subsisted after "three centuries of oppression" appeared as an obvious contradiction. Thus, the very same topic that served as the basis for revolutionary discourse also seemed to deprive it of a foundation, a discernable subject on whose behalf it could speak. The nation also would then appear as something to be constructed by artificial, political means. It is then that the revolution itself would become a myth of origin. It would be seen as marking a new aurora of liberty, uncontaminated by residues of a past from which it intended to break away.

The point is that the desire for a violent break with the past will prevent seeing to what extent this very desire had been prepared by previous conceptual developments that would eventually make a concept conceivable which had, until then, been simply absurd to imagine, and without which, independence would also have been unthinkable: the idea of a sovereignty detached from sovereign authority, a vague, ethereal sovereignty that exists everywhere and nowhere in particular.

It is true, however, that these previous developments do not yet explain or anticipate the way in which they would be articulated to give rise to a revolutionary discourse. This was the arrival point of a sinuous itinerary, in which the superficial recurrences of ideas hide drastic reversals of meaning resulting less from the semantic innovations than from the way ideas would be mutually articulated to produce new ideological constellations. During these successive reconfigurations, conceptual horizons would be opened up that were unthinkable at the starting point of this process. Far from following a logical, linear development, this historical-conceptual process entailed a permanent reversal upon itself to undermine those very assumptions that had set this series of transformations into motion. In sum, Halperin Donghi's recreation of the process that led to the revolutions of independence in Latin America illustrates why the issue of the "ideological origins" must be set aside, as it is leads nowhere, and that deciding it is simply irrelevant. However, his approach represents a much more radical methodological challenge than the traditional approaches of the history of ideas.

154   HISTORIOGRAPHICAL APPROACHES

As we have seen, Halperin Donghi's perspective breaks with the schematism of the models of thought and orients itself to tracing *ideological processes*; that is, how a given discursive field becomes successively reconfigured. It can be seen as a movement from a history of ideas to a history of political discourse. And this contains a much more fundamental—and less perceivable—reformulation of the ways intellectual history is conceived. That methodological shift actually results, in turn, from the redefinition of its very object. In effect, Halperin Donghi's perspective translates the whole issue from the subjective realm (the ideas of the subjects) into the objective realm. It meant the dislocation of the very epistemological ground on which the entire tradition of the history of ideas was erected: a philosophy of consciousness. The changes in discourses do not spring from the individual's consciousness. As Halperin Donghi says in connection with Giménez Fernández's interpretation of Suárez's ideas: "In that honourable name [Suarez's] Giménez Fernández condenses a long-lasting effort that could not be strictly individual. What was born from it was not, therefore, a personal doctrine, either."[40] The detachment of the nation from the body of the king was not something that someone thought up, something that a given thinker proposed or devised. Lastly, it meant a reconfiguration of the horizons within which ideas deployed—the conditions for their public articulation. Hence, even though the ideas of subjects remained unchanged, then they acquired a new meaning.

To go back to Tocqueville's expression, quoted by Guerra in connection to the Cortes at Cádiz, when he stated that, from the very moment the constitution of the nation became a matter of controversy, the ancient régime had ended. Guerra interprets this as affirming that the best expression of this change was the victory of the liberal party, led by Manuel Quintana, in the election of the deputies to the Cortes. However, this is not what Tocqueville meant, but rather the opposite: even the victory of the absolutist party would not have altered the fact that *from the very moment the constitution of the nation became a matter of controversy, the ancient régime had ended*. In effect, as Halperin Donghi has shown, the very emergence of a constituent power implied the collapse of the logic that articulated that discourse. The constitution of the nation was a problem that did not have any conceivable place within the framework of the political language of the ancient régime. Yet, it was not a merely ideological change, as it spread across the whole ideological

[40] Halperin Donghi, *Tradición política española*, 31.

spectrum. Lastly, changes in political language do not refer to the *ideas* of the subjects, but to the kind of *problems* which subjects eventually find themselves confronting. In fact, the ideas of the subjects in 1830 were probably not very different from those in 1800; however, the issues at stake had mutated, and this altered the entire political discourse.

We can understand now why traditional approaches, focused on the ideas of the subjects, are radically unsuitable to comprehend complex ideological processes, the transformation produced on the level of the conceptual ground on which ideas deploy. In the end, by focusing on ideas and models of thought, they cannot conceive what Halperin Donghi intended to understand: how traditional ideological frameworks could have led to a result that was not only the opposite of what they were originally intended to produce, but also inconceivable within them. That is, more precisely, what Blumenberg meant by a "history of effects" or *Wirkungsgeschichte*. And Halperin Donghi's work illustrates the crucial turn this entails in the writing of Latin American intellectual history.

6

From Tradition to Modernity?

Historical Revisionism and Political-Conceptual History

The bicentennial of the revolutions of independence has given rise to a new "revisionist" current whose main representative is François-Xavier Guerra (who was inspired, in turn, by the "revisionist" writings of the French Revolution by François Furet),[1] which is illustrative of recent orientations in Latin Americanist historiography. This revisionist current gave birth to a critical vision of the romantic-nationalist perspectives that emerged in the nineteenth century and were imbued with a teleological concept. According to Guerra, these perspectives place at the starting point of the revolutionary process what could actually only be found at its point of arrival: the modern nation.[2] As he asserts:

> Confusing the *post hoc* with the *propter hoc*, although conceptually indefensible, had the advantage of giving a simple explanation for a very complex phenomenon, but also of legitimizing with incontestable modern references the access of new countries to the concert of nations. The problems posed by this teleological vision of the revolutionary process are so great that, in fact, they make it untenable.[3]

---

[1] Fançois Furet, *Penser la Révolution Française* (Paris: Folios, 1978)]. On this, see Elías Palti, "Guerra y Habermas: Ilusiones y realidad de la esfera pública latinoamericana," in *Conceptuar los que se ve. François-Xavier Guerra historiador. Homenaje*, ed. Alicia Salmerón and Erika Pani (Mexico: Instituto Mora, 2004), 461–483.

[2] According to José Carlos Chiaramonte, the consolidation of an idea of "nationhood" is a development that took place only later in Latin America, in the second half of the nineteenth century. José Carlos Chiaramonte, *El mito de los orígenes en la historiografía latinoamericana* (Buenos Aires: Instituto Dr. Emilio Ravignani, 1993). According to Jeremy Adelman, besides, there was not necessarily a contradiction between the principle of nationhood and the Imperial political formations. See Jeremy Adelman, *Sovereignty and Revolution in the Iberian World* (Princeton: Princeton University Press, 2006).

[3] François-Xavier Guerra, "La desintegración de la Monarquía hispánica: Revolución de Independencia," in *De los imperios a las naciones: Iberoamérica*, ed. Antonio Annino, Luis Castro Leiva, and François-Xavier Guerra (Zaragoza: Ibercaja, 1994), 197.

Misplaced Ideas?. Elías J. Palti, Oxford University Press. © Oxford University Press 2024.
DOI: 10.1093/oso/9780197556641.003.0006

FROM TRADITION TO MODERNITY? 157

In this fashion, this new revisionist school intends to offer a more accurate historical perspective, uncontaminated with retrospective projections.[4] One of Guerra's fundamental contributions is to have re-appreciated the importance of the symbolic dimension of historical processes, thus rescuing intellectual history from the ill-reputation of the old history of ideas. And this allows him to reconsider the traditional views of the crisis of the colonial order in Latin America.

In the first place, Guerra, like Halperin Donghi, departs from the scheme of "ideological influences." From his perspective, what triggered the cultural mutation he analyzes was not the reading of imported books but the series of transformations that objectively altered the conditions of enunciation of discourses. The convergence with France at the level of political languages, he assures, "is not about phenomena of fashion or influences—although these also exist—but, fundamentally, of the same logic arising from a common birth to modern politics [the 'modernity of rupture']." Guerra thus discovers an *internal* link between both levels—the discursive and the extra-discursive. The "context" thus ceases to be an external setting for the development of "ideas" and becomes an inherent aspect in discourses, determining the logic of their articulation from within. And this leads to the second displacement that he produces.

In the second place, Guerra connects conceptual transformations with alterations at the level of political practices associated with the emergence of new realms of sociability, such as political clubs, and ambits of publicity, such as the periodical press.[5] The semantic displacements that then took place thus become meaningful in the function of their new means and places for the articulation of ideas, which did not pre-exist the political crisis but arose as a result of it, and which paved the way for the formation of an incipient "public sphere."

---

[4] "Consciously or unconsciously," affirms Guerra, "many of these analyses are impregnated with moral or teleological assumptions due to their reference to ideal models. It has been implicitly estimated that, everywhere and always—or at least in modern times—society and politics should respond to a series of principles such as equality, the participation of all in politics, the existence of authorities emerged from the people, controlled by them and moved only for the general good of society . . . It is not known if this 'should' corresponds to an ethical requirement, based on the nature of man or society, or if evolution of modern societies inexorably leads to this situation." François-Xavier Guerra, "El soberano y su reino," in *Ciudadanía política y formación de las naciones. Perspectivas históricas de América Latina*, ed. Hilda Sabato (Mexico: FCE, 1999), 34.

[5] The most influential book in this regard has been François-Xavier Guerra and Annick Lempérière, eds., *Los espacios públicos en Iberoamérica. Ambigüedades y problemas. Siglos XVIII–XIX* (Mexico: FCE, 1998).

158   HISTORIOGRAPHICAL APPROACHES

All this allows Guerra to overcome the dualism between Spanish traditionalism and American liberalism. As he shows, the revolutionary process was a global phenomenon that encompassed the whole Spanish Empire, and, as a matter of fact, had its epicenter, precisely, in the peninsula. It was actually the most directly impacted by the crisis of the monarchical system and where the most important political innovations were first produced and only subsequently transmitted to the colonies. These developments took place during what he calls "the two crucial years" from 1808 to 1810; that is, from the royal vacancy as a result of the Bayonne abdications and the summoning of the Cortes at Cádiz, which would end up with the sanction in 1812 of the first constitution in the world that defined itself as "liberal." However, it is here that problems appear in this new "revisionist" school.

The criticism of the epic perspective that postulates the revolutions of independence as the product of the arrival of French ideas of the Enlightenment, the ideals of freedom, self-determination, etc., ends up leading Guerra to reverse it, remaining, however, within its own conceptual frameworks. And this takes us to the antinomy between "tradition" and "modernity."

Whereas the epic vision holds the modernity of Latin American conceptual references against Spanish traditionalism, Guerra's revisionism inverts the terms to oppose Spanish ideological modernism to Latin American traditionalism. At this point, his view gathers a traditional motif of the Catholic, pro-Hispanic historiography.[6] Guerra believes to see the clearest symptom of the respective natures of these two competing discourses (the Latin American traditionalist and the Hispanic modernist) in the use of two key terms: those of *pueblos*, in plural, and *pueblo*, in singular. The use of the former would tell us about the persistence of a traditional and holistic view of society, composed by the concrete groups, the collective subjects (the bodies) of the old régime. The use of the latter, on the contrary, would make manifest the presence of a modern social imaginary that would conceive the nation as an abstract and homogeneous entity. Thus, the persistence of the first would explain the process of political disintegration produced in Hispanic America after independence. This would be the product of the inability to conceive a unified idea of nation.

---

[6] Actually, there is a fundamental difference between that historiographical tradition and Guerra's perspective. For the former, there was no such dichotomy between the ideological processes in the peninsula and the colonies: both were similarly attached to the Neo-Scholastic tradition. Guerra actually combines the liberal Hispanic perspective, whose best representative is Miguel Artola's *Orígenes de la España contemporánea* (Madrid: Instituto de Estudios Políticos, 1975), and the Latin American catholic historical view.

The opposition between the terms "pueblos" and "pueblo" appears, indeed, at the Cortes at Cádiz. There the deputies from the colonies would always speak of *pueblos*, in plural, while the peninsular ones will insist on the appellation of *pueblo*, in singular. For Guerra, this is a clear symptom of the greater traditionalism of the former. However, this interpretation is clearly arbitrary. If the deputies from the colonies spoke of *pueblos*, it was because they questioned the authority of the Cortes to dictate any measure if it was not first endorsed by the populations involved, by the *pueblos*. It was so because they considered that the Cortes were vitiated in their origin because of the adopted system of representation. The convocation to Cortes endorsed a principle of proportionality according to population size. However, the castes were excluded from the census, so the representation from the colonies was greatly diminished. The fallacy in Guerra's approach consists in taking political positions as expressions of the social or cultural nature of the agents, when, in reality, as we see in the case of the Cortes, the alignments of the deputies responded to a strictly political logic. And they varied according to the circumstances. In fact, from another perspective, it could be affirmed that the deputies from the colonies were much more "modern" than the peninsular ones because they upheld a principle of equalitarian, individual representation.

As a matter of fact, as Bernard Bailyn showed, and Guerra ignored, the same happened in the case of the North American Revolution. While the British Parliament endorsed a unified concept of nation, thus affirming to be the representative of the whole of it, the American colonists insisted on the plural constitution of the nation. And this would demolish that other opposition in the literature of the period: that between the "modernity" of the conceptual references of the revolutionary process in the North and their "traditionality" in the South. The point, however, is not to determine who was more "modern" and who was more "traditional" (the Northern or the Southern revolutions of independence, the political process in the Spanish peninsula or in the colonies). What these examples show is that both views are equally arbitrary; that everything can be seen as either modern or traditional depending on how one looks at it.

In short, this reveals the futility of this debate. Ultimately, it makes manifest problems of a deeper theoretical-methodological nature, which Halperin Donghi's text—analyzed in Chapter 5—helps us to understand. In the first place, the opposition between tradition and modernity assumes that there was only one conceptual mutation in Western intellectual history, which is

160 HISTORIOGRAPHICAL APPROACHES

the one that occurred by the end of the eighteenth century. In this way, it leads to ruling out the possibility of any subsequent, or preceding, conceptual ruptures. Everything that came after the aforementioned break is thus grouped together under the common label of "modernity," and, in the same way, everything that came before, under the label of "tradition." They are thus conceived as two perfectly coherent wholes, internally homogeneous and in mutual opposition. And this entails a rather static view of both "tradition" and "modernity." As we have seen in Chapter 5, if we do not dislocate this static vision of the colonial past, if we lose sight of the series of political-conceptual transformations that occurred over the three centuries in which it unfolds, in sum, if we do not put aside the scheme of "models," and the search for "influences," and try to reconstruct political-conceptual *processes*, it is impossible to understand how the revolutions of independence took place.

In effect, this static view of the colonial past, ignoring the series of political and conceptual transformations that preceded independence, has led Guerra and the members of his school to emphasize incidental events (mainly the monarchical acephaly as the consequence of the Bayonne abdications), as the determinant for the break of the colonial system. However, similar dynastic crises had already taken place in the past, as during the War of Succession, between 1701 and 1713, but then no one in the colonies was thinking of becoming independent. That approach cannot explain why similar events that a century before had had no consequences, this time led to the disintegration of the empire, what happened in the meantime so that similar events now had the consequences that they had. Furthermore, the emphasis on the peculiar circumstances that led to the dissolution of the Spanish Empire misses the fact that, at that moment, all the Empires created in the sixteenth and seventeenth centuries (the French, English, Portuguese, and Spanish) collapsed in such a completely synchronic fashion that it cannot be merely incidental.[7]

As a consequence of the former point, an even more serious problem arises. Seen from this dichotomous perspective, contradictions in intellectual history necessarily appear as the result of a kind of conceptual asynchrony, the accidental overlapping of two different historical epochs. Anything that deviates from the liberal "ideal type" can only be interpreted as an expression

---

[7] Carlos Marichal Salinas shows, besides, that the political decomposition of the Spanish Empire also comprehended public finances, and the two, in turn, were closely linked to the crisis of the system of international relations in the second half of the eighteenth century. See Carlos Marichal Salinas, *Bankruptcy of Empire. Mexican Silver and the Wars Between Spain, Britain and France, 1760–1810* (Cambridge: Cambridge University Press, 2007).

FROM TRADITION TO MODERNITY? 161

of the persistence of traditionalist views that stubbornly refuse to disappear. Tradition and modernity thus lose their character as concrete historical periods to become transhistorical essences that traverse the entire local intellectual history and explain its entire course up to the present.

Thus, the static view of the colonial past would also be prolonged to the independent period. For the revisionist school promoted by Guerra, as for Hale and the members of the "culturalist school," Latin America would continue to live in the old régime, attached to its colonial heritage from the time of the Conquest to the present. As Guerra pointed out in his doctoral thesis, whose very title is already enlightening, *Mexico: From the Old Regime to the Revolution*, in which he studies the Mexican revolution of 1910: "the essential division was, then, the one that separated a 'holistic' society formed by collective actors from the supporters of a concept that assigned to the individual the role of reference, both political and social."[8]

Here we see the arbitrary nature of this interpretive scheme based on this kind of eternal antinomy between organicism and individualism. Everything that happened in the region is explained according to the same mold: a struggle between the organicist tendencies rooted in the local culture and the modern individualistic ones. Independence, the revolutions of the twentieth century, and indeed the present controversies, all would have the same origin. Now, it is clear that a proposal that explains everything in the same manner explains nothing, nor does it permit one to think anything. All we are going to find, at each moment and place, is what we know beforehand: the eternal struggle between organicism and individualism, between tradition and modernity.

In sum, while this recent revisionist school began as an attempt to break the teleologism of the traditional interpretations of the revolutions of independence, it nevertheless ended up reinforcing it. Ultimately, the very topic "from tradition to modernity" within which that school inscribes its interpretations already contains an implicit teleological concept of history. The fact that the teleological assumption implicit here (the ideal of a modern liberal society) in this case functions simply as a counterfactual; that

---

[8] François-Xavier Guerra, *México: Del Antiguo Régimen a la Revolución* (Mexico: FCE, 1985), 23. For him, this problem is common to all Third World societies" (ibid., 24). It is paradoxical that exactly the same thesis was held by Arno Meyer in the case of Europe as a whole. See Arno Meyer, *The Persistence of the Old Regime: Europe to the Great War* (New York: Pantheon Press, 1981). Again, it reveals the fruitlessness of the very search for the "Latin American" peculiarity.

162   HISTORIOGRAPHICAL APPROACHES

is, pointing out what did not happen in this region, but what should have happened, is irrelevant, and it does not alter the essence of the question.

On the other hand, it must be said that if we understand the revisionist enterprise in its most elementary sense as an attempt to dismantle the conventional genealogical accounts of nationality, the novelty of its contribution would, in reality, be highly doubtful.[9] In this, it simply gathers a deeply rooted motif in local historiography (which is, ultimately, what explains the wide acceptance that Guerra's work had, as it converged with a kind of set wisdom in the field, allowing his hypotheses to appear intuitively plausible to historians).

Revisionism in Two Times

In actual fact, during the decade of 1960, a long series of studies propelled by the diffusion of Marxist thought and social history,[10] and also by the growing presence in the field of foreign, non-Latin American historians,[11] de-stabilized the Manichean traditional frameworks (albeit, it is true, without eliminating them from the scholarly milieu), introducing nuances and precisions that would set into question the very entity of the national states emerged out of the break with colonial ties. In fact, it seems hard to

---

[9] The present study somehow takes up the question raised by Guillermo Palacios in his "Introduction" to *Ensayos sobre la nueva historia política de América Latina, siglo XIX*, ed. Guillermo Palacios (Mexico: El Colegio de México, 2007). It must be said that the present work does not intend to be an exhaustive review of all the studies on the topic of the revolutions of independence in Latin America, which is far beyond the reach of this essay, but, more modestly, to review the main lines and some of the derivations of the "revisionist" impulse of the traditional approaches to the topic of the ideological foundations of the modern nations in the region, focusing, particularly, on the debates on the issue of the continuities and changes between the colony and the independent periods.

[10] See Maria Helena Rolim Capelato, ed., *Produção histórica no Brasil* (São Paulo: Xamá, 1995), F. J. C. Falcon, *História e historiografia nos anos 50 e 60* (Niterói: Editora da Universidade Federal Fluminense, 2004); W. Griffith, "The Historiography of Central America Since 1830," *Hispanic American Historical Review* 40, no. 4 (1960): 548–569;L. Pérez Cabrera, *Historiografía de Cuba* (Mexico: Instituto Panamericano de Geografía e Historia, 1962); Thomas Skidmore, "Studying the History of Latin America: A Case of Hemispheric Convergente," *Latin America Research Review* 33, no. 1 (1998): 105–127; Stanley Stein, "The Historiography of Brazil, 1808–1889," *Hispanic American Historical Review* 40, no. 2 (1960): 234–278.

[11] On the professionalization of historical studies see Marshall Eakin, "Latin American History in the United Status: From Gentleman Scholars to Academia Specialists," *The History Teacher* 31, no. 4 (1998): 539–561. The importance of the historiographical contribution to Latin American history by European and North American scholars was underlined in the reviews by Alan Knight, "Latinoamérica: un balance historiográfico," *Historia y Grafía* 10 (1988): 165–207 and Brian Hammet, "Tema y proceso: el problema de la periodización en la historia latinoamericana," in *Historiografía latinoamericana contemporánea*, ed. Ignacio Sosa and Brian Connaughton (Mexico: Centro Coordinador y Difusor de Estudios Latinoamericanos, UNAM, 1999), 31–54.

FROM TRADITION TO MODERNITY?   163

find in the work of this new revisionist school any original topic that was not already posed by the previous historiography. As Alfredo Ávila and Virginia Guedea remark, all the themes around which the historiography in the area revolve can be observed already perfectly established in the decades of 1960 and 1970.[12]

A first critical impulse of the nationalist-evolutionist historical versions of the nineteenth century came from the proliferation of regional perspectives that, although often impregnated with some kind of irredentist vocation, would serve, nonetheless, to reveal a much more complex and heterogeneous picture of the revolutions of independence than that proper to the "official stories," highlighting the presence of alternative projects to those that were eventually imposed. Studies of social history that sought to explore the social bases of the insurgency would also point in the same direction. These would try to give voice to the ideas and programs of different groups, beyond the narrow circles of the Creole elite, which had a role in the process of political rupture.[13] Ultimately, even though it was not their goal, both tendencies would contribute to undermine the idea of independence as an ineluctable destiny. And this is closely associated, in turn, with the emergence of dependency theories.[14]

[12] See Alfredo Ávila and Virginia Guedea, "De la Independencia nacional a los procesos autonomistas novohispanos: Balance de la historiografía reciente," in *Debates sobre la independencia iberoamericana*, ed. Manuel Chust and José Antonio Serrano (Madrid: AHILA/Iberoamericana Vervuert, 2007), 255–276. One fundamental impulse for the emergence of this "first revisionism" was the concern for the underdevelopment of the region. As Ignacio Sosa and Brian Connaughton said, "in general terms, it can be said that the diagnosis on the need to write a new history, in order to explain the causes of underdevelopment, either from the Marxist orthodox perspective, or from the critical view of social scientists, was elaborated, almost in its totality, in the period between 1967 and 1972." Sosa and Connaughton, *Historiografía latinoamericana contemporánea*, 17.

[13] This includes studies from the perspective of ethnicity and gender, although the latter proliferated in a later period to this "first revisionism." As Sarah Chambers says: these studies "first appeared in the late 1970s and 1980s and initially tended to focus on national case studies. Probably for that reason, overviews of the theme for the region as a whole began to appear only in the 2000s once there was enough literature to survey." Sara Chambers, "Scholarly Studies of Women and Gender during Latin American Independence," https://www.oxfordbibliographies.com/view/document/obo-9780199766581/obo-9780199766581-0260.xml. For a more recent study on the role of women during the revolutions of independence, see Asunción Lavrin, "Women in the Wars of Independence," in *Forging Patrias: Iberoamerica, 1810–1824: Some Reflections*, ed. Guadalupe Jiménez Codinach, vol. 2 (Mexico: Fomento Cultural Banamex, 2010), 541–565.

[14] In his balance of recent historiography, which appeared in the ninth volume of the *General History of Latin America* published by the UNESCO, Jurandir Malerba is drastic in his judgment: "In rigor, we can say that what is new in Latin American historiography is in the past, and that the present is full of pastiche—a copy. What Latin American intelligence produced as new, genuine, were the dependency theories, aborted with the coming of post-structuralism, which denied function having any theory." Jurandir Malerba, "Nuevas y viejas perspectivas," in *Teoría y metodología de la historia en América Latina*, ed. Estevão de Rezende Martin and Héctor Pérez Brignoli (Paris: UNESCO/Trotta, 2006), 88. On the dependency theory, see Fernando Henrique Cardoso and Enzo Falleto, *Dependencia y desarrollo en América Latina* (Mexico: FCE, 1969); Fernando Henrique Cardoso and Francisco

164   HISTORIOGRAPHICAL APPROACHES

These theories questioned the self-generated character of the revolutionary process, pointing out the impossibility of explaining it exclusively through an analysis of the forces at play in local settings. It is true that this point would rarely lead to drawing what its logical conclusion was: the need to place this phenomenon on a broader stage (the general dislocation of the international system of relations in the second half of the eighteenth century), limiting itself, instead, to serving as a basis for criticizing the performance of the ruling elites. At this point, however, the interpretations would bifurcate, giving rise to two conflicting interpretations (an ambiguity that, as we will see, would be transferred to the more recent revisionist perspectives).[15]

One current would minimize the revolutionary character of the process of rupture with the metropolises (Spain and Portugal), highlighting, instead, the continuity, after independence, of the social and economic structures inherited from the colony. Some interpretations inscribed in this current, clinging to their vision of local societies as adhering to traditionalist cultural patterns, would also cast doubt on the liberal-Enlightenment character of their ideological frameworks. In some cases, which are not limited to Marxist-inspired studies, but also include, as we have seen, a wide range of "culturalist" interpretations, endorsed something that until then had been one of the central topics of conservative pro-Hispanic historiography: the persistence of hierarchical class visions of the social more typical of Neo-Scholastic contractarian doctrines than of the modern Enlightenment ideal.[16]

Weffort, eds., *América Latina: Ensayos de intepretación sociológica-política* (Santiago: Editorial Universitaria, 1970); Agustín Cueva, *El desarrollo del capitalismo de América Latina* (Mexico: Siglo XXI, 1977); André Gunder Frank, *Capitalism and Underdevelopment in Latin America: Historical Studies of Chile and Brazil* (New York: Monthly Review Press, 1967); Celso Furtado, *La economía latinoamericana desde la conquista hasta la revolución cubana* (Mexico: Siglo XXI, 1969); Helio Jaguaribe et al., *La dependencia político-económica de América latina* (Mexico: Siglo XXI, 1973); Osvaldo Sunkel, "Capitalismo trasnacional y desintegración nacional en América Latina," *Estudios Internacionales* 16 (1971): 3–61. For a comprehensive analysis of the dependency theory, see Daniel Camacho et al., eds., *Debates sobre la teoría de la dependencia y la sociología latinoamericana* (San José: EDUCA, 1979); R. Chilcote, "Issues of Theory in Dependence and Marxism," *Latin American Perspectivas* 8, no. 3–4 (1981): 3–16; Cristóbal Kay, *Latin American Theories of Development and Underdevelopment* (London: Routledge, 1989), Tulio Halperin Donghi, "'Dependency Theory' and Latin American Historiography," *Latin American Research Review* 17, no. 1 (1982): 115–130.

[15] This split perspective was somehow connected to the famous Dobb–Sweezy debate on the transition from feudalism to capitalism, which was initiated after the publication of Maurice Dobb, *Studies in the Development of Capitalism* (London: Routledge, 1946).

[16] For a systematic elaboration of that thesis, see O. C. Stoetzer, *The Scholastic Roots of the Spanish American Revolution* (New York: Fordham University, 1979).

FROM TRADITION TO MODERNITY? 165

Another current, instead, insisted on the modern and revolutionary character of the process opened up by the crisis of the Iberian colonial empires. In some versions, this would be linked to the vocation of a wing of leftist thinking to appropriate its legacy and patriotic symbology. In any case, the visions of the time naturally converged toward the topic of the "unfinished revolution." Creole intervention, which would soon assume control of said process, displacing the other social forces that, it is claimed, had set it into motion, would succeed in diluting its democratic and revolutionary potential, which would remain, nonetheless, as an unfulfilled promise, waiting for its future redemption.

No doubt these perspectives were still imbued with a normative drive. As Guerra pointed out, the writing of history continued to be conceived "more than as a university activity, as a political act in the etymological sense of the word: that of the citizen defending its polis."[17] However, this would start to change shortly after. The most notable phenomenon that has occurred since the 1980s is the growing professionalization of the local historiographical milieu, which, along with the expansion of Latin American studies in the United States and Europe, would result in an important development an expansion of the approaches to the subject. This is expressed not only in a more systematic exploration of the documentary repositories but also, and fundamentally, in the diversification of the themes and objects of study.

Perhaps where this more general shift in the focus of historians' interest is best expressed is the new centrality that political history acquired. As some studies in this field show, the transition from subjects to citizens, beyond the contradictions and obstacles it would face, would have to fundamentally redefine the systems of power relations and the ways in which different social components interacted, and also how social agents reacted before those changes.[18] This renewed interest in political history is expressed more clearly, although not exclusively, in the large number of recent studies devoted to the systematic analysis of electoral processes and other forms of collective

---

[17] François-Xavier Guerra, "El olvidado siglo XIX," in *Balance de la historiografía sobre Iberoamérica Balance de la historiografía sobre Iberoamérica (1945–1988). Actas de las IV Conversaciones Internacionales de Historia*, ed. V. Vázquez de Prada and Ignacio Olabarri (Pamplona: Ediciones Universidad de Navarra, 1989), 595.

[18] Probably the work that most brilliantly shows these transformations is, again, Tulio Halperin Donghi's *Revolución y guerra. Formación de una elite dirigente en la Argentina criolla* (Buenos Aires: Siglo XXI, 1972).

166 HISTORIOGRAPHICAL APPROACHES

participation associated with the development of new spaces of political sociability.[19]

This political history will be intertwined, in turn, with regional, social, and cultural history. In consequence, a wide range of studies would emerge not limited to simply showing the plurality of lines of antagonism that tore apart Latin American societies, and that would be expressed in the coexistence of conflicting political projects, but also how, in the midst of this complex network of particular situations, new political practices expanded in which highly heterogeneous actors and social segments, both in terms of their material conditions of existence and in their ways of symbolically relating to them, would participate. Particularly revealing in this regard are the studies dedicated to analyzing the forms of military recruitment and mobilization, as well as the changing political adherence of peoples and communities.[20]

This imbrication between political history, social history, regional history, and cultural history has not only opened the field of studies on the action of the different social actors, including the so-called subaltern. Particularly productive has been the expansion of research into areas hitherto practically ignored, such as the action of the royalist side and the areas that remained loyal to the crown. Today we have a much clearer idea of the complexity hidden behind the counterinsurgent forces,[21] and also of how the

[19] See Antonio Annino, ed., *Historia de las elecciones en Iberoamérica, Siglo XIX. De la formación del espacio político nacional* (Mexico: FCE, 1995); Xioamara Avendaño Rojas, "De súbditos a ciudadanos: las primeras elecciones en la provincia de Guatemala, 1812–1822," in *Memorias del II Congreso de Historia Centroamericana (1995)*, ed. Víctor Hugo Acuña (Guatemala: USAC, 2000); Carlos Malamud, ed., *Legitimidad, representación y alternancia en España y América Latina: Las reformas electorales (1880–1930)* (Mexico: El Colegio de México/FCE, 2000); Marco Morel, *As transformações dos espaços públicos: imprensa, atores políticos e sociabilidades na Cidade Imperial (1820–1840)* (São Paulo: Hucitec, 2005); Luis Moulián, *La independencia de Chile. Balance historiográfico* (Santiago: Factum, 1996); Víctor Peralta, "Elecciones, constitucionalismo y elección en el Cusco, 1809–1815," *Revista de Indias* 206 (1996): 99–133; Eduardo Posada Carbó, "Malabarismo electorales: una historia comparativa de la corrupción del sufragio en América Latina, 1830–1930," in *Naciones, gentes y territorios. Ensayos de historia e historiografía comparada de América Latina y el Caribe*, ed. Víctor Manuel Uribe Urán and Luis Javier Ortiz Mesa (Medellín: Universidad de Antioquia, 2000); Sabato, ed., *Ciudadanía política y formación de las naciones*; Guillermo Sosa, *Representación e independencia. 1810–1816* (Bogota: Instituto Colombiano de Antropología e Historia, 2006); Marcela Ternavasio, *La revolución del voto. Política y elecciones en Buenos Aires, 1810–1852* (Buenos Aires: Siglo XXI, 2002); Mark Thurner, *Republicanos andinos* (Cuzco and Lima: CBC/IEP, 2006).

[20] See Peter Guardino, *Peasant, Politics and the Formation of Mexico's Nacional State. Guerrero, 1800–1857* (Stanford: Stanford University Press, 1996); Claudia Guarisco, *Los indios del valle de México y la construcción de una nueva sociabilidad política, 1770–1835* (Mexico: El Colegio Mexiquense, 2003); Eric Van Young, *The Other Rebellion: Popular Violence, Ideology, and the Mexican Struggle for Independence* (Stanford: Stanford University Press, 2001).

[21] See Christon Archer, "Politicization of the Army of New Spain During the War of Independence," in *The Evolution of the Mexican Political System*, ed. Jaime Rodríguez O. (Wilmington: Scholarly Resources, 1993); Anthony McFarlane, "Guerras e independencias en las Américas," in *Las revoluciones en el mundo Atlántico*, ed. María Teresa Calderón and Clément Thibaud

FROM TRADITION TO MODERNITY? 167

very attempt to preserve the traditional order would paradoxically lead its defenders to profoundly alter the systems of social, political, and economic relations on which that order was founded.[22]

The most decisive event in this process of historiographic renewal is the appearance of studies that seek to address the dissolution of the Iberian colonial empires from a global perspective, within which we must include the efforts made by Spanish (and also Latin American) historians to understand the links between the first Hispanic liberalism and the revolutions of independence in the colonies. It is also here that the most important contribution of the school initiated by Guerra lies. As we have pointed out, the result was a vision of the crisis of independence as part of a larger revolutionary process that encompassed the Spanish empire as a whole, a perspective that had been blocked by the traditional vision founded on the antinomy between Hispanic despotism and American liberalism.

Although it is certainly true that this is not an unheard-of undertaking, it departs from the previous analogous ones. In effect, albeit authors like John Lynch and Jaime Rodríguez O.[23] underlined the crucial importance of the crisis of the monarchical system in triggering the independentist movement, it is now interpreted not in a merely negative sense (the void of power then produced), but essentially positive: the role of the Spanish peninsula as the center from which new ideas and realities irradiated. It thus shifted the emphasis from the abdications in 1808 to the series of phenomena that immediately followed; particularly, the election process of deputies for the Cortes

---

(Bogota: Universidad Externado de Colombia/Taurus, 2006), 171–188; Juan Ortiz Escamilla, *Guerra y gobierno. Los pueblos y la independencia de México* (Sevilla: Universidad de Sevilla/El Colegio de México/Instituto Mora, 1997); Ortiz Escamilla, ed., *Fuerzas militares en Iberoamérica* (Mexico: El Colegio de México/El Colegio de Michoacán/Universidad Veracruzana, 2005); Víctor Peralta Ruiz, *En defensa de la autoridad. Política y cultura bajo el gobierno del virrey Abascal* (Madrid: CSIC, 2002); Julio Sánchez, "La independencia de la República Oriental del Uruguay: los realistas en la Banda Oriental," in *Bastillas, cetros y blasones: la independencia en Iberoamérica*, ed. Ivana Frasquet (Madrid: Mapfre, 2006), 57–92; Ana Ribeiro, *Los muy fieles. Leales a la corona en el proceso revolucionario rioplatense. Montevideo/Asunción, 1810–1820* (Montevideo: Planeta, 2013); José Antonio Serrano and Marta Terán, eds., *Las guerras de independencia en la América española* (Zamora: El Colegio de Michoacán, 2002); Clément Thibaud, *Repúblicas en armas. Los ejércitos bolivarianos en la guerra de Independencia en Colombia y Venezuela* (Bogota: Instituto Francés de Estudios Andinos/Planeta, 2003).

[22] The precursor studies on the topic are: Timothy Anna, *La caída del gobierno español en la ciudad de México* (México: FCE, 1981); Timothy Anna, *La caída del gobierno español en el Perú* (Lima: IEP, 2003) (originally published in 1979); Brian Hamnett, *Revolución y contrarrevolución en México y el Perú. Liberalismo, realeza y separatismo (1800–1824)* (Mexico: FCE, 1980).

[23] John Lynch, *Las revoluciones hispanoamericanas, 1808–1826* (Barcelona: Ariel, 1976); Jaime Rodríguez O., *La independencia de la América española* (Mexico: El Colegio de México/FCE, 1996).

168   HISTORIOGRAPHICAL APPROACHES

and the subsequent sanction of the Cádiz constitution, which generated a climate of political agitation hitherto unknown in the region.[24]

This new perspective is linked, in turn, to a theoretical-methodological shift. It is closely associated, as we have said above, with the new emphasis on the analysis of the conceptual dimension of historical processes and, more precisely, on its relationship with the alterations produced in the modes and places of enunciation of discourses. However, as we have also seen, it is here that deeper theoretical-methodological problems emerge. This vision is no less contaminated by retrospective projections than the one it criticizes. In this way, far from deepening the lines deriving from its own insights, the perspective of this school immediately relapses into a teleological vision of Latin American history that, however, stands in contradiction with its very object, and ends up diluting its own findings.

Ruptures and Continuities in History and Historiography

Going back to the question of whether the professionalization of historiography introduced an authentic renewal of our perspectives on independence or whether it was limited to deepening trends initiated by the previous revisionist wave that emerged in the 1960s and 1970s, as stated in the previous section, the point is not that easy to solve. The criticism of epic perspectives, which defines "revisionist" currents, including the most recent ones, is not an original undertaking nor does it indicate a radical novelty with respect to what different authors had been doing since at least half a century ago. The difficulties in understanding in what sense the former departed from the preceding revisionist currents are more clearly revealed in the recent debates around the question of whether or not the independence revolutions marked a break with the old régime.

---

[24] The precursor work on this topic is Nettie Lee Benson, *Mexico and the Spanish Cortes, 1810–1822: Eight Essays* (Austin: Texas University Press, 1966). For more recent studies, see: Márcia Regina Berdel, *A nação como artefato: deputados do Brasil nas Cortes Portuguesas* (San Pablo: Hucitec, 1998); María Teresa Berruezo, *La participación americana en las Cortes de Cádiz (1810–1814)* (Madrid: Centro de Estudios Constitucionales, 1986); Roberto Breña, *El primer liberalismo español y los procesos de emancipación de América, 1808–1824: una revisión historiográfica del liberalismo hispánico* (Mexico: El Colegio de México, 2006); Manuel Chust, *La cuestión nacional americana en las Cortes de Cádiz* (Valencia: UNED/Centro Francisco Tomás y Valiente, 1999); José María Portillo Valdés, *Crisis atlántica: autonomía e independencia en la crisis de la monarquía hispana* (Madrid: Marcial Pons/Centro de Estudios Hispanos e Iberoamericanos/Fundación Carolina, 2006); Marie Rieu-Millan, *Los diputados americanos en la Cortes de Cádiz* (Madrid: CSIC, 1998); Mario Rodríguez, *El experimento de Cádiz en Centroamérica. 1808–1826* (México: FCE, 1984).

FROM TRADITION TO MODERNITY? 169

At this point, these new studies appear, in principle, less innovative than what many of their authors would be willing to admit: the now dominant vision only gathers one of the central topics of the first revisionism, which, in opposition to epic visions, emphasized continuities, in terms of social and economic patterns, after independence, which would thus be reduced to a strictly political phenomenon. And the same can be said with respect to the contingent (political) nature of the foundations of American nationalities: the idea that, in Latin America, the state preceded the nation was already commonplace in the literature on the subject long before recent works corroborated it.

However, this consensus hides fundamental divergences which are rarely made explicit. The consideration of the Brazilian case offers a good example. The first Brazilian revisionism takes shape from a series of criticisms of the book *Formação do Brasil comtemporâneo* (1942), by Caio Prado Jr.,[25] which points out the so-called myths of the origins of Brazilian nationality.[26] The criticism of that book actually did not undermine the consensus around the idea, present in Prado Jr.'s work, that the continuity of the monarchical legitimacy (and the consequent less traumatic character that the breaking of the link with the metropolis assumed there) would have been decisive to preserve, in essence, the characteristics of the colonial society, and, in particular, its two nuclear institutions: monarchy and slavery. However, some leftist authors would then begin to question this interpretation, which, they claimed, tended to dilute the revolutionary event, thus losing sight of its deep nature, stripping it of its character as such. This would thus seek to highlight how institutional continuities would hide deep ruptures with the old régime.

This contained a paradox: while in Spanish America historical revisionism (both the old and the new) have emerged as a reaction against the epic views of independence that saw it as a radical rupture with the past, in Brazil the revisionist perspectives would be associated with the project of undermining the image of transhistorical stability deeply rooted in local historiography. Thus, starting from analogous premises, Brazilian revisionism would, however, move in a direction opposite to that which the revisionist currents would follow in its neighboring countries. Undoubtedly, the peculiarities of the independence process in that country help to understand this paradox,

---

[25] Caio Prado, Jr., *Formação do Brasil comtemporâneo* (São Paulo: Brasiliense, 1942).
[26] See Fernando A. Novais and Carlos G. Mota, *A Independencia do Brasil* (São Paulo: Moderna, 1986); João Paulo G. Pimenta, "A Independencia do Brasil: Un balanço da produção historiográfica recente," in Chust and Serrano, *Debates sobre las independencias iberoamericanas*, 143–157.

170 HISTORIOGRAPHICAL APPROACHES

although they do not suffice to explain it fully. And this brings us back to the previous question: what does recent revisionism take from its predecessor, and how does it differ from it?

The truth is that in Spanish America the answer will also differ depending on which the point is taken as reference. When trying to delimitate their own perspectives with respect to that of the old revisionist historiography of Marxist inspiration, positions differ depending on what versions of the former are taken as a target, whether the versions that insisted on the "merely political" character of the revolution of independence or, on the contrary, that other that emphasized its character as such. Thus, what some conceive as a continuation of well-known hypotheses (the persistence of colonial patterns), for others it appears as a fundamental historiographic innovation, and vice versa. Ultimately, the new revisionist interpretations would end up inheriting from the previous revisionist tradition, not only a series of common motives that run through both, but also a certain inconsistency regarding the sense of their critical enterprise of standard nationalist views.

This would blur its true object. Rather than proposing a new interpretation of the transition from tradition to modernity (which, in truth, has nothing novel about it), what this new revisionism would be setting into question, in actual fact, is the validity of the very scheme "from tradition to modernity" as a framework to analyze the nature of the fracture then produced.[27] What these studies actually disclose is the impossibility of clearly determining in that context what was "traditional" and what was "modern." In the Ibero-American countries of the early nineteenth century, continuities and changes would overlap with each other to the point of becoming indiscernible. But this "hybridity," rather than expressing a "Latin American peculiarity," as it is usually interpreted, indicates, on the contrary, a characteristic feature of these phenomena of historical rupture. More importantly, the anxiety for distinguishing what was traditional and what was modern leads to missing what effectively changed at that moment, the actual political and social transformations resulting from the break of the colonial system.

The studies referring to the aforementioned process of reversion of sovereignty, after the royal vacancy, to the *pueblos* are particularly revealing not only of the complexity, but also of the profundity of the break brought about by the dissolution of all transcendent authority (i.e., one located in a position

---

[27] On this, see Palti, *El tiempo de la política*.

FROM TRADITION TO MODERNITY? 171

of preeminence with respect to the society over which it rules), beyond the "modernity," or not, of the conceptual references of the actors.

This forces us to complicate the picture that shows the political and territorial fragmentation produced after independence as a result of the mere emergence in the political plane of a pre-existing corporative structure. Even though traditional jurisdictional powers did not disappear, from the very moment they became political actors, they would assume unprecedented powers and characteristics that were previously unthinkable.[28] And neither would their structures remain unaltered before their functional changes. The most notorious phenomenon was the decomposition of what had been the characteristic feature of the old régime society: its pyramidal structure.[29] In fact, as Antonio Annino shows,[30] these territorial jurisdictional powers did not pre-exist the crisis of the monarchical system but were its byproduct.[31]

As Annino indicates, the articulating principle of the new societies would not be that of *will* or *opinion*, but that of *justice* (which was proper to the corporative structure of the old régime). However, and this is the crucial point, the question of what is just or unjust at that moment would, it itself, become a matter *opinion*. The loss of the figure of transcendental authority, like that of the monarch, inevitably made the condition of the subjects and the corresponding system of rights and duties become matters of controversy, properly *political* issues. In this fashion, the idea that they plunged their foundations into nature itself, although was not abandoned, then became undermined, in actual practice, giving rise to conflicts and struggles for its definition.

We find here a torsion, characteristic of this type of historical rupture phenomena, by which a traditional principle folds upon itself to end up finding another that was no longer so. We thus go back to what Halperin Donghi

[28] Guerra adopted the idea of the persistence in Latin America of the traditional jurisdictional powers elaborated by Bartolomé Clavero and his school. See Bartolomé Clavero, *Antidora. Antropología católica de la economía moderna* (Milan: Giuffre Editore, 1991).

[29] See Antonio Annino, Luis Castro Leiva, and François-Xavier Guerra, eds., *De los imperios a las naciones. Iberoamérica* (Zaragoza: Ibercaja, 1994); Carlos Garriga and Marta Llorente, *Cádiz 1812. La Constitución jurisdiccional* (Madrid: Centro de Estudios Constitucionales, 2007); Beatriz Rojas, "Las ciudades novohispanas ante la crisis: Entre la antigua y la nueva constitución, 1808–1814," *Historia Mexicana* 229 (2008): 287–324; José Antonio Serrano, *Jerarquía territorial y transición política, Guanajuato 1790–1836* (Mexico: El Colegio de Michoacán/Instituto Mora, 2001).

[30] Antonio Annino, "Imperio, constitución y diversidad en la América hispana," *Historia Mexicana* 229 (2008): 179–227.

[31] An interesting analysis of how this inflection was produced is that of María Teresa Calderón and Clément Thibaud, "De la majestad a la soberanía en la Nueva Granada," in *Las revoluciones en el mundo atlántico*, ed. María Teresa Calderón and Clément Thibaud (Bogotá: Universidad del Externado de Colombia/Taurus, 2006), 365–401.

172   HISTORIOGRAPHICAL APPROACHES

pointed out and we analyzed in Chapter 5. Ultimately, what these studies reveal is the extent to which new societies will inevitably emerge out of rearticulations produced within pre-existing realities, however, taking on, in their course, meanings and functions that are already very different from the traditional ones, and indeed, many times simply hitherto unthinkable.

What precludes the new revisionist approaches drawing all the consequences of their own findings, relapsing into a little innovative perspective that emphasizes the continuities between the colonial and the independent periods, are, lastly, their re-inscriptions into the same teleological matrix that these approaches intended to dislocate and that saw in the origin of the process under consideration what can only be found at the end of it. They differ from older teleologies only in the reference point that each of them takes to produce these retrospective projections: the fully constituted national states, in epic visions; the political fragmentation that occurred immediately after the rupture, by the revisionists. However, what emerges from their own historical analyses is a different perspective, much less linear and deterministic. Just as independence was not the inevitable result of already constituted nations that sooner or later were destined to obtain their self-government, but the outcome of a series of events (such as the royal vacancy, the convocation of Cortes, etc.) that could perfectly well not have happened, nor was the political fragmentation that followed independence a fatal result of the breakdown of the colonial ties, which would simply have given rise to the political emergence of the corporate elements that formed the fabric of the society of the old régime. The latter event was also the product of the particular—equally contingent—circumstances in which the rupture took place, such as the long war to which it gave rise or the fact that the independence ended up consummating in a political climate already hostile to it, dominated by the ideas of the Restoration.

The conclusion that must be drawn from what we have observed so far is not that the rupture–continuity dilemma is irrelevant, but rather that it is ill posed. More precisely, what could be reconsidered is the framework of assumptions within which such a dilemma (in principle, perfectly legitimate) is embedded. Ultimately, the revisionist critique of the 1960s and 1970s intended to counter the teleologism of the traditional perspectives of the revolutions of independence by opposing another form of teleologism, different in its content but not very diverse in its nature. And something similar has happened with the more recent revisionist currents. Lastly, their perspectives remain inscribed within the frameworks of the interpretative

FROM TRADITION TO MODERNITY? 173

scheme of "models" and "deviations." In this case, it is no longer the Soviet revolution (or, rather, an image of it that we now know to be decidedly mythical) but the ideal of a modern individualistic society (or rather an image of it no less mythical than the previous one) which occupies the place of the presupposed "ideal type" that serves as a parameter to measure how close to it the process in question came.[32]

Thus, beyond their divergences, in every case the question about continuities and ruptures ends up surreptitiously displacing or covering up another: to what extent the concrete historical phenomenon satisfies or not the expectations that have been, in each case, projected upon it. The point, however, is that, as we have already remarked, these revisionist interpretations collide with their very findings. In its present format, the disjunctive rupture–continuity does not account for the complexities they intended to disclose. To avoid the simplification of their own perspectives, and the resulting conceptual anachronisms, it is necessary to detach them from the teleological frameworks in which they are currently embedded. But that requires a radical reformulation of the topic "from tradition to modernity;" which involves, in turn, the previous work of critical undermining of the ideal-type approaches; in the end, to strip the "models" of their appearance of perfect consistency and rationality and penetrate and disclose the radical contingency of their foundations.

This leads us to what constitutes the "hard core" that underlies these expressions of historical teleologism, which permeates indeed the perspectives that propose breaking with it: the concept of "modern democracy." It constitutes the heart of all teleological perspectives insofar as it appears as the ultimate goal, the ideal toward the realization of which all political developments after the revolutions of independence tended, or at least, should have tended. Ultimately, if we do not critically undermine this assumption, if we do not detach the veil of naturalness and perfect rationality with which the concept of "modern democracy" is presented to us, we will inevitably end up relapsing into some form of teleologism. As we will see in the pages that follow, the type of challenges that the new ruling elite in Latin America faced were infinitely more complex than that of the progressive realization of an ideal type of modern democracy, as normally asserted

---

[32] The fall of the Berlin Wall reinforced this perception of "liberal democracy" as a kind of final destiny of mankind. On this see Diego von Vacano, "The Scope of Comparative Political Theory," *Annual Review of Political Science* 18 (2015): 465–480.

174 HISTORIOGRAPHICAL APPROACHES

(and it would be blamed for failing to do that). In this critical, revolutionary period, the "models" themselves would be called into question, revealing inconsistencies that were inherent in them, and not merely a matter of their "applicability" of "adequacy" to the local context, as is asserted in the studies in the field by both nationalists and revisionists, in all their versions. Yet, it is not that easy to discover. It demands an arduous intellectual effort to uncover the radical contingency of the assumptions on which our own present political systems rest, the set of certainties whose validity appears to us as self-evident, as it occurs with the principle of "popular sovereignty" on which the concept of "modern democracy" is founded.

Modern Democracy as the Final Goal: A Long Road to the Realization of the Ideal Type?

The concept of "modern democracy" represents, in actual fact, the ultimate limit against which the attempts to dislocate teleological perspectives crash. Even in those cases in which the ideal of modern democracy looks as unfeasible, as would supposedly be the case of Latin America, according to the revisionist perspectives, it remains perceived as the last goal to which all political developments should lead. The process of naturalization of the concept of "modern democracy" has made it rob itself of its possible thematization, it appears today as the unquestionable premise at the basis of all historical narratives. In sum, the approach to the issue of democracy in Latin America from the perspective of conceptual history confronts us with what constitutes the unsurpassable limit of the attempts to overcome the teleological assumptions underlying the approaches to its political and intellectual history. The concept of the "ideal type" of modern democracy remains as the unthought-of premise for all studies in the field.

It actually has historical-conceptual foundations. Democracy appears today as the only political horizon that may claim ecumenical legitimacy. Yet, as John Dunn remarks in *Democracy: A History*,[33] in a complex and diverse world, this convergence around a term coined two-and-a-half millennia ago as a poor remedy to solve a local illness in a Greek city, and which then had more critics than supporters, is somehow surprising, The vastness and massiveness of this phenomenon darkened the fact that this is, in actual

---

[33] John Dunn, *Democracy: A History* (New York: Atlantic Monthly Press, 2005).

FROM TRADITION TO MODERNITY? 175

fact, a very recent development. Only after 1945 did the term acquire such ascendency. The UNESCO report, written in 1951 in the context of the Cold War, is eloquent in this regard:

> For the first time in the history of the world, no doctrines are advanced as antidemocratic. The accusations of antidemocratic action or attitude are frequently directed at others, but practical politicians and political theorists agree in stressing the democratic elements in institutions they defend and theories they advocate.[34]

However, at that very moment in Latin America, a series of bloody military coups followed one another as the result of the introduction of the region in the center of the Cold War after the Cuban Revolution. Thus, paradoxically, the same factor that served in Europe to consolidate the prestige of democracy (the instauration of the Cold War) made it unviable in practice in Latin America.

This paradoxical situation (the affirmation in the West of the democratic consensus and the expansion in Latin America of military dictatorships) was, in turn, retrospectively projected, lending credibility to the idea of the existence of an innate incompatibility between the traditionalist local culture and modern, universal principles of democracy. As we have seen, this pessimistic mood regarding the prospect of democracy in the region indeed deeply imbued the "revisionist" historiographical wave that spread in the 1960s and 1970s in the context of the diffusion there of Marxist thought and the so-called dependency theories. In their view, democracy there was a "misplaced idea." Actually, in this fashion, the "revisionists" only continued and deepened a perception that had emerged right after independence. As we have seen, as early as in the nineteenth century the idea that the whole political and intellectual history of Latin America was that of a persistent divorce between the ideal and reality, the long march toward the realization of a putative model of modern democracy, ever frustrated in actual reality, was already widely spread. From that perspective, students of the Latin American case should dedicate to disclose the vicissitudes that the ideal of democracy underwent in the region, but it would have nothing to tell us about its concept

---

[34] Richard McKeon, *Democracy in a World of Tensions* (Paris: UNESCO, 1951), 522, quoted by Russell L. Hanson, "Democracy," in *Political Innovation and Conceptual Change*, ed. Terence Ball, James Farr, and Russell L. Hanson (Cambridge: Cambridge University Press, 1995), 68–89.

176 HISTORIOGRAPHICAL APPROACHES

itself (the putative goal), which could be determined with complete independence from these circumstances. They would denote merely local anomalies
with no relevance for politico-conceptual history at large.

This perspective, which stains the entire local political history with teleologism, today seems to be self-evident. Who could sensibly question, for
example, that the consecration of universal suffrage marked an undeniable
institutional progress, compared to how all previous election systems looked
like mere deficient anticipations? Indeed, the critics of the "bourgeois democracy" accepted it as the implicit goal after independence. Unlike what
happens today with the rest of modern political concepts, like those of representation, public opinion, nation, people, etc., the democratic idea seems to
resist its historicization. The naturalization process it underwent during the
past half-century (which the collapse of the "really existing socialism" seemed
to reinforce) rendered the debates produced in the past around its concept
incomprehensible under any other assumption than that of the expression of
a persistent misunderstanding of its true meaning or the distorted application in practice of principles whose sense is assumed as perfectly transparent.
This category would thereby erect itself as the ultimate limit set to the enterprise of historicization of modern political thinking to which researchers in
the field are currently committed. What is certain is, as we have said, that if
we want to get rid of the teleological perspectives that indeed imbue the so-
called revisionist views of Latin American political history, we must confront
that limit and undermine its apparent naturalness.

Democracy as a Problem in Post-Colonial Latin America

According to most studies on the topic, a fundamental cause (although certainly not the only one) of the failure to establish truly democratic systems of
government in nineteenth-century Latin America was the anti-democratic
prejudices of the ruling elite of the time. And, certainly, at that moment democracy had a rather bad reputation (actually, not only in Latin America,
but all around the world).[35] Yet we must say that the study of primary sources
forces us to introduce some nuances in that statement. By analyzing them,
what we observe is some characteristic ambiguity. On the one hand, we

[35] On the anti-democratic prejudices of the "Founding Fathers" in America, see Sanford Levinson,
*Our Undemocratic Constitution: Where the Constitution Goes Wrong (and How We the People Can
Correct It)* (Oxford: Oxford University Press, 2006).

FROM TRADITION TO MODERNITY? 177

find repeated vindications of democracy as the distinctive feature of Latin American institutional system. Even conservative organs, like *El Orden* of Buenos Aires, could state, with no need for further clarification, that "there are certain principles on which doubt is not allowed to republicans without becoming guilty of *lesa democracy*."[36] Yet, on the other hand, this vindication of democracy as the characteristic seal of these nations coexisted, almost with no transition, with bitter and reiterated criticism to it. However, this does not contradict what we have stated above regarding the presence of an almost universal consensus around it. The true challenge for a historical approach to the issue of democracy in nineteenth-century Latin America is to understand this apparent paradox, the normative ambiguity of which it was an object. For this, we must recreate the semantic field in which that concept was inscribed and observe the meaningful (and not merely normative) fluctuations that it underwent during the period under consideration.

Here we must introduce a distinction between two terms that are closely associated to the concept of democracy: the voices *populus* (*people*) and *plebs* (*low people*). As we know, the latter bears pejorative connotations. However, beyond the opposite appraisals the two terms have had, there was a *conceptual* difference between them, which is much more significant, but that historians tend to obliterate by interpreting as simply an expression of the anti-popular and anti-democratic prejudices of the local elites. The idea of *populus* entailed a principle of totality. The concept of *plebs*, instead, referred to a particular sector of society, the one that the ancient Greeks designated with the term *demos*.

In its origin, the idea of democracy was inscribed within a theory of the forms of governments, and this theory would provide the framework for political debates until the mid-nineteenth century.[37] It was articulated around the question of which part of the community should rule over the rest: either one, or several or many, being that the rule of the many was not at all evident to be the best of the three alternatives. The association between democracy and the rule of the poor people hinged, in the last instance, on the assumption that one part of society must rule over the other. That all could simultaneously govern and be governed was simply inconceivable, an absurdity.

---

[36] *El Orden* (1858), "La verdad de la oposición y la sentencia de los partidos," # 899, Buenos Aires.

[37] As a matter of fact, following the premises of the ancient theory of the forms of government, all theorical-political debates in the early nineteenth century revolved around the issue of what the most suitable form of government was for each particular society. For the classical formulation of this theory, see Aristotle, *Politics* (New York: Barnes & Noble, 2005).

178 HISTORIOGRAPHICAL APPROACHES

The identification of a particular section of society (the *poor people*) with the social whole (the *people*) could then be established only by rhetorical means, but, for the political actors of the epoch, they kept their character as such. We will have to wait many years before these rhetorical uses of the term become naturalized in political language and stripped of their clearly ideological content.

Yet, by the nineteenth-century, a very different concept of democracy became superimposed on this. Analyzing the primary sources of the time, we can observe a two-fold semantic thread, leading, on the one hand, to understanding democracy as the index of popular sovereignty, and, on the other, as a specific form of government. These two meanings would never coalesce and mutually identify. In the former case, as the expression of popular sovereignty, democracy would be the generic content of *every form of post-traditional government*. Once deprived of their transcendent warranties, the new governments that emerged out of revolution could found their legitimacy only in the consent of their subjects. However, for that very reason, this generic democratic content accepted diverse translations on the institutional plane. As Juan Bautista Alberdi said: "democracy resides in popular sovereignty, *a principle that is conciliable with all forms of government*."[38] "The very hereditary quality of power," he continued, "does not contradict democracy, provided the succession has been instituted and can be abolished by the people."[39]

Nevertheless, the problematic nature of democracy lies in the fact that its generic content is what makes it accept diverse translations on the institutional level, and at the same time prevents its complete congruency with any of them. Lastly, the institution of a political order, whatever it is, entails the cancellation, or at least the temporary suspension of democracy *qua* expression of popular sovereignty. Conversely, its manifestation would mean annulling authority. According to Mariano Moreno, sovereignty is, by definition, "indivisible and inalienable," "hence," he concludes, "every time that the people managed to make manifest its general will, all the powers that previously regulated it came to a halt."[40]

Lastly, democracy would refer back to a plane preceding any instituted form of government; in sum, it would be identified with the constituent

---

[38] Juan Bautista Alberdi, *Escritos póstumos*, vol. 12 (Buenos Aires: Imprenta Cruz Hnos, 1899), 113.
[39] Alberdi, *Escritos póstumos*, 12:256.
[40] Mariano Moreno, "Sobre la misión del Congreso," in *Escritos políticos y económicos* (Buenos Aires: La Cultura Argentina, 1915), 284.

FROM TRADITION TO MODERNITY? 179

power, the emergence of which would involve the destitution of the existing order. There would thus be an intrinsic incompatibility between democracy and government. As immediately after Moreno says:

> under an instituted regime, sovereignty can be exercised only on the private realm; never on the public arena, where the citizen remains subjected to Law, and, ultimately, to the will of its bearer, the established authority. Hence, in private actions, and within its territory, a member of a federation behaves independently as a legislator of itself, but in public business, as a subject he obeys the laws and decrees passed by the national authority.[41]

Every institution of government involves the end of equality, necessarily entails a scission operated at the bosom of society by means of which subjects are divided into governors and governed. The double nature of the concept of democracy thus hides another, more fundamental, paradox: if democracy is the generic essence of every form of post-traditional government, so is aristocracy. As Cornelio Saavedra stated in his reply to Moreno: "These considerations, distinctions and the rewards of public services [on whose basis governments are established], are the ones that constitute the true honour of men, *whatever the dominant regime in society may be.*"[42]

After independence, democracy would thus become at the same time a destiny and a problem. As the expression of popular sovereignty, it would constitute the generic content of every post-traditional government, which, by definition, however, would never find expression on the political realm (as Alberdi ironically showed, in democracy "the majorities have the Platonic government of the world, while the minorities have the actual government").[43] Insofar as the institution of a political system entails the partition of society, democracy will appear as something always invoked, but always elusive, ungraspable, and inexpressible. And this is not merely due to factual matters, to its impossible materialization in actual political practice, but in regard with its very concept. This is inevitably equivocal to the extent that it would refer simultaneously to two different planes: the foundations of power and the means of exercising it.

---

[41] Moreno, *Escritos políticos y económicos*, 299–300.
[42] Cornelio Saavedra, *Memoria autógrafa* (Buenos Aires: Carlos Pérez Editor, 1969), 9–10.
[43] Alberdi, *Escritos póstumos*, 12:264.

180   HISTORIOGRAPHICAL APPROACHES

This explains the apparently contradictory coexistence in our primary sources (sometimes in the very same paragraph) of vindication and criticism of democracy. The negative view of it, that historians normally interpret as a demonstration of the persistence of anti-democratic prejudices, would refer, precisely, to those attempts to suppress that ambiguity intrinsic to its concept; that is, to the enterprise (understood as permanently unrealizable, by definition) of giving that generic content an unequivocal expression on the political-institutional realm.

Here we find the fundamental reformulation introduced by an approach to the topic of democracy in a post-colonial context from a historic-intellectual point of view. In actual fact, democracy would refer to nothing that could be defined in a determinate or determinable fashion. It has no object, it does not refer to any given set of principles, maxims, or institutions that could be listed (which is the aim of the history of ideas). It rather designates a *problem: how to operate the transition to the institution of a coercive power, how to produce the partition of society, without dislocating the egalitarian substratum that, in a post-traditional context, constituted its premise.* And this would not be that easy to solve.

To do so, it would be first necessary for the concept of democracy to be stripped of the dual nature it had in its origins. And this entails, in turn, a two-fold operation by means of which, on the one hand, its concept would narrow its content, cutting out its generic tie with popular sovereignty and becoming reduced to merely a form of government (the crystallization of popular sovereignty would thus turn into a mere matter of political engineering: universal suffrage, a party system, and so forth), and, on the other, it would widen its sense and become the only legitimate form of government: once the former reduction has been produced, the opposite term to democracy would no longer be aristocracy or monarchy (which were considered alternative forms of legitimate government), but authoritarianism (a radical illegitimacy). The whole universe of political forms would be exhausted in the dyad of these two asymmetric counter concepts. The latter then appears as only the reverse of the former, the one upon which all the negative attributes that were stripped from it will be projected.[44]

We can also appreciate here the extent to which teleological perspectives prevent historical comprehension. Rather than the progressive discovery, and realization, of an eternal truth, the "authentic" meaning of modern

[44] See Koselleck, *Future Past*, 159–197.

representative democracy, the agents of the period under consideration faced a much harder task: to occlude the inconsistencies inherent in its very concept and develop the blind spots on which stood the kind of idealizations that allowed to naturalize expressions that were originally simply self-contradictory, such as "representative democracy."[45] A more rigorous reconstruction of the political language of the times, of the meaning that the categories at stake had, compels us to reformulate the questions with which we approach the topic. The issue that emerges here is no longer why the agents of the epoch did not manage to understand (or make effective in actual practice) a modern ideal of representative democracy, whose concept is assumed as self-evident, but rather how to explain the *fault* in the process of naturalization of the concept by means of which it would lose the double nature it had in its origins. This reframes the issue, placing the question of democracy in nineteenth-century Latin America in a properly historical perspective. This means leaving aside the approaches that focus on "ideal types," transcending the perspectives that conceive the entire political-intellectual history as a mere succession and overlapping of "models of thought," and penetrating that aporetic core that, in each case, underlies the contradiction among competing ideologies. That is, to disclose the traumatic core that, in each case, underlies it, making of antagonism an inherent dimension in political practice. In sum, as Pierre Rosanvallon says, the point is "not to try to solve the enigma [of the modern political regime of government] by imposing on it a normativity, as if a pure science of language or law could show men the rational solution to which they must adjust themselves," but rather to consider "its problematic nature [. . .] in order to understand its concrete functioning."[46]

---

[45] See Bernard Manin, *The Principles of Representative Government* (Cambridge: Cambridge University Press, 1997).

[46] Rosanvallon, *Pour une historie conceptuelle du politique*, 27.

Conclusion
The Quest for an Identity

The Pseudo-Problem as a Historical-Intellectual Problem

For Borges, the question of national identity was not only insoluble. Its very formulation was absurd, something that could only yield "pathetic developments." As he stated in "The Argentine Writer and Tradition":

> I want to formulate and justify some skeptical propositions about the problem of the Argentine writer and tradition. My skepticism does not refer to the difficulty or impossibility of solving it but to the very existence of the problem. I believe that it confronts us with a rhetorical issue, apt only for pathetic developments. Rather than a real mental difficulty, I understand that it is an appearance, a simulacrum, a pseudo-problem.[1]

This observation by the always lucid author of *The Aleph* still did not manage to explain the fundamental point: Why such a "simulacrum," a "pseudo-problem," obsessed generations of thinkers in Latin America so persistently. "Rarely," said Zea, "have there been societies that have wondered so much about their destiny, that have searched so hard for the traits of their identity."[2] Interpreting this as merely denoting some kind of intellectual pathology that would affect local thinkers could only result in developments no less "pathetic" than those that Borges questioned.

If the question of identity is, in effect, as Borges said, a pseudo-problem, the question about the question itself is not so at all. Understanding how it arose; what generated such a persistent concern for defining the own identity; what was at stake, in each case, behind that question; what anxieties it

---

[1] Jorge Luis Borges, "The Argentine Writer and Tradition," in *Obras Completas (1939–1941)*, vol. 1 (Buenos Aires: Emecé, 1974), 267–272.

[2] Leopoldo Zea, ed., *América Latina en sus ideas* (Mexico: Siglo XXI, 1986), 12. On this, see also Aimer Granados and Carlos Marichal, eds., *Construcción de las identidades latinoamericanas. Ensayos de historia intelectual siglos XIX y XX* (Mexico: COLMEX, 2004).

Misplaced Ideas?. Elías J. Palti, Oxford University Press. © Oxford University Press 2024.
DOI: 10.1093/oso/9780197556641.003.0007

CONCLUSION   183

conveyed; in short, what it tells us of the particular historical-conceptual context or contexts in which that question emerged as a central concern that worried thinkers of such diverse political persuasions, cultural backgrounds, intellectual formations, etc. Such a phenomenon is certainly intriguing. In fact, it contains fundamental keys for the understanding of local intellectual history. However, paradoxically, such a question only becomes meaningful from the moment it is revealed, as Borges said, as "a pseudo-problem"; that is, that the concern for the own identity is stripped of its veil of naturalness and becomes a problem, one that demands an explanation of a historical-conceptual order.

The narrative construction of a given image of Latin America, its culture, and its intellectual tradition involved, in each case, a series of intellectual operations, and set in motion conceptual and rhetorical devices, presupposing a given cognitive framework. All this, in turn, at the point of departure, had implicit a series of assumptions about both the nature of the object and the sense of undertaking its study. And, at the intended point of arrival, the aspiration to intervene in a dialogic space where both real and supposed interlocutors would participate, as they would become constituted as such interlocutors within the very discursive field where reflection takes place. Both aspects, the semantic and the pragmatic dimensions of discourses, constitute together that field, which possesses, in turn, a given structure and logic of operation—a form.

We have defined here our research program. It aims to unravel and recreate, in each case, the discursive field where different ideas, theories, and historical perspectives could eventually display; the terrain that established the various possible directions for their unfolding, and delimited the range of the conceivable and the sayable in each particular historical-conceptual context. And this inevitably leads us beyond the realm of the "history of ideas." None of this can be done if we limit ourselves to analyzing the "ideas" of the authors under consideration, if we focus exclusively on the referential contents of their discourses, or, eventually, look for their sources, the "influences" to which they responded.

"Influences" are usually made explicit in the texts we analyze. It is not necessary to be exceedingly smart or subtle to have discovered the importance of Ortega y Gasset in the thought of Leopoldo Zea, or that Kusch's vision was impregnated with Heidegger's ontology, or that Dussel founded his idea of the Latin American being on the Levinasian philosophy of the otherness, or, even, that Guerra's idea of the continuity of the old régime in Latin

184 MISPLACED IDEAS?

America was incited by the reading of François Furet's "revisionist" writings on the French Revolution. Instead, the particular ground of knowledge underlying these discourses, the series of conceptual assumptions that lay at their base, the set of rhetorical strategies and intellectual operations by which such discourses took their concrete form, are not at all simple to discover and recreate. They are, moreover, inarticulable within the frameworks of the very discourses in question, not even within their sources' discourses. And yet, they are already inscribed in their texts as their very condition of possibility. We just need adequate conceptual tools to disclose them. And it is here where the traditional frameworks of the history of ideas, and the series of antinomies that are intrinsic to it find their limit; they are revealed as completely insufficient to do that.

What I call a "conceptual history" or, more properly, an "archaeological approach," is founded, in turn, on a series of assumptions. It has at its base a certain vision of intellectual history. It departs from those perspectives that conceive it as a succession and opposition among "models of thought," which appear as self-enclosed and clearly delimited systems, at least ideally, beyond contaminations and "hybridizations" undergone in the course of their practical realization.

In effect, insofar as "models" are assumed as perfectly consistent, all the problems that appear historically in connection with them are thus reduced to merely empirical problems; that is, springing from the (external) milieu to which they were applied, the circumstances of their practical realization. These circumstances would thus have nothing to say about the models themselves. Models are immune to these problems and the "external" circumstances that allegedly produced them. The latter do not make their definition, which could be perfectly established with independence of them. Models are nourished from another substance, which is not that of time. They live in a realm of ethereal substances. Hence contingency is not an element inherent in them, but something that comes to them from outside, from the "external" milieu of their practical realization.

Here, we come to the kind of methodological turn that an "archaeological approach" produces. It intends to break the traditional antinomy between "ideas" and "realities," as if there were ideas generated independently, produced in a universe of pure ideas, and which only subsequently become inscribed into actual realities, in sum, as if they pre-existed the material means through which they could eventually become socially articulated and circulate. And, on the other hand, as if there were crudely, empirically

CONCLUSION 185

realities, social, political, and economic practices which are not always already traversed by symbolic webs.

Ultimately, what underlies an archaeological approach is the perception of the radical indefinability of fundamental political and social concepts. This arises from the fact that conceptual formations are not founded on pure reason or nature, but on a given set of assumptions and idealizations historically constituted. "All concepts in which an entire process is semiotically concentrated elude definition," affirmed Nietzsche in *The Genealogy of Morals*; "only that which has no history is definable."[3] It is, in sum, the ultimate indefinability of concepts that makes them properly historical entities; that is, those whose semantic contents are always precariously constituted.

The point is that only if we consider contingency as an inherent dimension in intellectual history, if we undermine the appearance of inner consistency and perfect rationality of the "models," only then can we make sense of the debates around them produced in the past. As Rosanvallon said in his conference entitled "For a Conceptual History of *The Political*," "it is a history whose function is to restore problems rather than describe models."[4] The concept of "modern democracy" that we have analyzed at the end of the last chapter contains a fundamental key in this regard.

As we have seen, the kind of problems that historically arose around that concept did not refer to merely factual circumstances attributable to a local pathological formation of the Latin American social milieu, as usually stated, but they are revealing of more fundamental problems of a conceptual nature. Ultimately, if the concept of "modern democracy" cannot be defined, it is because it designates nothing that can be defined, no given set of principles, institutions, or values that can be listed; however, it is basically an index of a problem. More precisely stated, what lies at its basis is an aporia, the paradox of how the very same subject can be at once its own sovereign, and the other way around.

And, as I have said, only to the extent that we manage to penetrate that aporetic core that underlies modern political discourse can we render meaningful the debates that have occurred in the past around those concepts. Otherwise, if we think that they accept unequivocal definitions, the fact that the agents of the past have debated on them, that they have problematized

---

[3] Friedrich Nietzsche, *On the Genealogy of Morals* (Cambridge: Cambridge University Press, 1994), 51.

[4] Pierre Rosanvallon, *Pour une historie conceptuelle du politique. Leçon inaugurale au Collège de France faite le jeudi 28 mars 2002* (Paris: Éditions du Seuil, 2003), 19.

186 MISPLACED IDEAS?

them, could only be interpreted as the result of some kind of misunderstanding regarding their true, essential meaning. If we lose sight of the profoundly dilemmatic nature of the issues they confronted, the whole history of past thought also loses all substantive sense, it becomes a kind of comedy of entanglements, a long and regrettable chain of misunderstandings.

This necessarily leads, in turn, to historical narratives with a clearly teleological imprint. Losing sight of the aporetic nature of fundamental political and social concepts, thinking that their semantic contents could be fixed, inevitably leads to the retrospective reconstruction of the entire history of thought as a mere series of approximations, of more or less deficient anticipations with respect to that "true" definition that the historian in question claims to possess, to the "ideal type" which thus appears as the final goal towards whose attainment the given historical process led, or should have tended to lead.

"Democratic life," says Rosanvallon, "is not one of the distance from some preexisting ideal model but one of the exploration of a problem to be resolved."[5] Producing this shift in perspective, however, entails an always arduous and risky task of reviewing our own most ingrained certainties because they are at the basis of our collective existence. Yet, it is only to the extent that we manage to strip the veil of naturalness with which our present presuppositions appear to us, that we manage to take critical distance from them, we can make sense of past debates. That is, we can understand that, if the subjects in question problematized concepts like democracy, freedom, etc., it was not because of a mere deficiency on their part, attributable to their lack of clarity or understanding of the "true" meaning of these concepts that we know, or believe to know, but because those concepts are, themselves, problematic. And only in this fashion could the history of Latin American thought be rescued from the place of a merely local anomaly and reintegrated as a constitutive part of modern political experience. In this fashion, the study of Latin American political-intellectual history, as I have tried to show, can serve as a basis for raising problems whose relevance transcends the merely local context, making up the very conceptual and methodological frameworks on which the discipline is currently founded, and, eventually, to demand their reformulation, as any other local case.

---

[5] Rosanvallon, *Pour une historie conceptuelle du politique*, 31.

Quoted Bibliography

Abellán, José Luis. *El exilio filosófico en América. Los transterrados de 1939*. Madrid: FCE, 1998.

Acuña, Víctor Hugo. *Memorias del II Congreso de Historia Centroamericana (1995)*. Guatemala: USAC, 2000.

Adelman, Jeremy. *Sovereignty and Revolution in the Iberian World*. Princeton: Princeton University Press, 2006.

Alberdi, Juan B. *Escritos póstumos*. Vol. XII. Buenos Aires: Imprenta Cruz Hnos, 1899.

Alberdi, Juan B. *Fragmento preliminar al estudio del derecho*. Buenos Aires: Biblos, 1984.

Alberini, Coriolano. *Precisiones sobre la evolución del pensamiento argentino*. Buenos Aires: Docencia, 1981.

Aljovin de Losada, Cristobal, and Mils Jacobsen, eds. *Cultura política en los Andes (1750–1950)*. Lima: Universidad Nacional Mayor de San Marcos, 2007.

Altamirano, Carlos. *La invención de Nuestra América. Obsesiones, narrativas y debates sobre la identidad de América Latina*. Buenos Aires: Siglo XXI, 2021.

Anna, Timothy. *La caída del gobierno español en el Perú*. Lima: Instituto de Estudios Peruanos, 2003.

Anna, Timothy. *La caída del gobierno español en la ciudad de México*. Mexico: FCE, 1981.

Annino, Antonio. "Imperio, constitución y diversidad en la América hispana." *Historia Mexicana* 229 (2008): 179–227.

Annino, Antonio, ed. *Historia de las elecciones en Iberoamérica, Siglo XIX. De la formación del espacio político nacional*. Mexico: FCE, 1995.

Annino, Antonio, Luis Castro Leiva, and François-Xavier Guerra, eds. *De los imperios a las naciones: Iberoamérica*. Zaragoza: Ibercaja, 1994.

Arantes, Paulo Eduardo. *Sentimento da dialética na experiencia intelectual brasileira. Dialética e dualidade segundo Antonio Candido e Roberto Schwarz*. São Paulo: Paz e Terra, 1992.

Ardao, Arturo. *Espiritualismo y positivismo en el Uruguay*. Montevideo: Universidad de la República, 1968.

Ardiles, Oswaldo, ed. *Hacia una filosofía de la liberación latinoamericana*. Buenos Aires: Bonum, 1973.

Aristotle. *Politics*. New York: Barnes & Noble, 2005.

Arpini, Adriana. *Tramas e itinerarios. Entre la filosofía práctica e historia de las ideas en Nuestra América*. Buenos Aires: Teseo, 2020.

Artola, Miguel. *Los orígenes de la España contemporánea*. Madrid: Instituto de Estudios Políticos, 1975.

Austin, John. *How to do Things with Words*. Cambridge, MA: Harvard University Press, 1975.

Bailyn, Bernard. *The Ideological Origins of the American Revolution*. Cambridge, MA: Harvard University Press, 1992.

Bailyn, Bernard. *The Peopling of British North America: An Introduction*. New York: Random House, 1989.

188 QUOTED BIBLIOGRAPHY

Ball, Terence, James Farr, and Russell L. Hanson. *Political Innovation and Conceptual Change*. Cambridge: Cambridge University Press, 1995.

Bentivegna, Giuseppe. "Zea, Ortega y Gasset y la circunstancia hispanoamericana." *Revista de Filosofía* 142 (2017): 9–34.

Beorlegui, Carlos. *Historia del pensamiento latinoamericano. Una búsqueda incesante de la identidad*. Bilbao: Deusto, 2010.

Berdel, Márcia Regina. *A nação como artefato: deputados do Brasil nas Cortes Portuguesas*. San Pablo: Hucitec, 1998.

Berruezo, María Teresa. *La participación americana en las Cortes de Cádiz (1810–1814)*. Madrid: Centro de Estudios Constitucionales, 1986.

Bethell, Leslie, ed. *The Cambridge History of Latin America: From c.1870 to 1930*. Vol. IV. Cambridge: Cambridge University Press, 1989.

Biagini, Hugo, ed. *Orígenes de la democracia argentina. El trasfondo krausista*. Buenos Aires: Legasa, 1989.

Blumenberg, Hans. *Das Lachen der Thrackerin. Eine Urgeschichte der Theorie*. Frankfurt am Main: Suhrkamp, 1987. English translation: *The Laughter of the Thracian Woman: A Protohistory of Theory*. New York: Bloomsbury Academic, 2015.

Blumenberg, Hans. *The Genesis of the Copernican World*. Cambridge, MA: MIT Press, 1987.

Bosi, Alfredo. *Dialética da colonização*. São Paulo: Companhia de Letras, 1992.

Botana, Natalio. *La libertad política y su historia*. Buenos Aires: Sudamericana, 1991.

Botana, Natalio. *La tradición republicana. Alberdi, Sarmiento y las ideas políticas de su tiempo*. Buenos Aires: Sudamericana, 1984.

Breña, Roberto. *El primer liberalismo español y los procesos de emancipación de América, 1808–1824: una revisión historiográfica del liberalismo hispánico*. Mexico: El Colegio de México, 2006.

Calderón, María Teresa, and Clément Thibaud, eds. *Las revoluciones en el mundo atlántico*. Bogota: Universidad Externado de Colombia/Taurus, 2006.

Camacho, Daniel, ed. *Debates sobre la teoría de la dependencia y la sociología latinoamericana*. San José: EDUCA, 1979.

Campos, Haroldo de. *De la razón antropofágica y otros ensayos*. Mexico: Siglo XXI, 2000.

Candido, Antonio. *O discurso e a cidade*. São Paulo: Duas Cidades, 1993.

Cardoso, Fernando H. *Capitalismo e escravidão no Brasil Meridional. O Negro na sociedade escravocrata do Rio Grande do Sul*. Rio de Janeiro: Paz e Terra, 1977.

Cardoso, Fernando H., and Enzo Falleto. *Dependencia y desarrollo en América Latina*. Mexico: FCE, 1969.

Cardoso, Fernando H., and Francisco Weffort, eds. *América Latina: Ensayos de interpretación sociológica-política*. Santiago: Editorial Universitaria, 1970.

Carvalho Franco, Maria Sylvia de. "As idéias estão no lugar." *Cadernos de Debate* 1 (1976): 61–64.

Carvalho Franco, Maria Sylvia de. *Homes livres na ordem escravocrata*. São Paulo: USP, 1997.

Castro-Gómez, Santiago. *Crítica de la razón latinoamericana*. Bogota: Pontificia Universidad Javeriana, 2011.

Caturelli, Alberto, ed. *Temas de Filosofía contemporánea*. Buenos Aires: Sudamericana, 1971.

Cevasco, Maria Elisa. "El significado de 'las ideas fuera de lugar.'" *Políticas de la Memoria* 10/11/12 (2011–2012): 21–24.

QUOTED BIBLIOGRAPHY 189

Chambers, Sara. "Scholarly Studies of Women and Gender during Latin American Independence." https://www.oxfordbibliographies.com/view/document/obo-978019 9766581/obo-9780199766581-0260.xml.

Chaunu, Pierre. *La independencia de América Latina*. Buenos Aires: Nueva Visión, 1972.

Chiaramonte, José Carlos. *El mito de los orígenes en la historiografía latinoamericana*. Buenos Aires: Instituto Dr. Emilio Ravignani, 1993.

Chilcote, R. "Issues of Theory in Dependence and Marxism." *Latin American Perspectivas* 8, no. 3–4 (1981): 3–16.

Chust, Manuel. *La cuestión nacional americana en las Cortes de Cádiz*. Valencia: UNED/ Centro Francisco Tomás y Valiente, 1999.

Chust, Manuel, and José Antonio Serrano, eds. *Debates sobre la independencia iberoamericana*. Madrid: AHILA/Iberoamericana Vervuert, 2007.

Clavero, Bartolomé. *Antidora. Antropología católica de la economía moderna*. Milan: Giuffre Editore, 1991.

Crapanzano, Vincent. *Hermes' Dilemma and Hamlet's Desire*. Cambridge, MA: Harvard University Press, 1992.

Cueva, Agustín. *El desarrollo del capitalismo de América Latina*. Mexico: Siglo XXI, 1977.

De Andrade, Oswald. "Manifesto Antropófago." *Revista de Antropofagia* 1, no. 1 (1928): 1–5.

De Rezende Martin, Estevão, and Héctor Pérez Brignoli, eds. *Teoría y metodología de la historia en América Latina*. Paris: UNESCO/Trotta, 2006.

Derrida, Jacques. *Margins of Philosophy*. Chicago: University of Chicago Press, 1972.

De Ruggiero, Guido. *The History of European Liberalism*. Gloucester, MA: Peter Smith, 1981.

Devés Valdés, Eduardo. "El pensamiento latinoamericano a comienzos del siglo XX: la reivindicación de la identidad." *Anuario de filosofía argentina y americana* 14 (1997): 11–75.

Devoto, Fernando, and Nora Pagano. *Historia de la historiografía argentina*. Buenos Aires: Sudamericana, 2009.

Devoto, Fernando, and Nora Pagano, eds. *La historiografía académica y la historiografía militante en Argentina y Uruguay*. Buenos Aires: Biblos, 2017.

Dilthey, Wilhelm. *The Formation of the Historical World in the Human Sciences*. Princeton: Princeton University Press, 2002.

Dobb, Maurice. *Studies in the Development of Capitalism*. London: Routledge, 1946.

Donnantuoni Moratto, M. "La categoría de 'normalidad filosófica' en Francisco Romero y su dimensión histórica." *Anuario De Filosofía Argentina y Americana* 33 (2020): 93–115.

Ducrot, Oswald. *El decir y lo dicho*. Buenos Aires: Hachette, 1984.

Dunn, John. *Democracy: A History*. New York: Atlantic Monthly Press, 2005.

Dunn, John. *An Historical Account of the Argument of the "Two Treatises of Government."* Cambridge: Cambridge University Press, 1995.

Dussel, Enrique. *El humanismo semita. Estructuras radicales del pueblo de Israel y otros semitas*. Buenos Aires: Eudeba, 1969.

Dussel, Enrique. *Filosofía de la liberación*. Bogota: Editorial Nueva América, 1977.

Dussel, Enrique. *Historia de la filosofía y filosofía de la liberación*. Bogota: Editorial Nueva América, 1994.

Dussel, Enrique. *Método para una filosofía de la liberación*. Buenos Aires: Ágora, 1974.

Dussel, Enrique. *Para un ética de la liberación latinoamericana*. Buenos Aires: S.XXI, 1973.

190 QUOTED BIBLIOGRAPHY

Dussel, Enrique. *La posmodernidad a debate*. Bogota: Universidad Santo Tomás Aquino, 2002.

Dussel, Enrique. *Siete ensayos de filosofía de la liberación. Hacia una fundamentación del giro decolonial*. Madrid: Trotta, 2020.

Eakin, Marshall. "Latin American History in the United Status: From Gentleman Scholars to Academia Specialists." *The History Teacher* 31, no. 4 (1998): 539–561.

El Orden (Buenos Aires, 1858).

Entin, Gabriel. "Tulio Halperin Donghi y la revolución como exploración." *Prismas. Revista de Historia Intelectual* 15 (2011): 185–188.

Entin, Gabriel, ed. *Rousseau en Iberoamérica. Lecturas e interpretaciones entre monarquía y revolución*. Buenos Aires: SB Editores, 2018.

Falcon, F. J. C. *História e historiografia nos anos 50 e 60*. Niterói: Editora da Universidade Federal Fluminense, 2004.

Fenández Sebastián, Javier, dir. *Diccionario político y social del mundo iberoamericano. Conceptos políticos fundamentales, 1770–1870. 10 vols.* Madrid: Centro de Estudios Políticos y Constitucionales/Universidad del País Vasco, 2014.

Fernández Albaladejo, Pablo. *Materia de España. Cultura política e identidad de la España moderna*. Madrid: Marcial Pons, 2007.

Foucault, Michel. *Archaeology of Knowledge*. London: Routledge, 2002.

Foucault, Michel. *The Order of Things: An Archeology of Human Sciences*. New York: Vintage, 1970.

Frasquet, Ivana, ed. *Bastillas, cetros y blasones: la independencia en Iberoamérica*. Madrid: Mapfre, 2006.

Fresia, Iván Ariel. "La filosofía de la liberación como filosofía del pueblo. La experiencia del grupo argentino: La línea Kusch, Cullen, Scannone." *Cuadernos de Filosofía Latinoamericana* 39, no. 118 (2018): 77–94.

Furet, Fançois. *Penser la Révolution Française*. Paris: Folios, 1978.

Furtado, Celso. *La economía latinoamericana desde la conquista hasta la revolución cubana*. Mexico: Siglo XXI, 1969.

Furtado, Celso. *Formação económica do Brasil*. Río de Janeiro: Editora Fundo de Cultura, 1959.

Garramuño, Florencia, and Adriana Amante, eds. *Absurdo Brasil*. Buenos Aires: Biblos, 2001.

Garriga, Carlos, and Marta Llorente. *Cádiz 1812. La Constitución jurisdiccional*. Madrid: Centro de Estudios Constitucionales, 2007.

Goldman, Noemí. *El discurso como objeto de la historia*. Buenos Aires: Hachette, 1989.

Goldmann, Lucien. *Cultural Creation*. Saint Louis: Telos Press, 1976.

González Marcelo, and Luciano Maddonni. *La explosión liberacionista en la filosofía latinoamericana. Aportes iniciales de Enrique Dussel y Juan Carlos Scannone 1964–1972)*. Buenos Aires: Teseo, 2020.

Granados, Aimer, and Carlos Marichal, eds. *Construcción de las identidades latinoamericanas. Ensayos de historia intelectual siglos XIX y XX*. Mexico: COLMEX, 2004.

Griffith, W. "The Historiography of Central America Since 1830." *Hispanic American Historical Review* 40, no. 4 (1960): 548–569.

Guardino, Peter. *Peasant, Politics and the Formation of Mexico's National State. Guerrero, 1800–1857*. Stanford: Stanford University Press, 1996.

Guarisco, Claudia. *Los indios del valle de México y la construcción de una nueva sociabilidad política, 1770–1835*. Mexico: El Colegio Mexiquense, 2003.

QUOTED BIBLIOGRAPHY   191

Guerra, François-Xavier. *México: Del Antiguo Régimen a la Revolución*. Mexico: FCE, 1985.
Guerra, François-Xavier, and Annick Lempérière, eds. *Los espacios públicos en Iberoamérica. Ambigüedades y problemas. Siglos XVIII–XIX*. Mexico: FCE, 1998.
Gunder Frank, André. *Capitalism and Underdevelopment in Latin America: Historical Studies of Chile and Brazil*. New York: Monthly Review Press, 1967.
Hale, Charles. "The History of Ideas: Substantive and Methodological Aspects of the Thought of Leopoldo Zea." *Journal of Latin American Studies* 3, no. 1 (1971): 59–70.
Hale, Charles. *Mexican Liberalism in the Age of Mora, 1821–1853*. New Haven, CT: Yale University Press, 1968.
Halperin Donghi, Tulio. "'Dependency Theory' and Latin American Historiography." *Latin American Research Review* 17, no. 1 (1982): 115–130.
Halperin Donghi, Tulio. *Revolución y guerra. Formación de una elite dirigente en la Argentina criolla*. Buenos Aires: Siglo XXI, 1972.
Halperin Donghi, Tulio. *Tradición política española e ideología revolucionaria de Mayo*. Buenos Aires: Prometeo Libros, 2009.
Hamnett, Brian. *Revolución y contrarrevolución en México y el Perú. Liberalismo, realeza y separatismo (1800–1824)*. Mexico: FCE, 1980.
Harris, Marvin. *Cultural Materialism: The Struggle for a Science of Culture*. New York: Random House, 1980.
Hartz, Louis. *The Founding of New Societies: Studies in the History of the United States, Latin America, South Africa, Canada, and Australia*. New York: Harvest/HBJ, 1964.
Hartz, Louis. *The Liberal Tradition in America: An Interpretation of American Political Thought since the Revolution*. New York: HBJ, 1955.
Hawkings, Stephen J. "Fundamental Ambiguities: Metaphor, Translation, and Intertextuality in Hans Blumenberg's Metaphorology." PhD diss., University of Michigan, 2014.
Heidegger, Martin. *The Question Concerning Technology and Other Essays*. New York; Harper & Row, 1977.
Hernández Flores, G. *Del circunstancialismo filosófico de Ortega y Gasset a la filosofía mexicana de Leopoldo Zea*. Mexico: UNAM, 2004.
Hewes, G. W. "Mexican in Search of the 'Mexican' (Review)." *American Journal of Economics and Sociology* 13, no. 2 (1954): 209–222.
Hobsbawm, Eric, and Terence Ranger, eds. *The Invention of Tradition*. Cambridge: Cambridge University Press, 1992.
Husserl, Edmund. *The Crisis of European Sciences and Transcendental Phenomenology; an Introduction to Phenomenological Philosophy*. Evanston: Northewestern University Press, 1970.
Husserl, Edmund. *Ideas Pertaining to a Pure Phenomenology and to a Phenomenological Philosophy. First Book: General Introduction to a Pure Phenomenology*. The Hague: Martinus Nijhoff Publishers, 1983.
Jaguaribe, Helio, Aldo Ferrer, Miguel S. Wionczek, and Theotonio Dos Santos. *La dependencia político-económica de América latina*. Mexico: Siglo XXI, 1973.
Jiménez Codinach, Guadalupe. *Forging Patrias: Iberoamerica, 1810–1824. Some Reflections. 2 vols.* Mexico: Fomento Cultural Banamex, 2010.
Kantorowicz, Ernst. *The King's Two Bodies. A Study in Mediaeval Political Theology*. Princeton: Princeton University Press, 1981.
Kay, Cristobal. *Latin American Theories of Development and Underdevelopment*. London: Routledge, 1989.

192   QUOTED BIBLIOGRAPHY

Knight, Alan. "Latinoamérica: un balance historiográfico." *Historia y Grafía* 10 (1988): 165–207.

Koselleck, Reinhart. *Critique and Crisis: Enlightenment and the Pathogenesis of Modern Society*. Oxford: Berg, 1988.

Koselleck, Reinhart. *Future Past: On the Semantics of Historical Time*. Cambridge, MA: MIT Press, 1985.

Kozel, Andrés. *Dos tratamientos de lo trascendente en el latinoamericanismo clásico: Ezequiel Martínez Estrada y Leopoldo Zea*. [online]. Buenos Aires: Universidad Católica Argentina, 2013. https://repositorio.uca.edu.ar/bitstream/123456789/4818/1/dos-tratamientos-trascendente.pdf

Kozel, Andrés. *La idea de América en el historicismo mexicano. José Gaos, Edmundo O'Gorman y Leopoldo Zea*. Buenos Aires: Teseo, 2017.

Kusch, Rodolfo. *América profunda*. Buenos Aires: Biblos, 1999.

Kusch, Rodolfo. *Esbozo de una antropología filosófica latinoamericana*. Buenos Aires: Castañeda, 1991.

Kusch, Rodolfo. *Obras completas*. Vol. III. Rosario: Fundación Ross, 1975.

Lacan, Jacques. *The Object Relation: Seminar of Jacques Lacan. Book IV*. New York: Polity Press, 2021.

Lecuna, Vicente, and Lewis Bertrand, eds. *Selected Writings by Simón Bolívar*. New York: Colonial Press Inc., 1951.

Lee Benson, Nettie. *Mexico and the Spanish Cortes, 1810–1822. Eight Essays*. Austin: Texas University Press, 1966.

Levene, Ricardo. *Las Indias no eran colonias*. Madrid: Espasa Calpe, 1973.

Lévinas, Emmanuel. *Totalité et Infini, Essai sur l 'exteriorité*. Paris: Kluwer Academic-Martinus Nijhoff, 1971.

Levinson, Sanford. *Our Undemocratic Constitution: Where the Constitution Goes Wrong (and How We the People Can Correct It)*. Oxford: Oxford University Press, 2006.

Lynch, John. *Las revoluciones hispanoamericanas, 1808–1826*. Barcelona: Ariel, 1976.

López Morillas, J. *El krausismo español*. Mexico: FCE, 1956.

Lotman, Iuri M. *La semiosfera I: Semiótica de la cultura y del texto*. Barcelona: Cátedra/Universitat de València, 1996.

Lotman, Iuri M. *La semiosfera II: Semiótica de la cultura, del texto, de la conducta y del espacio*. Barcelona: Cátedra/Universitat de València, 1998.

Lovejoy, Arthur. "Reflections on the History of Ideas." *Journal of the History of Ideas* 1, no. 1 (1940): 3–23.

Lukács, György. *The Destruction of Reason*. Atlantic Highlands, NJ: Humanities Press Inc., 1981.

Lukács, György. *Die Seele und die Formen*. Berlin: Egon Fleischel, 1911. English translation: *Soul and Form*. New York: Columbia University Press, 2010.

Lukács, György. *La novela histórica*. Mexico: Era, 1971.

Malamud, Carlos, ed. *Legitimidad, representación y alternancia en España y América Latina: Las reformas electorales (1880–1930)*. Mexico: El Colegio de México/FCE, 2000.

Manin, Bernard. *The Principles of Representative Government*. Cambridge: Cambridge University Press, 1997.

Marchart, Oliver. *Post-foundational Political Thought in Nancy, Lefort, Badiou and Laclau*. Edinburgh: Edinburgh University Press, 2007.

Marichal Salinas, Carlos. *Bankruptcy of Empire. Mexican Silver and the Wars Between Spain, Britain and France, 1760–1810*. Cambridge: Cambridge University Press, 2007.

QUOTED BIBLIOGRAPHY 193

Marini, Ruy Mauro, and Márgara Millán, eds. *La teoría social latinoamericana. Textos escogidos. Tomo II: La teoría de la dependencia.* México: UNAM, 1994.

Martínez, José Luis, ed. *El ensayo mexicano moderno.* Mexico: FCE, 1958.

Martínez Marina, Francisco. *Discurso sobre el origen de la monarquía y sobre la naturaleza del gobierno español.* Madrid: Centro de Estudios Constitucionales, 1988.

Marx, Karl. *The Eighteenth Brumaire of Louis Bonaparte.* London: Pluto Press, 2002.

Medin, Tzvi. *Leopoldo Zea: ideología, historia y filosofía de América Latina.* Mexico: UNAM, 1983.

Medin, Tzvi. *Ortega y Gasset en la cultura hispanoamericana.* Mexico: FCE, 1994.

Medin, Tzvi. *Entre la jerarquía y la liberación: Ortega y Gasset y Leopoldo Zea.* Mexico: FCE, 1998.

Meyer, Arno. *The Persistence of the Old Regime: Europe to the Great War.* New York: Pantheon Press, 1981.

Mignolo, Walter. *The Darker Side of the Renaissance: Literacy, Territoriality, and Colonization.* Ann Arbor: University of Michigan Press, 2003.

Mignolo, Walter. *La idea de América Latina. La herida colonial y la opción decolonial.* Barcelona: Gedisa, 2005.

Miró Quesada, Francisco. "Universalismo y latinoamericanismo." *Isegoría* 18 (1998): 61–78.

Montaigne, Michel de. "The Apology of Raymond Sebond." In *The Complete Works: Essays, Travel Journals, Letters,* Book II, chapter XII. Translated by Donal M. Frame. New York: A. A. Knopf, 2003.

Morel, Marco. *As transformações dos espaços públicos: imprensa, atores políticos e sociabilidades na Cidade Imperial (1820–1840).* São Paulo: Hucitec, 2005.

Moreno, Mariano. *Escritos políticos y económicos.* Buenos Aires: La Cultura Argentina, 1915.

Morgan, Edmund. *Inventing the People: The Rise of Popular Sovereignty in England and America.* New York: W. W. Norton, 1988.

Morse, Richard. *New World Soundings: Culture and Ideology in the Americas.* Baltimore: Johns Hopkins University Press, 1989.

Moulián, Luis. *La independencia de Chile. Balance historiográfico.* Santiago: Factum, 1996.

Murilo de Carvalho, José. "História intelectual no Brasil: a retórica como chave de leitura." *Topoí* 1 (2000): 123–152.

Naxara, Márcia, and Virginia Camilotti, eds. *Conceitos e linguagens: construções identitárias.* São Paulo: Intermeios, 2014.

Nietzsche, Friedrich. *On the Genealogy of Morals.* Cambridge: Cambridge University Press, 1994.

Novais Fernando A., and Carlos G. Mota. *A Independencia do Brasil.* São Paulo: Moderna, 1986.

O`Gorman, Edmudo. "Latinoamérica: así no." *Nexos* 123 (1988): 12–17.

O`Gorman, Edmudo. *México. El trauma de su historia.* Mexico: UNAM, 1977.

Ortiz Escamilla, Juan. *Guerra y gobierno. Los pueblos y la independencia de México.* Sevilla: Universidad de Sevilla/El Colegio de México/Instituto Mora, 1997.

Ortiz Escamilla, Juan, ed. *Fuerzas militares en Iberoamérica.* Mexico: El Colegio de México/El Colegio de Michoacán/Universidad Veracruzana, 2005.

Pachón Soto, Damián. *Filosofía de la liberación y teorías descoloniales. Textos reunidos.* Colección Nuevas Ideas 5. Bucamaranga, 2018.

Palacios, Guillermo, ed. *Ensayos sobre la nueva historia política de América Latina, siglo XIX.* Mexico: El Colegio de México, 2007.

194 QUOTED BIBLIOGRAPHY

Palti, Elías J. *An Archeology of the Political: Regimes of Power from the Seventeenth Century to the Present*. New York: Columbia University Press, 2017.

Palti, Elías J. *El tiempo de la política. El siglo XIX reconsiderado*. Buenos Aires: Siglo XXI, 2007. Portuguese edition: *O tempo da política. O século XIX reconsiderado*. Trans. Romulo Monte Alto. Belo Horizonte: Autêntica, 2020.

Palti, Elías J. *Intellectual History and the Problem of Conceptual Change. Skinner, Pocock, Koselleck, Blumenberg, Foucault, Rosanvallon*. Cambridge: Cambridge University Press, forthcoming.

Palti, Elías J. ed. *Mito y realidad en la cultura política latinoamericana*. Buenos Aires: Prometeo, 2010.

Palti, Elías J. "The Nation as a Problem: Historians and the 'National Question.'" *History and Theory* 40 (2001): 324–346.

Palti, Elías J. "The Return of the Subject as a Historical-Conceptual Problem." *History and Theory* 43 (2004): 57–82.

Palti, Elías J. *Verdades y saberes del marxismo. Reacciones de una tradición política ante su "crisis."* Buenos Aires: FCE, 2007. French edition: *Vérités et savoirs du marxisme. Réactions d'une tradition politique à sa crise*. Trans. Luis Dapelo. Paris: Editions Delga, 2018.

Peralta Ruiz, Víctor. "Elecciones, constitucionalismo y elección en el Cusco, 1809–1815." *Revista de Indias* 206 (1996): 99–133.

Peralta Ruiz, Víctor. *En defensa de la autoridad. Política y cultura bajo el gobierno del virrey Abascal*. Madrid: CSIC, 2002.

Pérez Cabrera, L. *Historiografía de Cuba*. Mexico: Instituto Panamericano de Geografía e Historia, 1962.

Piaget, Jean. *Biology and Knowledge: An Essay on the Relations Between Organic Regulations and Cognitive Processes*. Chicago: University of Chicago Press, 1971.

Pocock, John. *The Machiavellian Moment: Florentine Political Thought and the Atlantic Republican Tradition*. Princeton: Princeton University Press, 1975.

Pocock, John. *Politics, Language and Time: Essays on Political Thought and History*. Chicago: University of Chicago Press, 1989.

Pocock, John. *Virtue, Commerce and History*. Cambridge: Cambridge University Press, 1991.

Portillo Valdés, José María. *Crisis atlántica: autonomía e independencia en la crisis de la monarquía hispana*. Madrid: Marcial Pons/Centro de Estudios Hispanos e Iberoamericanos/Fundación Carolina, 2006.

Prado, Jr., Caio. *Formação do Brasil comtemporâneo*. São Paulo: Brasiliense, 1942.

Quijano Velasco, Francisco. *Las repúblicas de la Monarquía: pensamiento constitucionalista y republicano en Nueva España 1550–1610*. Mexico: UNAM, 2017.

Raat, William D. "Ideas e historia en México, un ensayo sobre metodología." *Latinoamérica: Anuario de Estudios Latinoamericanos* 3 (1970): 175–188.

Rancière, Jacques. *Key Concepts*. London: Acumen Publishing, 2010.

Ramos, Samuel. *El perfil del hombre y la cultura en México*. Mexico: UNAM, 1934.

Ribeiro, Ana. *Los muy fieles. Leales a la corona en el proceso revolucionario rioplatense. Montevideo/Asunción, 1810–1820*. Montevideo: Planeta, 2013.

Rieu-Millan, Marie. *Los diputados americanos en la Cortes de Cádiz*. Madrid: CSIC, 1998.

Rodríguez, Mario. *El experimento de Cádiz en Centroamérica. 1808–1826*. Mexico: FCE, 1984.

QUOTED BIBLIOGRAPHY 195

Rodríguez O., Jaime, ed. *The Evolution of the Mexican Political System.* Wilmington: Scholarly Resources, 1993.

Rodríguez O., Jaime. *La independencia de la América española.* Mexico: El Colegio de México/FCE, 1996.

Rodríguez de Lecea D., and T. Koniecki, eds. *El krausismo y su influencia en América Latina.* Madrid: Fundación Ebert/Fe y Secularidad, 1989.

Roig, Arturo Andrés. *Historia de ideas, teoría del discurso y pensamiento latinoamericano.* Bogota: Universidad Santo Tomás, 1993.

Roig, Arturo Andrés. *Los krausistas argentinos.* Puebla: José M. Cajica, 1969. https://ens ayistas.org/filosofos/argentina/roig/krausismo/3.htm.

Roig, Arturo Andrés. *Teoría y crítica del pensamiento latinoamericano.* Mexico: FCE, 1981.

Roig, Arturo Andrés. *El pensamiento latinoamericano y su aventura.* 2 vols. Buenos Aires: CEAL, 1994.

Rojas, Beatriz. "Las ciudades novohispanas ante la crisis: Entre la antigua y la nueva constitución, 1808–1814." *Historia Mexicana* 229 (2008): 287–324.

Rolim Capelato, Maria Helena, ed. *Produção histórica no Brasil.* São Paulo: Xamá, 1995.

Romero, Francisco. *El hombre y la cultura.* Buenos Aires: Espasa-Calpe, 1950.

Romero, José Luis. *Las ideas políticas en Argentina.* Buenos Aires: FCE, 1975.

Rosanvallon, Pierre. *Pour une historie conceptuelle du politique. Leçon inaugurale au Collège de France faite le jeudi 28 mars 2002.* Paris: Éditions du Seuil, 2003.

Saavedra, Cornelio. *Memoria autógrafa.* Buenos Aires: Carlos Pérez Editor, 1969.

Sabato, Hilda. *Republics of the New World: The Revolutionary Political Experiment in Nineteenth-Century Latin America.* Princeton: Princeton University Press, 2018.

Sabato, Hilda, ed. *Ciudadanía política y formación de las naciones. Perspectivas históricas de América Latina.* Mexico: FCE, 1999.

Said, Edward. *Orientalism.* London: Routledge/Kegan Paul Ltd., 1980.

Salazar Bondy, Augusto. *¿Existe una filosofía de Nuestra América?* Mexico: Siglo XXI, 1968.

Salmerón, Alicia, and Erika Pani, eds. *Conceptuar los que se ve. François-Xavier Guerra historiador. Homenaje.* Mexico: Instituto Mora, 2004.

Samper, José María. *Ensayo sobre las revoluciones políticas.* Paris: Imprenta de Thumot, 1861.

Sánchez Albornoz, Claudio. *España, un enigma histórico.* Buenos Aires: Sudamericana, 1956.

Santiago, Silviano. *Uma Literatura nos trópicos.* São Paulo: Editora Perspectiva, 1978.

Sasso, Javier. *La filosofía latinoamericana y sus construcciones históricas.* Caracas: Monte Ávila Editores Latinoamericana, 1997.

Scannone, Juan Carlos, and Ignacio Ellacuría, eds. *Para una filosofía desde Latinoamérica.* Bogota: Universidad Javeriana, 1992.

Schmidt, Henri. *The Roots of Lo Mexicano: Self and Society in Mexican Thought, 1900–1934.* College Station: Texas A&M University Press, 1978.

Schmitt, Carl. *The Concept of the Political.* Chicago: University of Chicago Press, 2007.

Schwarz, Roberto. "Las ideas fuera de lugar: algunas aclaraciones." *Políticas de la Memoria* 10/11/12 (2011–2012): 25–30.

Schwarz, Roberto. *Misplaced Ideas.* London: Verso, 1992.

Schwarz, Roberto. *Que horas são? Ensaios.* São Paulo: Companhia das Letras, 1997.

Schwarz, Roberto. *Seqüências brasileiras. Ensaios.* São Paulo: Companhia das Letras, 1999.

Seoane, María Cruz. *El primer lenguaje constitucional español.* Madrid: Moneda y Crédito, 1968.

196 QUOTED BIBLIOGRAPHY

Serrano, José Antonio. *Jerarquía territorial y transición política, Guanajuato 1790–1836*. Mexico: El Colegio de Michoacán/Instituto Mora, 2001.

Serrano, José Antonio, and Marta Terán, eds. *Las guerras de independencia en la América española*. Zamora: El Colegio de Michoacán, 2002.

Serulnikov, Segio. "Tulio Halperin Donghi y la independencia hispanomaericana." *Boletín del Instituto de Historia Argentina y Americana "Dr. Emilio Ravignani."* Número Especial (2018): 132–154.

Shanker, S. G., ed. *Gödel's Theorem in Focus*. London: Routledge, 1981.

Skidmore, Thomas. "Studying the History of Latin America: A Case of Hemispheric Convergence." *Latin America Research Review* 33, no. 1 (1998): 105–127.

Skinner, Quentin. "Meaning and Understanding in the History of Ideas," *History and Theory* 8, no. 1 (1969): 3–53.

Skirius, John, ed. *El ensayo latinoamericano del siglo XX*. Mexico: FCE, 1981.

Sosa, Guillermo. *Representación e independencia. 1810–1816*. Bogota: Instituto Colombiano de Antropología e Historia, 2006.

Sosa, Ignacio, and Brian Connaughton, eds. *Historiografía latinoamericana contemporánea*. Mexico City: CCYDEL-UNAM, 1999.

Stein, Stanley. "The Historiography of Brazil, 1808–1889." *Hispanic American Historical Review* 40, no. 2 (1960): 234–278.

Suárez, Francisco. *Defensa de la Fe Católica y Apostólica contra los Errores del Anglicanismo (Defensio Fidei)*. Madrid: Instituto de Estudios Políticos, 1971.

Suárez, Francisco. *De Legibus: De natura legis. Book I*. Madrid: CSIC, 1971.

Stoetzer, O. C. *The Scholastic Roots of the Spanish American Revolution*. New York: Fordham University, 1979.

Sunkel, Osvaldo. "Capitalismo trasnacional y desintegración nacional en América Latina." *Estudios Internacionales* 16 (1971): 3–61.

Terán, Oscar. "Sobre la historia intelectual", in *De utopías, catástrofes y esperanzas. Un camino intelectual*. Buenos Aires: Siglo XXI, 2006, pp. 61-69.

Terán, Oscar. *Historia de las ideas en Argentina, Diez lecciones, 1810–1980*. Buenos Aires: Siglo XXI, 2008.

Ternavasio, Marcela. *La revolución del voto. Política y elecciones en Buenos Aires, 1810–1852*. Buenos Aires: Siglo XXI, 2002.

Ternavasio, Marcela. "Los enigmas de Halperin. Comentario al artículo de Fabio Wasserman." *Boletín del Instituto de Historia Argentina y Americana "Dr. Emilio Ravignani."* Número Especial (2018): 86–98.

Thibaud, Clément. *Repúblicas en armas. Los ejércitos bolivarianos en la guerra de Independencia en Colombia y Venezuela*. Bogota: Instituto Francés de Estudios Andinos/Planeta, 2003.

Thurner, Mark. *History's Peru: The Poetics of Colonial and Postcolonial Historiography*. Gainesville: University Press of Florida, 2011.

Thurner, Mark. *Republicanos andinos*. Cuzco: CBC/IEP, 2006.

Uribe Urán, Víctor Manuel, and Luis Javier Ortiz Mesa, eds. *Naciones, gentes y territorios. Ensayos de historia e historiografía comparada de América Latina y el Caribe*. Medellín: Universidad de Antioquia, 2000.

Van Young, Eric. *The Other Rebellion: Popular Violence, Ideology, and the Mexican Struggle for Independence*. Stanford: Stanford University Press, 2001.

Vázquez, Josefina, ed. *Recepción y transformación del liberalismo en México. Homenaje al profesor Charles A. Hale*. Mexico: El Colegio de México, 1991.

QUOTED BIBLIOGRAPHY   197

Vázquez de Prada Vallejo, V., and Ignacio Olábarri Gortázar. *Balance de la historiografía sobre Iberoamérica (1945–1988)*. *Actas de las IV Conversaciones Internacionales de Historia*. Pamplona: Ediciones Universidad de Navarra, 1989.

Velasco Gómez, Ambrosio. *La persistencia del humanismo republicano en la formación del estado y la nación en México*. Mexico, UNAM, 2009.

Véliz, Claudio. *The Centralist Tradition of Latin America*. Princeton: Princeton University Press, 1980.

Villoro, Luis. "¿Es posible una comunidad filosófica iberoamericana?" *Isegoría* 18 (1998): 53–60.

Villoro, Luis. *México, entre libros. Pensadores del siglo XX*. Mexico: El Colegio Nacional/ FCE, 1995.

Villoro, Luis. *Perfil de México en 1980*. México: Siglo XXI, 1972.

Villoro, Luis. *Sobre el problema de la filosofía latinoamericana*. Mexico: Siglo XXI, 1983.

Von Vacano, Diego. *The Color of Citizenship: Race, Modernity and Latin American/ Hispanic Political Thought*. Oxford: Oxford University Press, 2011.

Von Vacano, Diego. "The Scope of Comparative Political Theory." *Annual Review of Political Science* 18 (2015): 465–480.

Wasserman, Fabio. "Intelectuales, sociedad y política en los siglos XVIII y XIX: la historia intelectual en el espejo de Halperin Donghi." *Boletín del Instituto de Historia Argentina y Americana "Dr. Emilio Ravignani."* Número Especial (2018): 59–74.

Weber, Max. *Economy and Society*. Vol. 1. Berkeley: University of California Press, 1978.

Weinberg, Liliana. *El ensayo entre el infierno y el paraíso*. Mexico: FCE/UNAM, 2001.

Weinberg, Liliana. *Situación del ensayo*. Mexico: CCYDEL-UNAM, 2006.

Wiarda, Howard, ed. *Politics and Social Change: The Distinct Tradition*. Amherst: University of Massachusetts Press, 1982.

Wood, Gordon. *The Creation of the American Republic*. Chapel Hill: University of North Carolina Press, 1969.

Zea, Leopoldo. *Conciencia y posibilidad del mexicano*. Mexico: Porrúa, 1952.

Zea, Leopoldo. *Dialéctica de la conciencia americana*. Mexico: Alianza, 1976.

Zea, Leopoldo. *Filosofía de la historia americana*. Mexico: FCE, 1978.

Zea, Leopoldo. *La filosofía como compromiso y otros ensayos*. Mexico: FCE, 1952.

Zea, Leopoldo. *La filosofía latinoamericana como filosofía sin más*. Mexico: Siglo XXI, 1969.

Zea, Leopoldo. *El pensamiento latinoamericano*. Barcelona: Ariel, 1976.

Zea, Leopoldo. *El positivismo en México*. Mexico: El Colegio de México, 1943.

Zea, Leopoldo, ed. *Pensamiento positivista latinoamericano*. Caracas: Ayacucho, 1980.

Zea, Leopoldo, ed. *América Latina en sus ideas*. Mexico: Siglo XXI, 1986.

Žižek, Slavoj. *Tarrying with the Negative: Kant, Hegel, and the Critique of Ideology*. Durham: Duke University Press, 1993.

Index

For the benefit of digital users, indexed terms that span two pages (e.g., 52–53) may, on occasion, appear on only one of those pages.

Tables and figures are indicated by *t* and *f* following the page number

Age of Forms, 69–70, 85
Alberdi, Juan Bautista, 43, 133, 178, 179
Alberini, Coriolano, 37
Alphonso of Castile, 130–31
Annino, Antonio, 171

Bacon, Francis, xii
Bailyn, Bernard, 13–14, 16–17, 159
Blumenberg, Hans, ix–xi, 139
Borges, Jorge Luis, 182
Bourbon dinasty, 146

Cadiz Cortes, 148
Candido, Antonio, 105
Carvalho Franco, Maria Sylvia, 99–102
Castro-Gómez, Santiago, 23–24, 66–69
    Foucault, Michel, 66
    preconceptual, 67
Crapanzano, Vincent, 74
Cullen, Carlos, 90–91
cultural nationalism, 1

democracy, 174
    origins, 177–78
    popular sovereignty, 178
dependency theory, xv–xvi, 95–96
De Ruggiero, Guido, 6–7
Dilthey, Wilhelm, 45
Dobb, Maurice, 164n.15
Ducrot, Oswald, 118n.42
Dunn, John, 174–75
Dussel, Enrique, 28, 78–93
    analectics, 83–84

ego cogito, 80, 82
    incarnation, 81
    rupture, 87–88
    specular logic, 90
    Trinitarian pattern, 86
    uniprinciple, 67–68

Escalante Gonzalbo, Fernando, 6–7

Fernández Albadalejo, Pablo, 147n.29
Fernández Retamar, Roberto, 27
Feuerbach, Ludwig, xiii, 80
Furet, François, 156
Furlong, Guillermo, 134

Goldman, Lucien, 105
Guerra, Fançois-Xavier, 6, 148, 154–55,
    156–62, 165
    concepts of *Pueblos* and *Pueblo*, 158–59
    critique of ideological influences, 157
    nationalist teleologism, 156
    public sphere, 157
    scheme from tradition to
        modernity, 159–60

Hale, Charles, 4, 6–8, 10–11
    Hispanic Ethos, 8
Halperin Donghi, 136–55
    concept of nation, 144–46, 149–51
    critique of history of ideas, 138
    first Spanish liberalism, 149
    historical constitutionalism, 153
Hartz, Louis, 8–9, 16–17

200 INDEX

Hebbel, Friedric, 108n.27
Heidegger, Martin, 72, 82–83
Hiperión group, 29
History of Latin American Ideas, xv
Husserl, Edmund, xn.2, 70–71

Kantorowicz, Ernst, 59–60
Knight, Alan, 13
Korn, Alejandro, 37
Koselleck, Reinhart, 50–51, 152
Krause, K. Ch. F., 38
Kusch, 61–77
   being-there, 63–64
   ground, 64–66

Lacan, Jacques, 81n.51
La Fontaine, Jean de, xiii
Lakebrink, Bernhard, 78
Latin American philosophy, xv–xvi
Latin American Revolutions of
     Independence, xvi
Levene, Ricardo, 134–35
Lévinas, Emmanuel, 78, 79
Lo Mexicano, 4
López Lisperguer, Francisco, 147–48
Lotman, Iuri, 120–22
Lynch, John, 167–68

Malerba, Jurandir, 163–64n.14
Marichal Salinas, Carlos, 160n.7
Martínez Marina, Francisco, 147n.30
Marxist historiography, 162–63
metahistory of ideas, x
Mignolo, Walter, 85n.59
Miró Quesada, Francisco, 58
misplaced ideas, xvi–xvii
Montaigne, Michel de, xii–xiii
Moreno, Mariano, 178
Morgan, Edmund, 146
Morse, Richard, 8–10, 12–13

Nietzsche, Friedrich, xiii

O'Gorman, Edmundo, 14

Ortega y Gasset, José, 2

Piaget, Jean, 122
Pocock, J. G. A., 15–16
Plato, ix
Prado Jr., Caio, 169

Reyes, Alfonso, 33
Rodó, José Enrique, 1–2, 27
Rodríguz O., Jaime, 167–68
Roig, Arturo A., 36–57
   Hegelian rupture, 52
   historical *a priori*, 46–47
   ideology, 89n.64
Rosanvallon, Pierre, 180–81

Saavedra, Cornelio, 179
Said, Edward, 23–24
Salazar Bondy, Augusto, 29
Santiago, Silviano, 109
Sanz del Río, Julián, 39
Scannone, Juan Carlos, 28
   Mediator, 86
Schwarz, Roberto, 96–127
   1824 Brazilian Constitution, 125
   Alencar, Jose de, 106
   critic of nationalism, 98
   Fabio Zerpa's Syndrome, 117
   "French philosophers," 110–11
   history of ideas, methodology, 113–16
   Machado de Assis, Joaquim
     Maria, 107–8
Skinner, Quentin, 44
Solórzano, Juan de, 143
Suárez, Francisco, 134, 141
Sweezy, Paul, 164n.15
synderesis, 144n.23

Thales of Miletus, ix
Toqueville, Alexis de, 148, 154–55
Toynbee, Arnold, 64n.14

Véliz, Claudio, 10–11
Villoro, Luis, 32–33

Vitoria, Francisco de, 142
Voltaire, F.-M. A., xiii
Von Vacano, Diego, 11

Weber, Max, 71
Wiarda, Howard J., 10

Zea, Leopoldo, xv, 2–6, 29–37, 182
  derivative culture, 3
  logic of *justaposition*, 34–35
  "models" and "deviations," 4
  positivism, 32
Žižek. Slavoj, 61n.6